Fire Captain Bill Lavin has written a story that entwines his past, present, and future into a narrative filled with tremendous sorrow, buckets of love, deep compassion, and mountainous heroism. Four major US tragedies, spanning from 2001 to 2012 are the backdrop for his heartwarming tale. We happen to be part of this book in a most unfortunate and horrific way. However, Bill's dream, to give children safe and grand places to play in honor of our daughter, her friends, classmates, and educators, has lent a healing balm to our family's' wounded hearts. We cherish this project as we cherish our nation's children and their need to play.

Jennifer, Jeremy, and Imogen Joy Richman
Parents and Sister of Avielle Richman

Where Angels Live Work and Play

The Story of the Sandy Ground Project

By

William J. Lavin
with Smitty Lavin

To the Angels from Sandy Hook Elementary School
and their Moms and Dads, spouses and families
who's grace, courage, strength and trust
continue to inspire the world.

To Charles and Elizabeth Lavin
who's love and example to me
and my 10 amazing brothers and sisters
laid the foundation for Where Angels Play.

To Kathy, Smitty, Kelly and MaryKate,
four incredible reasons I've had a wonderful life!

To Mark Virag and Dennis Bourke
who proved you can go from the Angels army
to the army of angels and never miss a beat.

And finally,
To every firefighter, police officer, military personnel,
EMT, nurse, teacher and public servant
who ever felt unappreciated or disrespected.
It is your unconditional service to our children
and our seniors that makes you great,
let no one take that away from you.

Smitty and Teddy Lavin, "A Playground's view
to a hopeful, peaceful and joyous future."

Note from the Co-Author

I had never considered writing anything in a voice other than my own. Not until the story of The Sandy Ground Project needed to be told by my father and he asked for my help. Consciously or not, I have been speaking in his voice, with his mannerisms and expressions, my entire life. So I felt uniquely qualified for the job.

Over the next couple years, in fits and starts, we held dozens of hours worth of interviews. In cars and in diner booths; at a food court or across the dining room table. As I asked questions and listened back to the answers over and over, I waited patiently for the lull… For the part that was ho-hum, business-as-usual.

As we got towards the end I realized how silly that was. Because for something like the Sandy Ground to come together, it was all going to be special. The families, the towns, the volunteers, the stars of this story—they were going to make each step a truly remarkable one. They were always going to throw a perfect game.

I am far from a religious guy. But I do believe that the people we love are present beyond life here on Earth. They live on in our hearts and minds and, therefore, live forever. Throughout this process I have thought much about Fred Middleton and Chris Danchisko—my own personal saints—who have had, and continue to have, a great impact on me in one way or another.

I have also thought much about those most responsible for any type of success of mine, with completing this book and otherwise…

To Dayna
my amazing, beautiful partner in all things—who holds our world together and has always believed that writing is what I oughta be doing.

To Teddy and Juniper
who've made our lives complete. For teaching me that
the greatest adventures will require more endurance and
more love than you ever thought you could muster.

To my Dad
for living a life worth writing about.
And for trusting me to be the one to tell the story.

Smitty Lavin
June 5, 2016, Toms River, NJ

Team Kowalski

Foreword

by Rebecca Kowalski

I think every American can remember where they were on September 11, 2001. I vividly remember that day. I was 8 days away from my due date with our second child. It was an exceptionally beautiful day. I was getting our oldest daughter ready for her first day of pre-school.

The first phone call was from the director, canceling school. The second was from my husband telling me to turn on the television. As we all learned of the attacks on NYC and on our country, we were in disbelief. How could this happen?

Then we thought of family. We had just been in one of those buildings back in February for Stephen's grandmother's 85th birthday party at Windows on the World. Our Uncle Michael worked on the 85th floor. Panic set in. I stayed glued to the television, trying to get some information about Uncle Michael.

That was one of the most emotional days I think I had ever experienced. The heartbreak I felt for the babies that wouldn't have a mommy or daddy come home was terrible. Here I was, about to give birth in just eight days, and my husband would be with me. Every time I write down my daughter Erin's birthday, I think of those babies and how blessed I was to not have lost a family member.

Fast forward to Superstorm Sandy. We now have three children and a wonderful life. We have our ups and downs, just like any middle class family, but still very happy, healthy, and blessed. We were without power for maybe a week—no biggie. We used a small generator to get things running, the house was in tact, and the family was safe.

It was nothing more than an inconvenience and, honestly, the lack of power made for great family time. We passed the time doing puzzles and playing cards. It was a nice break... until we got our power back and saw on television how bad the shoreline was hit.

We watched in disbelief, once again worried about Uncle Michael, his family, and the houses in New Jersey. We had just spent a week that August at his home in Normandy Beach. We'd played games on the boardwalk that was now damaged. We'd ridden the roller coaster that was now standing, half-submerged, on the ocean floor.

Once again, disbelief. Once again our family was safe.

Fast forward several more weeks, to December 13th. Our beautiful family is intact. The Christmas card's complete, already at the post office. All of our Christmas gifts are purchased and wrapped. I've never been this organized and ready for Christmas so early. I was so looking forward to spending time with our friends and family at multiple parties we had coming up. Even the kids had a pretty busy weekend coming up.

One day later, my life, our life as a family, and the lives of 26 families was forever changed. Most of that day is a blur and I choose to remember and honor my son for who he was—not how he was taken.

Enter Bill Lavin, a firefighter from New Jersey who I'd never met or heard of until the idea of 26 playgrounds came into my home. We sat down with him and listened to what he had to say. What an amazing idea! Who knew that Bill would be such a go getter, and be able to get this done? Getting 26 grieving families to agree to anything was a major undertaking with all of us in our own places dealing with grief.

The idea of a playground built to honor the life of our loved ones was genius. What my family didn't realize at the time was how much working hand in hand with strangers, and building something for children, would help our healing process. The other thing we came to know about these big-hearted strangers—called the "Angels Army"—is that they would only be strangers for a brief moment. I can only speak for my family, but these men and women were a fuzzy warm blanket that hugged us from the first smile that was cracked.

We had gone to a few ribbon-cuttings at the start and said hi to the troops, but never got to know them until Chase's #8 build. When we would see Bill at other builds he would always come right over with a hug and a smile. He'd introduce us to the big guys at the ceremonies, but the Army kept their distance on the ribbon cutting days. They were a strong group, "stoic" I would say, but at each ribbon-cutting the biggest of men were a sniffling mess.

That all changed the day we rolled up on the Army in Normandy Beach. They had just finished preliminary work on Chase' playground and were hiding their beverages, trying to be "proper". Not having met us, they were timid. Stephen took one look and asked for a beer. We had been driving back from Virginia, at the Christening of the Benjamin Chase a few days prior to the playground build, and now it was "Miller Time".

From that point on we were swept up into the ranks of the Angels Army! The love we share with this group is amazing. I feel protected, loved, and honored. I feel like the baby sister to a bunch of big brothers and sisters. I could make a single phone call and know that whatever I needed I would have a minimum of ten people offering a helping hand. We have amazing support, fabulous friends, and this group just adds even more to that group with a little more character.

To say that firefighters are a different breed is an understatement. When you are blessed to join their family, it is an honor of the highest kind. "NO MAN LEFT BEHIND"—and they mean it. There isn't anything they wouldn't do for the ones they love. And for our family, that's just another way Chase has blessed us. His spirit is with us always, but it is the love he spreads through the people he has placed on our path in this journey through life without him physically here.

We weren't able to make every build or ribbon-cutting, but reading Bill's memories makes me feel like we were. I can hear the voices of all the parents that spoke at their playgrounds, the gratitude of having a good day, honoring the love we have for our beautiful children. It is not easy to have a good day when you grieve the loss of a loved one, but you do have a choice to do things out of love or fear. And this project came out of pure Love.

Whose love, you ask? Well, it depends on who you are. For me, it was my little Angel who was a part of an Angelic team of 26 that found a man who needed to learn how to find love again. He needed to not be so angry and to give from his broken heart so it could love again. Simply put—was this our modern day story of the Grinch? I find it hard to believe that Bill Lavin was ever a grinch, but I do know he is grateful that his heart grew bigger with each and every build.

For my family, we are grateful for an Army of men and women lead by an honest man that stayed true to their word and delivered much more. We say thank you for helping to heal our broken hearts just a little bit more every day. For every child that plays on these playgrounds, there are 26 Angels smiling down on a job well done. 26 Angels, proud that they chose Bill Lavin to be their champion.

Prologue

"December 2012"

It's beginning to look a lot like Christmas and I'm miserable. So I'm speeding southbound on the New Jersey Turnpike, alone. If I've ever been in a worse place mentally or emotionally in my entire life, I can't recall it. I have no idea where I'm going. All I know is I've got to get away.

So now I'm just driving. Trying to find the peace of mind that has eluded me for the past several years.

I've been a firefighter in the City of Elizabeth, New Jersey for 25 years. For 16 of those I've been the President of the New Jersey State FMBA—the state's largest firefighters' union. While I wear those labels proudly, right now I'm disgusted with all of it.

I am questioning what to do for my family, for the union I represent, and for my state. My role as a labor leader has placed me smack in the middle of perhaps the worst political atmosphere New Jersey has ever seen. And, if you know anything about Jersey, that's saying something.

I'm just intent to get away from all that being the head of a labor union involves. The Governor of New Jersey, the State Legislature, local mayors; I've fought many of them tooth and nail. I've lost so much sleep over broken promises. Maybe I should know better by now.

Dealing with these types of individuals—battling to do what is right for firefighters—has left me physically and emotionally drained. But I want justice for them. I want people to understand that firefighters deserve the very best of safety, training, health benefits, pensions… I've attended the funerals of far too many men who have made the ultimate sacrifice doing a job that is so often thankless.

· · ·

A little more than a month ago, our home state was hit by the worst hurricane in its history. Not even a hurricane... a *superstorm* they called it, Superstorm Sandy. As usual, my Vice-President Bob Brower and I attempted to save the world. I guess we are hard-wired with the idea that firefighters are supposed to go the extra mile no matter what the sacrifice. They save people, no matter what the emergency happens to be.

So there we were at the Jersey Shore, trying to rescue and rebuild and recover as best we knew how. We reached out to fellow firefighters, fire departments that had been decimated, private citizens, people simply in need of some gasoline or a generator or their flooded basement pumped out. Ultimately it is a task that will take several years, billions of dollars, and more man-hours than one can count. But that doesn't make it any less frustrating.

I guess that's what it is—the *frustration* that has built up and sent me on this aimless drive. The amount of despair I was surrounded by, and the lack of concern by those who were supposed to be leading. At this point I see a billboard for Parx Casino in Bensalem, Pennsylvania. It seems as good a place as any to drown in a sea of self-pity... so I follow the signs.

I've been to my fair share of casinos—and racetracks for that matter—but for the first time in my life I am gambling consequence-free. I don't care if I win or lose. The money doesn't mean a thing. The act of gambling is just a means of wallowing, and surrounding myself with those who would be obsessing over a horse race on a Friday at Noon.

Despite my current state of mind, the truth is that I have a wonderful life. The greatest wife, the greatest kids, the greatest parents, and a support system of four brothers and six sisters who will do anything for me. But these are the types of things you can't see clearly—or at all—when you're as spent as this.

As I sit at the track, aimlessly betting on random horses, I am aware that something very terrible is happening on the lobby televisions but I ignore it all. I have no room in my mind for any more bad news, so I refuse to look at the TV and continue throwing money away. It is December 14th and I'm catching bits and pieces of some sort of horrifying news from the television. A story is breaking and, as the world is learning about a tragedy of unspeakable proportions, I'm turning my back on the details. I'm focusing only on my own problems today, once again. No room for any more reasons to lose faith in this world.

Ironically this catastrophic day, and the events I am actively ignoring, will ultimately *restore* my faith. It will send me down a new road, with a new mission. All the problems that have brought me to this point will seem irrelevant. It will be the first day of the rest of my life.

William J. Lavin
Captain, Elizabeth Fire Dept.
President, NJ State FMBA

"If you threw your problems in a pile with everyone else's, you would fight to get yours back."

Elizabeth Dwelle Lavin

Ret. Fire Chief Lou Kelly with the Gulf Coast mailbox
connecting the EFD, 9/11 and Hurricane Katrina

Chapter One

Introduction

L ike so many other stories that have been told over the past 15 years, this one begins on September 11, 2001.

• • •

Just about four years to the day I was elected President of the New Jersey State Firefighters Mutual Benevolent Association, I drove the fifteen minutes from home to my office in Rahway, NJ. It was your average Tuesday—actually, better than average—sunny and clear and no sign of summer ever ending.

I was in a meeting with my good friend and colleague Larry Petrillo when the first plane hit the World Trade Center. We then watched on television as the second plane hit, and the towers fell one after the other. Larry's wife, Gail, was at work in the Security Exchange Commission Building which lies directly underneath where One and Two World Trade had just gone down. He had no idea if she was dead or alive. We stood next to each other in stunned silence. (Thankfully she survived.)

At that point, pretty much everyone in America was asking themselves the same question: What do I do now? Well, it is the very nature of a firefighter to rush towards an emergency—which runs contrary to a normal human being's instinct to flee. So I, like just about all my brother and sister firefighters in the area, and many nationwide, began making my way towards New York City. I stopped to see my wife and kids to say goodbye.

The first step was to grab my gear and go to the headquarters of my department in my home city of Elizabeth, NJ. Many other guys were beginning to show up, wondering what we could possibly do to aid in the unthinkable fight our FDNY brothers were now engaged in at Ground Zero. Instead of waiting for some orders to deploy, Deputy Chief John Syers and I got into his pick-up truck. We loaded up and headed towards a firehouse in the Red Hook section of Brooklyn, where Chief Syers happened to know some of the guys.

We spent the night riding out of Red Hook, which sits at the entrance of the Brooklyn Battery Tunnel just across from Lower Manhattan. It was all-hands-on-deck for the FDNY responding to the World Trade Center, so Red Hook was left unprotected. The firehouse was relatively empty. So a handful of us from New Jersey (guys from Plainfield and Springfield as well) filled in for the time being.

The tradition in the fire service is that no man is ever left behind. So the idea was for us out-of-towners to fill in at the firehouses while the New York firefighters went to the World Trade Center to, for better or worse, bring back their own. It did not work out quite that way. Television reports from Ground Zero continuously showed emergency responders showing up from other cities and states, working on the pile. All the while, some FDNY were ordered to stay at the firehouse and ride "shotgun" and assist out of town companies. They just wanted to go and get their own brothers.

• • •

The public's response to the incident was immediate and over-whelming. Our job became less about firefighting that night and more about collecting donations. People began showing up at the firehouse to bring food, water, clothes, supplies, anything and everything they had to give. The firehouse was completely full of donated goods well before dark. New Yorkers (and Americans) were coming together quickly, rallying for the emergency responders and searching for any way to pitch in.

But I will never forget the other segment of the public who came by the firehouse that night. They weren't there to drop off food or bottled water, but to check on their husbands and fathers and sons who were on duty when the planes hit. They wanted to know where they had gone or if we had heard anything. Nothing had been confirmed at that point of course, but we had a pretty good idea the news was not going to be good.

What do you tell someone at a time like that? Wait? Pray? Everything will be alright? It's impossible to know. Ultimately, many brother firefighters from that Red Hook firehouse had given their lives at the World Trade Center that morning.

It is strange to think of the things you can clearly recall. I don't remember when I returned home from New York City that week, or who I saw or spoke to first. But that night in Red Hook I do remember seeing a car speeding down the street with no tires. Just the rims grinding across the road, sending sparks in every direction. That's certainly something you don't see every day—but it just seemed to confirm the surreal world we were now living in.

We didn't sleep a wink the night of September 11th. Few Americans did, I'd imagine. All night long, we sat up listening to the fighter jets screaming overhead, protecting the airspace above New York City.

• • •

The following morning, Chief Syers and I were deployed to Lower Manhattan to aid in the ongoing search and rescue operations at what used to be the World Trade Center (already regularly referred to as "Ground Zero"). We went over and found unimaginable destruction. It was like there was a blizzard, a white-out of dust and dirt and smoke. We met up with a few crews from Elizabeth who had been sent over from Jersey with our trucks, equipment, etc.

Much of the FDNY's leadership, needless to say, was in complete chaos. The FDNY's leadership, their top brass, had been killed in the collapse of the first tower.

To illustrate the level of confusion at the scene... At one point a Battalion Chief from FDNY walked up to me and said, "What do you need me to do?"

What do *I* need *him* to do?! Here is a high-ranking officer on his own turf and I'm just a firefighter who's not even in his own state. And he wants to know what I need him to do?

That really sums up the atmosphere, I think. Everyone was ready and willing to do anything and everything to help, but the situation was so alien—and the devastation so widespread—that no one was quite sure exactly what to do or how to do it. The landscape was so surreal that it was hard to get a handle on where you even were. That first day was a complete scramble to get to, and rescue, survivors.

During that initial shift on the pile I remember seeing a giant, round object standing prominently amongst the rubble. It didn't occur to me to even think about what the object was as I stood and worked next to it—not until my memory was jogged weeks later by a news report telling about the landing gear from one of the planes being found mostly intact. It was a massive wheel that I'd seen and stood in the shadow of. That wheel was supposed to have landed in Los Angeles. Not in Lower Manhattan, smoldering next to me.

It was all an out-of-body experience. Almost like a weird dream where you remember snapshots of it, but you can't quite piece it all together. In the moment you are not even sure it's really happening. Nothing made sense. I don't know when that shift ended, or who told me to stop working, but that night I slept in the back of a bread truck that happened to be parked on a nearby street.

There was no set schedule or plan, so you just kind of worked until you were exhausted, fell asleep somewhere, then got up and did it all over again.

The Elizabeth Fire Department, myself included, responded in assistance of the FDNY for basically the next two months. Throughout that time, while dealing with a crisis, I got to see the very best come out of people. There were heroic efforts a thousand times over. Emergency responders working tirelessly for days and weeks on end, never asking for a breather. Volunteers helping out in every way imaginable, collecting food, water, clothes, supplies. The general population couldn't give their blood fast enough.

· · ·

Throughout my life, I have always felt guilt about never having served in the military. I used to go to events, whether it be for Veterans Day or something else around the city, and would feel inferior to all those who were being celebrated. I was extremely close to enlisting after high school to follow in my brother Bob's footsteps. Ironically he, who was a Navy veteran, was the one who discouraged me from going through with it the most.

Shortly after the 9/11 attacks my brother Bob, a Battalion Chief in our department, said to me, "Don't ever feel bad again about not serving in the military. This is as bad as it gets."

This coming from a guy who had been in Vietnam—and talked me out of joining the armed forces because of his experience—tells you all you need to know about what emergency responders went through in the wake of 9/11. It was hell. But at least the public appreciated the effort. For a little while anyway… But none of it changes the fact that I still wish I had served in the armed forces. I continue to hold veterans and all who serve our country in the highest regard.

• • •

In the eyes of the public, the attacks on September 11th certainly magnified what the job of firefighter (or police officer, or EMT) is really all about. Goodwill towards men was at an all-time high, and this was certainly the case with the fire service. Literally hundreds of families of New York City firefighters and civilians had been devastated by the 9/11 attacks. So, from my perspective as state union president, we turned our attention to fundraising for them.

In the days and weeks following the attacks, the NJFMBA, our guys on the Jersey side of the Lincoln Tunnel—at a department now known as North Hudson Regional Fire & Rescue—spent hours walking up and down the rows of stopped traffic with their boots. The drivers, upon seeing firefighters who had responded to the World Trade Center, were more charitable than ever before. All told, those few guys alone raised more than a million dollars with their boots.

And this was the sort of thing going on all across New Jersey, and across America I'm sure. Firefighters banded together to raise money with spaghetti dinners, coin tosses, 5K races, you name it. All geared towards giving as much support as we possibly could to the families of the fallen heroes.

. . .

"We Will Never Forget" was the mantra of the time. But I guess 'never' is a strong word, because in terms of the fire service's relationship with the community—and the government in particular—they would forget rather quickly. As the state union president, I had a unique and front-row seat for this. Firefighters (and police officers, EMS workers, and all the rest) were no longer asked 'How can we thank you?' Fewer than six months later, the question had become 'How much can we take back?'

This became most evident when the economy took its downward turn. Some of the politicians who had posed for pictures with us showed that they actually cared very little. We were made the scapegoats of the government's incompetency with money. We were now portrayed as greedy and lazy and sucking the public dry to line our own pockets. They tried and lobbied (and in some cases succeeded) to take away what they could from our health benefits, our sick time, and our pensions. Meanwhile we had paid our fair share—both in financial contributions and sacrificing our bodies and health—all along.

I guess September 11, 2001 just served to highlight the duplicity of the politics involved. The job never changed, but going from heroes to liabilities really showed the true colors of a lot of people. And the colors were, in many cases, not pretty at all.

But this story, ultimately, is one that proves love always wins.

. . .

It was one single act of love that first put the wheels in motion to affect so many. One act of kindness—from a distant part of the country—that is still echoing to this very day.

One of our Captains in Elizabeth, Jay Rice, has a niece who is a schoolteacher at North Bay Elementary School in the small coastal town of Bay St. Louis, Mississippi. In the aftermath of 9/11, another teacher, Jackie Wintruba and her class were looking to do something patriotic and positive to cheer up some of the first responders who had worked at Ground Zero.

So they decided to build a mailbox, and decorated it as if it were an American flag flying high on a flagpole. The mailbox came stuffed with all sorts of messages from the kids—drawings, letters, pictures—all with the simple goal of brightening our days.

Jackie had the mailbox delivered as a gift to the Elizabeth Fire Department. It was forwarded to Chief Lou Kelly, the head of the department at the time.

Right around this time, a brand new fire headquarters was being built on Irvington Avenue in Elizabeth. So Chief Kelly had the idea to prominently display the mailbox from Mississippi in the front office, and it was in place and accepting mail when the building was officially dedicated later that year.

· · ·

For the next four years or so, that mailbox simply became part of the landscape. You walked passed it when you visited the Chief's office. It served as a friendly reminder that someone out there cares. That what you're doing doesn't always go unnoticed. The cards and letters from those kids were also hung up in the firehouse.

Then, in late August of 2005, the mailbox—and all those cards and letters—took on a whole new meaning.

I'm not sure who put two-and-two together, but as Hurricane Katrina hit and became the single most devastating storm in world history, we realized that the friends who had reached out to us in the time of our greatest need were now in tremendous need themselves. Where was Bay St. Louis, Mississippi? Was this school okay? Were these kids okay?

We needed to find answers to these questions as fast as possible. And we needed to find a way to return the great favor they had done for us if at all possible.

Katrina devastates America's Gulf Coast

CHAPTER TWO

Hurricane Breakfast

All I had to do was glance at a map of Mississippi to know that the place where our one-of-a-kind mailbox originated from had taken a direct hit. The small town of Bay St. Louis, Mississippi was—to borrow a 9/11 phrase—at Ground Zero of the Hurricane Katrina devastation. I couldn't help but wonder if the very same teachers and students, who had been so kind to reach out to us in 2001, were flooded… or homeless… or injured… or worse. The images on all the news channels were painting a bleak picture to say the least.

Like most of the country, we focused our energy on raising funds for the Katrina victims. Through several different channels, we sought out information on our special friends at North Bay Elementary. Their homes, their school, their entire town—all of it completely turned upside-down and washed away. Many were living in FEMA trailers (and still would be years later). Some just left the area entirely to be with family in other cities and states. There was simply nothing of theirs left to stay for.

North Bay Elementary would, after some scrambling, resume classes inside a network of trailers parked on an empty stretch of land. Debris dominated every landscape. Life, clearly, would go on… but it would also never be the same again.

• • •

In the months following Hurricane Katrina, the New Jersey gubernatorial race was heating up. Political campaigns spend an obscene amount of money under normal circumstances, but in this particular race the dollar amounts were even more exorbitant. Here you had Americans on the Gulf Coast enduring inhuman conditions and struggling to survive, and all the while two multi-millionaires are throwing away gobs of money on ads to slander one another. To top it off, the 2005 New Jersey Governor's race featured my personal friend Jon Corzine as the Democratic candidate. Jon, a one-time Chairman and CEO of Goldman Sachs, was not shy about spending his own personal wealth to get his political message across. By the time it was all said and done, Corzine and his opponent (Republican Doug Forrester) had collectively spent over $73 million on the gubernatorial campaign that fall.

Considering the crisis the Gulf Coast was facing, I spontaneously reached out to Senator Corzine and asked if he would like to throw some of that money at a better cause. He was more than willing to help out.

So we put together an event called the "Hurricane Breakfast", a formal banquet-style affair to raise as much money as we could. The event was a great success, raising roughly $150,000 for Katrina relief. Much of the credit for this goes to Senator Corzine who not only sponsored the event, but brought in many donations on his own.

The one thing I remember most about that Hurricane Breakfast, however, was the personal generosity that Senator Corzine demonstrated. At the end of the event, Jon pulled me aside and said, "Here Bill, I want you to add this to whatever we raised today."

He had handed me a single check, folded in half. It was from him, personally, and made out to the amount of $250,000. So here I was, holding a quarter of a million dollars in my hand. For me, that is a dizzying amount to just fold back up and stuff into your pocket. He asked that I keep the donation anonymous.

Jon Corzine was perhaps the most misunderstood politician I ever met. He was one of the nicest people you would ever want to know in private, a true gentleman, extremely generous, and an all-around good guy. For whatever reason he was unable (or unwilling) to show that side of himself to the public. I have no doubt that things would have turned out different politically for him if everyone knew the kind of guy he really is. His humility as a man was actually a negative for him as a politician.

· · ·

So, all told, we now had $400,000 to donate to the overall Hurricane Katrina relief cause, but were not sure exactly where it would do the most good. At the time, my friend and colleague with the NJ State FMBA, Brian McGorty, was a great influence on me. While he served in many titles and on many committees, my unofficial title for him was the "Conscience of the Organization". He has always been a great ambassador for our union and for all firefighters, very disarming with his friendly manner and unmistakable gravelly voice.

Brian had done a lot of work personally with the group "Save The Children". They are an international non-governmental organization that promotes children's rights and provides relief and support to children both at home and abroad. We were looking to do something special for the kids of Bay St. Louis who had been so kind to us in the wake of 9/11. So Save The Children seemed to be the ideal partner for us in getting this money spent the right way.

· · ·

Through our contacts at the school and the team that "Save The Children" already had on the ground in Mississippi, we were invited to tour the Gulf Coast and visit North Bay Elementary. The devastation we witnessed throughout Louisiana and Mississippi that weekend was unbelievable. There were entire blocks, entire communities really, that were completely wiped away. No debris, no nothing. In many cases, just a concrete set of steps were left as a tombstone-like marking of where somebody's home once stood.

This was six months after Hurricane Katrina had made landfall, but it might as well have been six hours. The people, those who were still there, were in despair. A wall of water had come and gone and left them basically with nothing. The storm victims, by this time, had realized that FEMA was not in any way prepared for a storm of this magnitude. Clearly no one was coming to save the day.

The people could not have been more appreciative of our fund-raising efforts back in New Jersey. But by the time we made our way down to visit the teachers and students at North Bay Elementary, it was clear to me that $400,000 was going to be just a drop in the bucket compared to what was going to be needed. So I sat down to talk with Jackie Wintruba and Tammy Raymond, two teachers at the school and two of the most dedicated people I've ever met. And I asked them what else we could possibly do to help.

The answer was clear to them: They needed a playground. There was nowhere for the children to go. Nowhere safe where they could run around, and laugh, and play, and… be kids. Everywhere you went on the Gulf Coast, the landscape was covered with varying degrees of wreckage. Lots of gravel, glass, garbage, and an assortment of debris that the water drove in from God knows where. There wasn't even a nice green patch of grass for kids to play on. The land itself was still a menacing reminder of the storm. The overall feeling you took away during our visit was that there appeared to be an absence of life. No birds, no dogs, no sounds of nature, nothing growing—just a vacuum.

So we resolved to build them a playground. Something not only for the kids to play on, but also to serve as the symbol for a comeback. A rallying-point and a sign that good things will happen here again. And that symbol, that something good, could seemingly pop right out of the ground.

• • •

By the time our work had come to an end on Mississippi's Gulf Coast, we had logged two trips down to the area and left behind three beautiful, brand new playgrounds. One each in Bay St. Louis, Lakeshore, and Pearlington. They were the first fully handicapped-accessible playgrounds in the history of the State of Mississippi. We had certainly left our mark on the landscape down there. But it's nothing compared to the mark that the experience left on all of those who went and built.

Through each trip and each build there was an unexplainable sense of camaraderie every which way. Between the workers and volunteers, between the volunteers and the residents, between the children and their shiny new hangout. Unbreakable bonds were formed and great memories were made, all of it symbolized by the playgrounds themselves and the kids that have grown up on them ever since.

Thinking in terms of being State Union President back in New Jersey, I was used to dealing with complaints from firefighters. About their job, or their pay, or how they were being mistreated and short-changed and worked too hard. These playground builds were a refreshing distraction. The harder the volunteers were asked to work, the more they thanked me for letting them be a part of it.

One night we worked well into the night in Lakeshore, setting up floodlights so cement could be poured and left to set overnight. The work had begun at 8:00 that morning, but the volunteers had gotten a second wind, and then a third, and then a fourth…

Around 11 PM we shut down the lights and the work was done. Guys were caked in mud, sweaty, cement dust in their eyes and noses and mouths. It was January so the temperature was in the 30s, but nobody seemed to notice. They were kids playing on a playground of their own and gave the kind of effort that no paycheck could ever inspire.

After a good 14–15 hour building shift, the crew headed across the street to a local watering hole. A well-earned reward was in order. It is said that a man working outdoors feels more like a man if he can have a bottle of suds. How true that is. The reverie was at a fever pitch that night, with our New Jersey firemen celebrating alongside the local crowd. Buying each other drinks, an arm draped around the next guy's shoulder, a slice of Americana in every sense of the word. They told us their Katrina war stories and thanked us. We told them it would be okay and that we were with them.

The country music was blaring throughout the bar, which is not something that you come across very often in New Jersey. But we were fully assimilated by then. We were all Mississippians. We had all been victimized by the hurricane as Americans.

Then, somebody cut the music.

A young man, probably in his early thirties, announced that he had something to say. He was clearly not a public speaker and told us as much, but we heard him loud and clear that night. He expressed his thanks to us as only he could. He tearfully said he had lost his home, was in the process of rebuilding, and was so happy that his children would have a place to go while they recovered. He was in disbelief that it had all been done by a group of guys from New Jersey who he had never seen before and, after that weekend, would probably never see again.

Then he raised his glass and promptly threw back his whiskey. We all cheered him and did the same. Hugs all around.

This spontaneous moment, in a nutshell, was the true reward. So when people labeled this project as a selfless act of charity, the other volunteers and I know the truth. And the truth is that building playgrounds for the victims of Hurricane Katrina was the most selfish thing we had ever done. Primarily because it was US who were receiving far more than we were giving.

CHAPTER THREE

Katrina Comes Home

We flew home from New Orleans on a freezing cold Sunday morning in January, back from what would be our final Gulf Coast playground build. It was Championship Sunday in the NFL and we all rushed home to root for our new favorite team, the New Orleans Saints. We hoped they would continue their storybook run to the Super Bowl while inspiring the entire region in the recovery and rebuilding effort. Unfortunately, the Saints would get crushed by the Chicago Bears that day. (They would ultimately win it all a few years later.)

The exhausted gang of Mississippi playground builders was back in their New Jersey homes and settled in for a long, long winter's nap. And life just sort of… went on.

A unique bond was formed between the volunteers who had spent those weeks in Mississippi. Every time we would see each other—at a meeting, convention, barbecue, parade—we would reminisce about how great it all was. And we would talk about going back down, or doing another playground, or building something somewhere else. We were looking for another way to recapture that Mississippi magic, but nothing ever seemed to come to fruition. Maybe those three builds were just the ideal 'lightning-in-a-bottle' situation? It certainly seemed that way.

. . .

As the weeks turned into months, and months into years, the talk turned away from playgrounds and charitable efforts. We came all the way back to the drudgery of day-to-day life—where complaints were in abundance and friendship (particularly in political circles) was at a premium.

By the time our Mississippi project wrapped up in 2007, the worm had begun to turn against firefighters... and police officers... and just about anyone whose line of work was serving the public. Long forgotten were the heroes of September 11th and the synergy that had formed between citizens and those who were sworn to protect them. With the economy and general 'goodwill towards men' tanking drastically, we were starting to be seen as nothing more than a superfluous expense. A drain.

The same government officials who had made flowery, patriotic speeches about our heroism and service only a few years ago were now looking to take back anything they could. As long as it meant keeping them in office and padding their bottom line. Health benefits, pensions, manpower—the necessary safeguards of performing such a hazardous job were now considered excessive. And they would cast us as "greedy" and come after all of it.

All of this came to a head in November 2009 when the citizens of New Jersey elected Chris Christie as their Governor.

After penning a letter to all police and firefighters about how he would never touch their pensions or benefits, he wound up spearheading a campaign to do exactly that. He pitted middle-class New Jerseyans against one another in order to protect the wealthy. Cutting into our health benefits would mean not having to tax millionaires any further, and would subsequently boost his profile within his own party. He vilified all public workers, dismissed our unions as greedy, and even (through his sycophantic minions) called ME names that are too lewd for me to put in print.

Suffice to say that the stress of dealing with this situation was rapidly bringing me to a low point in my life. As I tried to advocate for my members and somehow educate the public on what was really going on, I had the highest-ranking (and most vocal) government official in our State berating me and anyone who dared take our side. This is when you find out who your real friends are and who is going to turn tail and switch sides when the chips are down.

As it turned out, at that time I didn't have as many real friends in government as I thought. Many of those who we had supported as a union, and many of those who I considered to be solid on a personal level, did not hesitate to jump ship. There was no shortage of folks ready and willing to bow down and kiss the ring of Governor Chris Christie.

But all of that is neither here nor there. Volumes have been written about the evil of politics (in New Jersey especially) and there will be more to come. Suffice to say that I was in an extremely frustrated, bitter, and disillusioned state by the end of 2012.

• • •

I had seen first-hand what Hurricane Katrina had done to the Gulf Coast. But on October 29, 2012, a Katrina-like catastrophe landed right on our doorstep in the form of Superstorm Sandy. Instead of watching the devastation on television, this time all I had to do was look out the window—or get a report from a friend or family member—to get a sense of what a Superstorm like this could really do.

Tons of help was needed throughout New Jersey, especially in our shore communities. Homes were destroyed, fires raged, roads were wiped out, people were left without power, and entire towns were inaccessible to emergency services due to the devastation. In many cases firehouses were completely destroyed. And where they were still standing, there was no one left in the area to man them. It was utter chaos.

So, like we always do when an emergency hits, the fire service sprang into action. More accurately, the New Jersey State Firefighters Mutual Benevolent Association, and its magnificent 5,500 members sprang into action.

One of the programs the NJFMBA started immediately was called "Adopt a Local Community". We had the more inland fire departments—ones with significantly less storm damage—essentially "adopt" one of the coastal communities that were completely over-whelmed with the recovery effort. For instance, Elizabeth and Linden Firefighters responded almost exclusively to the Point Pleasant area. Vineland and Trenton sent teams to Long Beach Island and Ocean City. And so forth and so on.

The majority of the efforts had very little to do with firefighting or even providing support for the actual departments at the shore. It was a lot of pumping out basements of peoples' homes, ripping out sheetrock, removing debris. We also transported tons of sup-plies—including food, water, and clothing—to the local communities and the temporary shelters that were popping up in the wake of the storm. Sometimes we just set up a makeshift soup stand for anyone that wanted to stop by and get a hot meal. With no fuel or electricity available in most places, a hot meal was not necessarily easy to come by at this point.

My job as President of the NJFMBA, the largest organized body of firefighters in New Jersey, I felt, was to place the resource with the need. Mostly people just needed cash—which is king in an emergency like this. So we did a lot of fundraising and tried to spread the proceeds around to the places it was needed most.

In some cases, the resources actually sought US out. The best example of this was Teddy Honcharik from the "Fuel Relief Fund". He had traveled to places like Haiti and Turkey and Tokyo after cata-strophic natural disasters, to provide fuel to where it was needed most. So we organized a handful of gasoline distribution events around the tri-state area. We were at a point where peoples' only means of powering their homes was via generators. Not to mention the lack of electricity had rendered any local fuel pumps inoperable.

I spent a lot of time with Teddy—and Joe Lee of the Boston Fire Department—getting fuel to local fire departments and citizens alike. And it's funny how, even when you are giving somebody something for free to try and help, they can still prove to be knuckleheads. You'd have people standing near the truck smoking and getting annoyed when you ask them to put their cigarette out. It's like, do you want gas or do you want to smoke? Most people would kill to get even a gallon of gas at that point.

I was scrambling around the tri-state area in an attempt to coordinate whatever type of relief the New Jersey State FMBA could possibly be a part of providing. My vice-president Bob Brower played a major role in the effort, specifically in the hard-hit town of Sea Bright, on an almost 24-hour basis. I was also trying to make sure my children, my brothers and sisters, and my friends were all taken care of. All the while I didn't have a generator at my own house.

The chaotic weeks that followed Superstorm Sandy were certainly a distraction from my political battles over pensions and benefits and staffing. But the evil shadow of state government was never too far away—at least not in my mind.

While our members toiled away, knee-deep in the flood waters, Governor Chris Christie was all over the television in his famous fleece jacket giving press conferences. He was taking credit for handling the emergency response, and the media cast him as the hero. Meanwhile, the very men whose livelihood he had worked so hard at eroding for the past three years were the boots on the ground. That is as demoralizing as it gets. He would be delivering speeches and hugging the victims while we pumped out their basements and shoveled mud from their houses.

· · ·

The circumstances surrounding Superstorm Sandy—and all that came with it—had me feeling very sorry for myself and frustrated to no end. By the time an unspeakable tragedy struck Newtown, Connecticut on December 14th, I was too out of it to pay attention. I consciously avoided it because I was so wrapped up in my own misery that I couldn't absorb any more. I remember hearing that a school principal had been shot in the foot, but that was about it before I went off the grid.

My mother used to say, "If you threw your problems into a pile with everyone else's, you would be fighting to get yours back." And that saying never rang more true to me than at this point in my life. As down as I was, in reality, I had no problems. My loved ones were all alive and well, and that is all that matters at the end of the day. It is a shame that it took a tragedy of such magnitude to be able to see that clearly, but I guess that is human nature.

• • •

And then, almost out of nowhere, I opened up an email from Chief Lou Kelly with a video attachment. Chief Kelly was one of the frontmen for the Mississippi playground builds and the video was a local news clip from Waveland, MS. Apparently the kids in the area had put together a Christmas toy drive to benefit New Jersey's little victims of Superstorm Sandy. And they were doing it because of the playground they had received six years prior. Help was on the way from our old friends.

One part of the video hit me like a bolt of lightning. It was a little girl, named Karli Coyne, reading a letter to the firefighters who had built her neighborhood playground back in 2007. It read:

Dear New Jersey Firemen:

Thank you so very much for building the same playground I've played on for three years. I know you did a lot to help us during Hurricane Katrina, and now we're helping you. We're sending gifts to you because you sent us a bigger gift. I'm not talking about the playground, I'm talking about the gift of you caring so much about us.

With all the storms and violence and overall despondency hanging over our country, here was a little girl looking to pay it forward in a positive way. And it all began with a playground that had allowed her to feel cared for and recover from Hurricane Katrina.

What if building more playgrounds could help everyone recover and rebuild once again? Maybe we could provide a small window of hope or healing or a symbol of recovery?

CHAPTER FOUR

The First Responders

It was right around Christmastime when the idea first occurred to me.

Building playgrounds in the most storm-ravaged areas had worked in Mississippi. It was a cathartic experience for the builders, a beacon of hope for the town, and a return to some sense of normalcy for the children who would play on it. But in the wake of the Newtown tragedy, I felt like there was a way to give these playgrounds an even deeper meaning. To create an even more profound bond between those who were struggling to cope with what had happened.

In a nutshell, this was my idea: We would build 26 playgrounds in the coastal towns of the tri-state area (New York, New Jersey, and Connecticut) that had been devastated by Superstorm Sandy. Lord knows the playgrounds were a hit in the towns that Katrina had leveled, so we would go with the same formula in our own back yard. The difference would be connecting the playgrounds with the Newtown tragedy as well. The reason we would build 26 is because each of the playgrounds would be built to honor one of the 20 children and 6 adults lost at Sandy Hook Elementary School. Each would be specially built to reflect that person's ongoing spirit. Their favorite color, a specific theme, a location that they would have loved, and so on…

A nice idea, but clearly too crazy to ever work. Or so I was told.

• • •

First I shared the concept with my wife, then my daughter MaryKate, and we kind of kicked around ideas and possibilities. What would the project be called? How could we raise the money? Was it even logistically possible? The particulars were a long, long way from being figured out but I could feel the excitement of something big about to start. I felt a sense of hope and optimism that I hadn't in a while.

I specifically remember being at the Elizabeth Fire Department's 4th-Tour Christmas party. I was excitedly telling the guys about the new idea, and they gave me a kind of look that I was starting to become more and more familiar with. A look that says, "Yeah, ok, great idea… but it's not like it could ever get done". Not long after I ran into the Mayor of the City of Elizabeth, Chris Bollwage, and I shared the idea with him as well. I thought maybe it was something he could support and help us get it off the ground. He basically rolled his eyes, said "Good luck with that", and turned and walked away. (To his credit, he acknowledged his skepticism at an event a year and a half later. Like many others, he thought it was impossible.) Chris Bollwage has been a believer and supporter ever since.

So, as far as motivating others to believe in the project, confidence was not necessarily high.

• • •

It wasn't until I started sharing the idea with the guys who had gone on the Mississippi builds that it started to gain some traction. They had seen first-hand what these playgrounds had done for the victims of tragedy, for their town, and for the builders themselves. The consensus was: We HAVE to do this. We have to at least try. The project, which was just hypothetical at this point, just had too much potential for good to not give it a try. Whether we were able to do all 26 playgrounds… or half that amount… or five… or even just one—we had to go forward.

Although there was not much to go on at this point, we started setting up meetings to try and figure out what could be done. When it came to the firefighters involved, my pitch to them was simple: No matter how badly we are treated—by Governor Christie, our municipalities, politicians, etc.—we have to stay true to what we do and who we are. We have to be there for people in their time of need. We have to be the ones who respond when no one else will. We have to be who we say we are, regardless of the forces trying to tear us down. When all the politics is geared toward dividing people, we can be the ones that unite them. This project was giving me a new focus, a new direction, that I sorely needed.

• • •

Clearly none of this could be put into action without the support of the 26 Newtown families. But how could I get in touch with them? And even if I could, would they embrace it? How would they feel about it? This is where the first of many miracles comes into play.

My mother-in-law, Phyllis Middleton, just so happened to have a relative, Terra Geissler, that was married to Principal Christopher Geissler of the middle school right there in Newtown, CT. She gave me the contact information and I put together a letter outlining the entire concept of what we would like to do. I asked that she get the letter to the local authorities and, in turn, the Newtown families themselves.

That letter was forwarded to Pat Llodra, who was the Newtown selectwoman in charge of filtering the deluge of media requests, gifts, letters, emails, donations, etc., etc. She was essentially the gatekeeper of what would get through to the people that the entire world was trying to reach out to. At the time she received my letter, they were averaging 800 emails a day. The town had taken receipt of over 80,000 teddy bears. My letter was basically a needle in an enormous haystack.

I don't know which of the 26 angels was responsible for this miracle, maybe all of them, but somehow Pat came across my letter and latched onto it. She felt it was something that the families could get behind. It wasn't looking to exploit the story, or politicize it, or throw money at… it was a chance to celebrate the lives of these teachers and children in a way that they would have liked, while at the same time helping others. Pat agreed to forward the letter onto the families and we would wait and see.

• • •

In the meantime (and probably a little prematurely), I began putting the pieces together to actually execute a playground build. Although we didn't quite know if we'd have even one family's blessing to build a playground in honor of their loved one, we needed to get the ball rolling in case they did. But who was going to build the playgrounds? How were we going to pay for them? And where would they go? At this point there were far more questions than answers, so we began tackling them one by one.

I reached out to Giordano Construction—more specifically Toni Giordano and Rich Picerno, the couple who run the business. They had guided the work on one of our Mississippi playgrounds and are a local company I could still get in touch with. When I spoke with Toni, she thought it was a great idea but had doubts about how it could all get done. At the time, she was hurting both personally and professionally. Business was not going particularly great and she had just lost her mother. They were also victims of Superstorm Sandy themselves, having basically lost their bayside home in Toms River, New Jersey.

We held a meeting at the State FMBA offices in January 2013 to set the wheels in motion. I invited anyone and everyone I thought could help get the project off the ground, including Toni and Rich. They were there to lend their building expertise, but soon Toni was standing up and speaking to the group about her own recent struggles. She gave a tearful speech about how the project, and the idea, felt very close to her heart and would have a healing effect for them as well. Toni and Rich decided that Giordano Construction would be going all in on the newly-named "Sandy Ground Project".

The name more or less comes from the names of the school, the storm, the towns, and the word playground itself. You had Superstorm Sandy, Sandy Hook Elementary, the 'sandy' element of the shore towns that were rebuilding… It just seemed to work.

While we were in that initial planning meeting, an email popped up on my phone. It was a response from one of the parents from Newtown—Nelba Marquez-Greene, mother of Ana Grace. I announced this to the rest of the group and an excitement spread throughout the room. It was only our first contact, asking for more information about the project, but it made everything seem all the more real. One parent being intrigued enough to take the time to follow up made our mission seem possible. While we would eventually build Ana Grace's playground, it turned out that Nelba wasn't ready just yet at that point. Many parents weren't, and understandably so. But I'll always remember her as being our first responder.

At the same time we were figuring out HOW to build these new playgrounds, we were also looking into WHERE to build them. One town that seemed to reveal itself as the perfect candidate was Sea Bright, New Jersey. The mayor there, Dina Long, was one of the earliest supporters of The Sandy Ground Project and the need in this community was certainly evident. Sea Bright was one of the hardest-hit shore locations during Superstorm Sandy and they had space for a playground—right on the beach behind the town's firehouse.

• • •

The Sandy Ground idea eventually got to an organization called "Save the Jersey Shore". This group—which was formed to raise funds for communities affected by Superstorm Sandy—was headed by Warren Diamond, the owner of the nationwide American Storage chain. At the time they were discussing putting on a fundraising concert and I was invited to do a presentation for them about our playground project. They were very excited about the idea and agreed to support a playground build in Sea Bright.

At this meeting was a gentleman named Brian D'Antoni. At the time he was a television promoter/developer who was there to lend his expertise in accessing celebrities who could help the fundraising effort. The Sandy Ground idea resonated with him, much like it did with Toni Giordano. He was looking for a way to change his life, to do good for others and in turn do good for his own soul. The idea was close to his heart as well.

I have to give Brian credit for pushing the project forward and urging me to just go to Connecticut and meet the Newtown families face-to-face. He believed in the power and spirit of the playground idea. And if we could only sit down with the people and connect with them on a personal level, they would see the benefit of it as well.

So we made it our mission to set up meetings with any of the families that wanted to hear more about the project at this point. We would go to them, present the idea, and the decision was theirs for whatever they wanted. Brian and I set up the first two meetings in Connecticut for the same day. While the idea was conceived several weeks earlier, this would turn out to be the day that The Sandy Ground Project was truly born.

We met with Ian and Nicole Hockley—parents of Dylan Hockley—at the Blue Colony Diner off of Route 84 in Connecticut. The location was a two-hour drive from my own home, but I realized I had been there several times before. This diner was a frequent stop on my way to and from the Connecticut Children's Burn Camp where I had volunteered as a counselor the past several summers. I took this coincidence as a sign. I had no idea the diner was in Newtown and only a mile or so from Sandy Hook Elementary School.

Our meeting with Ian and Nicole was tense. It's incredibly difficult to speak to strangers who had just lost their son in such a sudden way. But I would imagine it is nowhere near as difficult as it was for them to talk about it—and they did so with such openness and such grace. They spoke to me about Dylan, what he was like and what he enjoyed most in his life. They also spoke about their surviving son, Jake, who had been Dylan's best buddy and protector. Jake was left feeling helpless. His parents were busy with funeral arrangements (and a hundred other things, I'm sure) and he felt like he didn't have a purpose.

At this point I suggested that he work as the honorary foreman for Dylan's playground build. They loved the idea and loved the project as a whole. They agreed to speak to some of the other Newtown parents about it, and the siblings as the construction foremen became a theme throughout.

Ian and Nicole ultimately did decide that they would like to have a playground built in honor of their son Dylan. But they also wanted to have the playground in a nearby Connecticut town, and they wanted to wait until that was possible. They wanted it to be in a place where they could easily visit it.

I received a text a few hours after our meeting at the Blue Colony Diner. Jake had accepted the job as foreman.

· · ·

Later that same night, I would sit down with the family of teacher Anne Marie Murphy. I was originally scheduled to meet with her husband, Michael, that afternoon but he had gotten held up. So he invited me to his house later that night to meet with him and his children.

This meeting begins the incredible story of Playground #1. It would be the first of 26 playgrounds, 26 stories. Every single one of them a miracle in their own special way.

Two original "Mud Ducks", Brian McGorty and Brian Dolaghan

CHAPTER FIVE

Playground Celebrating the Life of Anne Marie Murphy

Sea Bright, New Jersey

They all sat down and ate London broil, graciously offering me to have dinner with them.

With our afternoon meeting canceled, Michael Murphy invited me into his home that evening to talk about The Sandy Ground Project. He, his son, and three daughters, all seemed very much at ease with Brian and I—two perfect strangers. It was pretty awkward for us at first, but Michael's hospitality and matter-of-fact demeanor made us feel like part of the family before long.

As we got to talking, I found myself awestruck by Michael's remarkable strength in dealing with what had happened. He said that he was, of course, devastated about his wife's death and all that had come with it. But he was very appreciative of the years that he and his wife had together. They loved each other very much and had built a life over the past thirty years. For this reason, he said, he could not compare his pain to that of the other Newtown families. The ones who had lost children. He felt for them and could not imagine what they were going through.

While sitting around the table during that first meeting, I had no idea that Michael had a very serious health issue of his own. He was going through treatment at the time and continues to. When I learned this, he explained to me in a very straight-forward way: "This is what I have and I'm getting all the best treatment I can. If I make it, great. If I don't, we are at least giving it our best try. They are doing all they can for me."

I learned fast that Michael has an uncanny ability for focusing on the silver lining of a situation. He told me a story about how, in the immediate aftermath of the Newtown tragedy, one of the math teachers at Newtown's high school could not handle returning to work and retired prematurely. When he did, Michael's daughter—a budding math teacher herself—was hired to a permanent position in his place. So, in a roundabout way, Anne Marie's death had opened a window for her daughter's career to begin.

You can never truly know how you will react in the face of a tragedy. Whether it's a catastrophic storm, terminal illness, death of a loved one, whatever the case may be. But the best anyone could hope for is to look at things in the way Michael Murphy does. And be the kind of man that he is.

Michael was also kind-of just looking for someone to vent to that night. He told me about how terrible the news media had been to the families in Newtown. One story was particularly bothersome; where a "journalist" deceived his in-laws and made them think he was a friend of Anne Marie's to gain entry to their home. They then used the opportunity to take pictures inside their house. They photographed pictures of her to use for a news story about the Newtown tragedy. Despicable to say the least.

This type of story, when Michael and his family were at their most vulnerable, is the sort of thing that could make a person lose faith in mankind. It can break your spirit and leave you wondering if there is any goodness left in the world. But Michael is not the kind of guy to lose heart. In respect to The Sandy Ground Project, I felt honored that he was even listening to me at this point. Or could trust me enough to support a playground build in his wife's name.

In short, Michael and his children loved the project. They didn't care when it was built or where. They would support it and cherish it and were supremely confident that Anne Marie would have found a playground in her name to be an amazing and fitting tribute. So the stage was set to kick off our project as soon as we could pull it together.

I had pitched the location of Sea Bright, NJ to both the Hockleys and Murphys that first day in Connecticut. Sea Bright was right in the eye of our storm in New Jersey and the administration there—headed by Mayor Dina Long—was very keen on The Sandy Ground Project. Mayor Long had attended many of the initial planning meetings and the need in the town was certainly there.

A crucial component of the entire project comes down to one thing: fundraising. With the first build approaching, we needed a way to quantify each playground in dollars and cents. There were, of course, many variables including: the location, materials of the playground structure itself, labor, shipping, the ground surface (sand/rubber surfacing/etc.), and the list goes on and on. With all of those initial expenses, plus feeding and accommodating the volunteers themselves, we put the number at $100,000 per playground. So all told, if we were going to get all 26 of the playgrounds built, we were going to have to find a way to raise roughly $2.6 million.

In addition to all the money, we also needed to be in communities with an administration that welcomed the project. They would have to accept the playground as a gift, insure it, maintain it, and provide the land. I had done a presentation for the City Council in Sea Bright in a makeshift council chamber set-up. It took place on a basketball court that was now serving as the town's main municipal offices. Just a small sampling of the disarray that Superstorm Sandy had caused.

The council members were enthusiastic about the new playground and the local businesses even came out to help do some fundraising. Needless to say, there were a lot of moving parts involved but I still somehow envisioned all of them coming together… 26 times over.

First thing's first though. The Sea Bright build was a valuable learning experience for the builders and organizers alike…

• • •

Thanks to extremely generous donations from 'Save the Jersey Shore', The RAINE Foundation and the Port Authority PBA, we knew we were ready to move forward with the planning and building of the first playground in Sea Bright. So on March 1, 2013, we held a ceremonial groundbreaking to kick things off. From a fundraising perspective, it was important to get as much press there as possible.

From a spiritual perspective, it was important to hold the ceremony at the break of dawn. This was, after all, a new beginning... The first formal public event for The Sandy Ground Project. The camaraderie was apparent right away.

At sunrise that morning, we had a large crowd gathered at the Sea Bright shoreline. It was a clear, but cold, day—still very much winter at the Jersey Shore. Shortly after sunup, Mayor Long said a few words to welcome everyone to town and thank us for kicking off the project in Sea Bright.

Then, we had 20 local children and 6 teachers, each one representing an angel, line up at the leveled patch of sand where the playground was about to be built. Each of them held a small bucket emblazoned with the name of one of the 26 Newtown angels. One by one, they stepped forward and scooped sand into their buckets and marched together to the waterline.

As fireworks lit up the dawn sky—and a fireboat cascaded red, white, and blue water on the horizon—the children lined up shoulder-to-shoulder facing the ocean. On the count of three they stepped up to the crashing waves and dumped their buckets into the water. Hundreds of onlookers cheered, or cried, or both. It suddenly wasn't so cold out.

This was done to symbolize what we all hoped The Sandy Ground Project would become. That one playground in Sea Bright would be the jumping-off point. And the spirit of healing and recovery, like the sand, would drift up and down the coast. And the playgrounds would sprout up on the shores of New Jersey, New York, and Connecticut.

The only thing missing that morning was the Murphy family. Michael had been going through a tough time with his medical treatments and his children did not want to visit the playground site for the first time without him. He resolved to keep fighting and eventually make it to the ribbon-cutting ceremony that would ultimately open the playground.

• • •

And then the building began. We didn't know whether or not we would all be working together on 26 playgrounds; in the moment we just thought it was cool to do one. The work itself was invigorating and I personally felt like I was finally doing something positive and therapeutic. After being bogged down with politics and all the negativity that goes along with it, this gave me a sense of belonging again. Deep down I knew this project was bringing me back to my roots.

One tradition we began on that first build was customizing the playground's theme to reflect the Newtown angel it was made to honor. In this case, Anne Marie Murphy enjoyed gardening and her dogs. So that first playground was adorned with flowers and some of the volunteers built a garden next to it using the 26 buckets from the groundbreaking ceremony. The structure itself would actually have permanent panels with the likenesses of her dogs etched onto them. This aspect of the build and the playground itself would become vital to the entire Sandy Ground Project. The work—and more importantly the final product—needed to be a tribute to each Newtown angel's spirit. It needed to be a living tribute expressing how they lived and will continue to live and inspire hope.

• • •

From a "nuts-and-bolts" standpoint, this was an extremely frustrating build. We took solace in the fact that this was the first time around and would be a learning experience; plus the reason behind the build kept everyone upbeat and positive. But there were a truly daunting number of questions to be answered and things to sort out.

Questions included, but were definitely not limited to:

Which of the volunteers can perform which tasks?

What kind of drills, bits, tools, etc. do we need?

How many people do we need for each job?

Who can use a screw-gun?

What size auger bit do we need?

Where is the nearest hardware store?

These few examples were only the tip of the iceberg. It was controlled chaos. But when it comes down to it, we were in no rush. It was important that Rich Picerno and his crew from Giordano Construction get a handle on the situation and get it right. We were looking at this build as something we would (hopefully) be doing at least 25 more times. This playground was a building block (albeit a crucial one) in the whole vast configuration of things. The Sandy Ground Project would prove to be a marathon, not a sprint. It took twice as long to build the first playground than it would take for any other.

After about four days of building, a shiny blue and white playground was standing strong amongst the sand dunes of Sea Bright. As we began planning a ribbon-cutting ceremony to officially open the playground to the public, we realized that there was nowhere to stage it and the playground was not easily accessible from the nearby parking lot.

As would become a theme of The Sandy Ground Project, we overcame any obstacle with a potent combination of hard work and the angels watching over us. In addition to the playground, our guys wound up building several hundred yards of brand new boardwalk along the Sea Bright beach. This not only gave us a place to view and access the playground, but it provided even more beachfront infrastructure for the people and businesses in downtown Sea Bright.

• • •

April 6, 2013, was a beautiful sunny day in Sea Bright—not a cloud in the sky, sunbeams sparkling off of the ocean. With Michael Murphy, his children, and many family and friends present, we cut the ribbon opening Anne Marie Murphy Memorial Playground. Speeches were made, church bells rang, bagpipes blared. And at the climax of the morning Michael stood in front of the entrance ramp to the playground, thanked everyone for the honor, and cut the ribbon. Children were running, sliding, and swinging in a matter of seconds.

I would be lying though if I said that everything went perfectly and as-planned. A valuable lesson was about to be painfully taught.

As part of the ceremony, two musicians had asked to play a song they had written to honor the Newtown victims. We agreed to have them perform it that morning, and I was left kicking myself for not vetting the actual song beforehand.

The refrain of the song contained a very negative word—one nobody wanted to hear on such a beautiful occasion—and the lyrics really beat you over the head with it.

"How will we survive the violence, the violence, the violence… How will we survive the violence, the violence, the violence…" and the line kept repeating and repeating and it certainly affected me in a negative way. I was mortified. To be honest I wanted to jump off of the boardwalk and run and hide. The singers were absolutely well-intentioned so I stood there stoically while that word—*violence*—became like nails on a chalkboard. I was cringing inside.

Apparently I wasn't alone in my thinking. During the planning of a subsequent ribbon-cutting, I began to ask one of the mothers if she would like that song performed. Before I could even finish the question, she answered with an emphatic, "No. Absolutely not." She had been in the audience at the first ribbon-cutting in Sea Bright and had herself recoiled when those lyrics were sung.

I wholeheartedly agreed. We live and learn. And the project would be better for it in the long run.

• • •

It was becoming clear that The Sandy Ground Project had an uncanny way of bringing people together. In the aftermath of the ribbon-cutting, a large 'Irish Breakfast'-type celebration was held at a nearby restaurant, Off the Hook—all organized by Karen and Joe Burke. Anne Marie Murphy was one of seven children in her family, and I am one of eleven. That day we were one big happy family and the celebration—that started off as a breakfast—went through the afternoon and into the night. All of us mixed together as brothers and sisters and toasting Anne Marie as one.

Just before the night started winding down, we asked the bartender to put on the CBS Sunday Evening News. At the end of the broadcast, there we were, a whole segment on Anne Marie's playground and The Sandy Ground Project. We all cheered and hugged and toasted this first of many accomplishments together.

With a brand new playground on the beach of Sea Bright opened and ready for business, there was a sense that something was just getting started. Something big. An unbelievably tight brotherhood of volunteers had been born. The emotional high of the ribbon-cutting and subsequent celebration had left everyone eager to do it again (and again… and again…)

We would get our chance very soon, and only a few miles up the coast.

Patti Dickens and Mike Faboozi from the RAINE Foundation

CHAPTER SIX

Union Beach, New Jersey

Perhaps this would be an appropriate moment to reflect on the many heroes and sources of inspiration mentioned, quoted, and described in this book. Many of the sources and examples of strength and trust and wisdom and grace will not be cited. Because while this story will include very personal accounts and delicate moments of pain and grief and sorrow, it will have to omit many others. This is not because any one miracle, or faithful comment, or act of selflessness is any more noteworthy than another. Rather it reflects the promise and commitment of the author and founder of the Where Angels Play Foundation to always, in every instance, place the privacy, concerns, and wishes of the families as our number one priority.

As you will read, the admiration and affection for each and every family member is quite evident. Those mentioned and those unmentioned share the same level of respect and love and the personal wishes of all the families was to be honored from the beginning and continues to this day.

The content of this book reflects those wishes and it is with the very best interest and love of these moms and dads, my heroes, that this book was written and edited.

With that said there are so many remarkable people who will need to be thanked for efforts that were herculean and part of the miracle that is the cornerstone of Where Angels Play and sits at the very core of our ability to bring joy to communities and families in such great need. Like Patti Dickens from the RAINE Foundation and Mike Fabozzi its president. Mayor Paul Smith from Union Beach who's leadership and generosity were incredible. Joe and Karen Burke whose attention to detail were priceless. Some of their personal stories will be left out for privacy sake but were remarkable and noteworthy none the less.

· · ·

In the wake of the playground build in Sea Bright, I began to see The Sandy Ground Project for the major undertaking that it was. And I needed to make it a priority. I was splitting my time between being the project's coordinator/spokesman and my two full-time jobs as State President of the New Jersey Firefighters Mutual Benevolent Association and an Elizabeth Fire Captain. The contrast between the three hats I was wearing made them no longer fit.

On one hand I was spearheading a beautiful, uplifting, charitable project that was restoring my faith in humanity and all things good. On the other hand I was fighting tooth-and-nail for my fellow firefighters against duplicitous New Jersey politicians. This was counter-acting the goodwill I was feeling from The Sandy Ground. For every hug and emotional tear shed with a Newtown family or with our loyal band of volunteers, there was another Senator, Assemblyman, or Governor betraying firefighters, deceiving the public, and turning their backs on our safety.

It was at this point I starting thinking about an exit plan after 16 long years as State Union President. In my heart of hearts I knew I was done. I had lost the desire to deal with the unscrupulous. I wanted to be working alongside angels instead.

· · ·

The small bay-shore town of Union Beach, NJ had taken a shine to the Where Angels Play Foundation—now our organization's official name. It is a close-knit, blue-collar community that was completely leveled by Superstorm Sandy.

The RAINE Foundation, led by Patti Dickens and Mike Fabozzi, took the lead for our playground build in Union Beach. They felt they had the means to raise the funds, a nice spot for the playground, and a community that would embrace it wholeheartedly. We were put in touch with them through Karen Burke who was, and is, an absolutely vital part of The Sandy Ground Project. She is the accountant responsible for managing all of the Foundation's finances and was instrumental in getting us 501(c)(3) status. Karen and her husband Joe are also great friends of mine as well as residents of Highlands, NJ who had lost their home during Sandy. Karen is a pivotal figure in that area and was key in pointing us towards people and places in need during our relief efforts.

The RAINE Foundation had a great location in mind—a waterfront spot that held a firemen's memorial and the ruins of a playground that was destroyed during Superstorm Sandy. Patti Dickens was an especially dynamic force for our Union Beach build and was responsible for garnering the support of the local government and businesses.

With all interested parties on board and enthusiastic about going forward with Playground #2, it was decided that a playground would be more than welcome in Union Beach and constructed at Fireman's Park right on the Raritan Bay.

The playground itself would be in the shape of a large football and its color scheme would be red, white, and blue. New York Giants colors.

The actual build was vastly different from the first one we had done in Sea Bright. Whereas Anne Marie's playground was built right on the beach using the sand as the surface, this style of playground was what we would come to know as a "surface mount" build. It started off with a significant amount of excavation. The remnants from the previous playground needed to be removed and other areas needed to be filled in. We partnered with the Union Beach Volunteer Fire Department, the Union Beach Department of Public Works, and Mayor Paul Smith—all of whom were tremendous in their efforts and generosity towards us.

• • •

After the ground was broken and foundation done, the playground apparatus itself was built on top of it. Once the playground structure was in place, it was finished off with a rubber surfacing covering the ground. This was by far a more challenging and more expensive build than the first one. Yet we were able to get it done in half the time. The volunteers were becoming a more cohesive unit from one minute to the next.

As the playground was going up, a couple who lived in a house in close proximity to the park stopped by. Their home had taken on major damage during Superstorm Sandy. The siding was still ripped off and half the homes around theirs were knocked right off their foundations. We got to talking and they told me that, a few weeks prior, they were all set to pack up their lives and leave Union Beach behind. They felt like there was nothing to stay for and would be better off starting over elsewhere. But the news of the playground—and seeing it come to life right in front of them—had compelled them to change course. They decided to stay. Because Union Beach is their home and it would be coming back better than ever. It was just the playground that helped them to realize it.

Another local resident I spoke to—an older woman from the same neighborhood—had a special, personal connection to the park where our playground was being built. Her husband had spent years and years coming to this very spot every single morning. It was where he had his coffee and read the newspaper; it was where he started his days.

He passed away shortly before Superstorm Sandy hit, and the woman was devastated that his favorite spot was gone. That she could no longer visit it safely. Now, she said, with the new playground going up it was a place that she could visit as it brought joy to others. She knew how happy her husband was, looking down to see his favorite spot restored.

The teamwork and family atmosphere in Union Beach was palpable. They had adopted the slogan "U.B. Strong" in Sandy's aftermath and the people there certainly were. They were in it together. The residents—as well as the business community there—are the salt of the earth, and I cannot say enough about their efforts and generosity. One nearby restaurant—"Jakeabob's"—was scrambling to set up at a new location after the storm damage had crushed their business. But the owner, Gigi, still could not do enough for us. They fed us, raised money, and hosted our celebration dinner. Union Beach knows how to treat its guests.

• • •

On May 4, 2013, the Union Beach playground was officially opened at a beautiful ribbon-cutting ceremony. The New York Giants sent Sean Landeta and David Wilson to represent the organization.

The forecast that morning read: "100% chance of rain". It was supposed to be a total washout. Even Brian D'Antoni, The Sandy Ground Project's unofficial "spiritual advisor", had conceded that we wouldn't be able to pull off the ribbon-cutting and wanted me to postpone it. But I insisted that we move ahead and let the Angels play their part in the festivities. And if it rained, it rained.

Lo and behold, the clouds parted to give us the sun we needed to get through the ceremony. There was literally a hole in the clouds, rain all around, and the sun shining down specifically on the playground. Almost like a Simpsons cartoon where the clouds part and God's voice booms down through a sunbeam. Patty Dickens from The RAINE Foundation put together an amazing ceremony involving the local kids, a dove release, music, and the whole thing went off without a hitch. It seemed like the entire town was there. As we ended the ceremony and the ribbon was cut, it began to rain again. It would pour the rest of the day, and that was fine. The Angels had blessed us and had already saved the day.

With the ribbon-cutting concluded and the Union Beach playground officially open, we gathered up to go celebrate at Jakeabob's—indoors and out of the now-driving rain.

With two playgrounds completed, and planning for a third in the works, I was beginning to see The Sandy Ground Project taking shape down the road. The volunteers—who would soon be known collectively as the "Angels Army"—were getting the bug. They craved the work, they embraced the cause, and the team chemistry was starting to gel. It was incredible to see that something other than money could still be the greatest motivator.

I had also seen the way the families had reacted to opening a playground in their loved one's name. They told me that this was the most fitting tribute imaginable. It was personal. It captured the spirit of how their loved one lived. It was helping others.

But what was the public perception in the towns? Would the neighborhoods embrace the playgrounds? Or would the parents want to avoid a reminder that something bad could happen? Would they get it?

About a week after the ribbon-cutting for our second playground, I had my answer in the form of a beautiful letter from a resident of a nearby neighborhood. The following is an excerpt from that letter.

"The tragedy of Newtown, CT affected me greatly—as it did most of America. It will forever be one of those moments you look back on years from now and still know where you were when you heard the horrible news. I shed many tears, not only for those little (and big) angels but for the families they left behind. So, when the news of the park came up, my first instinct was to avoid it. The park would dredge up such a painful moment, so why do that to myself if there were plenty of other parks to visit?

Then, one day, I saw my girls playing in our backyard on a beautiful spring day. The sun was shining, they were laughing, and life seemed perfect. It dawned on me that this is why The Sandy Ground Project was created—to memorialize all the angels that left us too soon that horrible day. While the event of their death was tragic and heart-breaking, the playgrounds were an opportunity to celebrate their life in such a way that it would bring hours of laughter and enjoyment to both parents and their children.

So, my husband and I packed up both girls and headed to the park. It was late, about 6:30 PM or so, and not many people were there. The first thing I sensed was a feeling of peace and quiet joy. Upon my first look at the park, I knew it was a place that we would return to again and again."

As the letter concluded, I wiped my eyes and thought, "Yes. This is everything we are trying to achieve." People were seeing the true value of the project. They were getting it. I've read the letter a hundred times since. It had become, in essence, the project's Mission Statement.

Mike Candelori surveys build at Union Beach

Catherine's Butterfly Garden

CHAPTER SEVEN

Playground Celebrating the Life of
Catherine Hubbard

Ansonia, Connecticut

I n regards to people "getting" the ultimate mission and reason for The Sandy Ground Project, maybe I got a little bit spoiled with the folks in Sea Bright and Union Beach. The local government, the mayors, and the public works staff—all of them could not have been more helpful or appreciative. No red tape, no bureaucratic mumbo-jumbo. They got it.

The same cannot be said for the Parks & Recreation Department in Staten Island, New York.

. . .

Playground #3 was originally planned to be built in the Midland Beach section of Staten Island. The Port Authority PBA, and president Paul Nunziato who had been extremely active and generous supporters of the project since it kicked off, wanted to sponsor an entire playground on their own. They also expressed a preference for having the build take place within New York City. And Staten Island's shores were hit incredibly hard during Superstorm Sandy. It all seemed to make sense.

I met personally with Borough President James Molinaro and he could not have been more excited for The Sandy Ground Project to take root on Staten Island. In fact, he wanted to have two of our eventual 26 playgrounds built on Staten Island and pledged his full support. However, he did warn me that we would have our hands full with New York City's Parks and Recreation Department. He described them as a very bureaucratic, Byzantine organization. In short, they would prove to be a nightmare for anyone interested in getting anything done.

I have to say, the man knew who he was dealing with.

• • •

Dina Long, the Mayor of Sea Bright, was the ideal partner as far as The Sandy Ground Project working hand-in-hand with local government. Ironically, Adena Long, Commissioner of Staten Island's Parks & Recreation, was the polar opposite. In every conversation we had I was told about a series of approvals, and processes, and this, and that. When I told her we were looking to put up a playground within the next month and a half, she actually laughed at me. Said it would be six months, minimum. Here was someone that definitely did not get it.

It was becoming clear that Staten Island was not going to work for us, at least not anytime soon.

• • •

From the beginning, the Staten Island playground had been earmarked to celebrate the life of Catherine Hubbard. I had met with her mother Jenny one afternoon, along with her son Freddy. Jenny is a very strong, sweet, and spiritual woman whose faith and resolve was remarkably strong in the wake of the tragedy at Sandy Hook Elementary. Jenny spoke with great conviction and frequently about Catherine being in heaven.

Jenny thought the playground was absolutely perfect and told me the story explaining why. The Hubbards had moved across town fairly recently and Jenny described Catherine as being upset about having to leave their old house because of the playground and rope swing in the back yard that she loved so dearly. Jenny took this project as a way for Catherine to get a playground of her own and her beloved rope swing back.

So of course we would work Catherine's rope swing into the plans for Playground #3. In addition, Jenny spoke about how much she cared about animals and loved everything to be pink and purple. They had even established a foundation for a nearby animal sanctuary in her name. And there we had our themes to customize Catherine's playground especially for her.

I knew that Jenny and the Hubbards would be extremely passionate about the project and the upcoming build. The last thing she said before our meeting ended that day was, "How amazing! Catherine is going to get her playground back, and her big brother is going to build it for her!"

Like the others, it was a very difficult and very touching meeting. I cried as I pulled away from their house, but I also had to smile at the thought of Freddy serving as honorary foreman on our third playground build. I was lucky enough to meet him that first day at the Hubbard's place and he accepted the job on the spot. Freddy has such an open, sociable way about him and a desire to create and work with his hands. I had the privilege of meeting him that day because school had closed due to a snowstorm. I just knew his enthusiasm would be infectious when the time came. All of us couldn't wait to get started.

• • •

Right around the time I was reaching the end of my rope in dealing with Staten Island's draconian parks people, I received a random letter from an elementary school principal in Ansonia, Connecticut. His name is Mr. Joseph Apicella and he described his school's playground as being one in dire straits. The wood was splintering. Kids were getting injured on it. It was infested with bees they could not seem to get rid of. Suffice to say it was in rough shape and there was no money available to fix it. They had even started a program to raise money for the playground and—after four years of trying—were still coming up far short of the fundraising goal.

He understood, he wrote, that he was not in a coastal town with any significant storm damage from Superstorm Sandy. But that did not mean his school wasn't in need. He had heard of The Sandy Ground Project and loved the spirit of our mission. So he figured there was nothing to lose by writing us a letter to see if there was anything we could do. I could certainly respect that, as it was my own 'Hail Mary' letter to Newtown that had gotten this program started in the first place.

I forwarded the letter to Jenny Hubbard and further explained the trouble we had been having in Staten Island. She felt that building the playground in Ansonia would be even better. It was very much needed and wanted, had children right nearby there in the school, and its close proximity to Newtown would allow them to visit it more often. It would be the ideal spot.

• • •

I went to Ansonia and met with Mr. Apicella and surveyed the grounds at John G. Prendergast School. I knew immediately that it would be a great fit for Catherine's playground and would be going ahead with it, but I played it cool—as if we were still deciding what to do. Our idea was to show up one morning and surprise Mr. Apicella and the kids, and just start building right away.

So I worked in conjunction with Vice-Principal Sherrod McNeill and the local Department of Public Works and Fire Department—who were all tremendous. Everything set up perfectly and on the morning of the ground-breaking we pulled the trucks in and Mr. Apicella realized his school was finally getting a new playground. It was a lot like the show "Extreme Home Makeover" when they move the bus out of the way and the family flips out. Mr. Apicella was overjoyed and brought to tears, and his 700+ students were all excited to watch the build take shape. (Unfortunately the press got a hold of the news early that morning and may have spoiled the surprise a little bit. But the principal's reaction was still classic.)

• • •

The build itself was, for me, kind of a throwback to the playgrounds we had built in Mississippi after Hurricane Katrina. In the way that the town—and the kids at the school in particular—were present for every aspect of the process. The students kept the workers going with a steady stream of cold drinks, food for energy, and high-fives to keep the momentum going. They were all fantastic and itching to get playing.

It was also a flashback to Mississippi because I was starting to see that we had a die-hard band of volunteer workers that were in it for the long haul. Ansonia is quite a hike for our Jersey guys (unlike Sea Bright and Union Beach) but they were not deterred in the least. They worked late into the night in Ansonia, headed home to sleep, then would be back first thing the next morning raring to go.

The workforce had been a concern of mine going into the Ansonia build, but from that point on I would never have to worry about it. The self-proclaimed "Angels Army" was born in Connecticut that week. A loyal, playground-building band of soldiers who would march together anywhere they were needed.

The Angels Army took their cue from Freddy Hubbard on that first Connecticut build. He brought his own loaded tool belt and take-charge attitude and truly inspired the crew. Freddy was involved with every aspect of the construction—digging, measuring, drilling, anything you could think of. To date he is probably the most dynamic foreman The Sandy Ground Project has ever seen.

• • •

There were many special moments during that Ansonia build, but one in particular sticks out in my mind. Since we were in Connecticut for the first time, and not too far from Newtown itself, a lot of the mothers who had also lost children at Sandy Hook came out to support Jenny Hubbard. Some of whom I hadn't even had the chance to meet with yet.

I saw them all just being themselves, drinking coffee and sharing a light moment together. Even if just for a day, or a few minutes, they were distracted with a positive project. They were simply enjoying a nice spring morning outdoors. It was heartening to witness this from afar and think that this playground was already serving its ultimate purpose.

. . .

Work-wise the build was extremely tough. Wherever we drilled we seemed to run into a layer of rock called "ledge" which is very difficult to penetrate. Because of the ledge-factor it made for a long, laborious job for the volunteers. We had to bring in jackhammers, pry-bars, poles, anything we could to break through. Yet, the harder the job was, the more positive the workers became. Eddie Donnelly (who would eventually succeed me as State FMBA President) commented after a jackhammer shift that he never felt so tired, yet so great about what he was a part of.

Another work-site conversation, this one with a Port Authority Police Officer, made me realize that there were a lot more than 26 families who had been impacted by the Newtown tragedy. His daughter was in her classroom at Sandy Hook Elementary School that day and survived. He was there to work for Catherine and the Angels, but for his daughter as well.

With the local fire department illuminating the darkness with their floodlights, we worked tirelessly into the night. The rubber surfacing was being poured and set first thing the next morning, so we HAD to finish, ledge or not. When it was all said and done, the work wrapped up around midnight. All the volunteers took a deep breath and enjoyed a cold one together under the lights.

. . .

May 31, 2013, was the day we would cut the ribbon and open Catherine's playground. It featured her favorite colors (purple and pink) and imprints of all the best animal drawings she had done at school; as well as a butterfly garden and a panel with an ark loaded with all kinds of animals. Mr. Apicella and every one of his students were there, eagerly awaiting the opening of their brand new playground.

We purposely planned the event for a Friday, a school day, so that the kids could be there to play as soon as possible.

Jenny Hubbard addressed the students and everyone in attendance that day. I remember thinking what amazing strength it must take for a mother to address all these children with such a positive message after losing one of her own. She told the crowd about Catherine and how her presence was definitely being felt that day. This playground was a gift from her.

She also gave everyone a bit of advice and quoted Catherine's principal, Dawn Hochsprung. The message was simple: Be kind. Be good to one another. And if you love someone, never hesitate or waste an opportunity to let them know about it. And no matter what, remember that everyone loves you.

We had arranged for a fly-over message to be displayed via airplane during the ribbon-cutting. It circled the playground and read: "TO PRENDERGAST… LOVE, CATHERINE".

The ceremony concluded with a huge balloon release that filled the clear blue sky with white balloons. Several minutes after the balloons were released, there was still one specific balloon that seemed to be hanging around while the kids played. It was just kind of bobbing around low in the breeze, having a look around.

More than one person pointed out this last balloon and stated matter-of-factly that it symbolized Catherine. She was having a look at her new playground. Just meandering throughout the grounds and not wanting to leave quite yet. We all were watching this with a sense of awe. It was a balloon after all. And yet it was so much more than that.

A few minutes later, it just up and floated away.

• • •

As we departed Ansonia it was clear that the Angels Army was itching for another build. There was no denying their energy and friendship. Everyone, I'm sure, had their own personal reasons for dedicating themselves so fully to The Sandy Ground Project. And all those reasons were intertwining and building like a ball of fire.

They came, they built, they gave of themselves, and left John G. Prendergast School with a new playground compliments of Catherine.

Catherine's story and Jenny's remarkable speech would serve as a vital part of our future presentations to families in need of hope and inspiration. There is no way to overstate the impact this beautiful little red-haired Angel continues to have on the Where Angels Play Foundation and everyone who would eventually benefit from it.

CHAPTER EIGHT

Playground Celebrating the Life of Dylan Hockley

Westport, Connecticut

Jake Hockley was the inspiration for one of the more fun and touching aspects of The Sandy Ground Project: the honorary foreman. He had lost his brother and his parents were mourning a son. Dylan was the light of their lives.

During my initial meeting with Ian and Nicole Hockley that centered on building a playground to honor Dylan, they spoke about his brother's struggles with all that had gone on. He felt like there was nothing for him to do. No role to play in the family. He had been Dylan's protector before, and now he just felt lost.

That's when it occurred to me to make him the foreman, charged with leading the Angels Army in building a playground for Dylan. His parents loved the idea, as did he. So much so that they declined being involved in The Sandy Ground Project's first build in Sea Bright. For Jake's sake, and their own desire to frequent Dylan's playground when it was done, they decided to wait until a town in Connecticut near their own was available.

That opportunity would reveal itself at Playground #4.

• • •

It is fair to say that Westport, Connecticut, is not a community in need. Far from it actually. It also didn't suffer all that greatly from Superstorm Sandy. But that does not mean the playground wouldn't serve its purpose and then some.

The Hockley's home sits only a half-hour drive from Westport, so they were thrilled at the possibility of Dylan's playground being built close (but not too close) to Newtown. Also, Dylan was an autistic child and Westport is well-known for being progressive in its advocacy for autism awareness. (It is where St. Vincent's Behavioral Health Services is based.) All things considered, Westport was the way to go.

• • •

Our contacts and supporters in Westport certainly helped things along as well, and it reassured us that we had made the right decision.

We had a great support system there, led by Bob Kepchar of the Westport Fire Department. I had known Bob through my work as a fellow counselor at the Connecticut Children's Burn Camp. He is a great supporter of The Sandy Ground Project and arranged for us to put-up about 15 to 20 members of the Angels Army at the fire department's dormitories. They not only housed, but *fed* our troops during their stay in Westport. All in all, I can't say enough about the generosity of the Westport Fire Department and its firefighters. They hosted and helped with subsequent builds in neighboring areas as well.

• • •

Much like in Ansonia, it was determined that Dylan's playground would be built on school grounds. This time it would be Long Lots Elementary School of Westport. Both the kids and teachers turned out to be staunch supporters of our efforts and a vital source of motivation to ramp up the construction process. It was getting to be mid-June by the time we pulled our trucks into town, so there was a slight sense of urgency to get these kids their playground before school let out for the summer.

When you're building on school grounds—like in Mississippi, Ansonia, and now at Long Lots—the students and teachers become an inspiration AND a support system. They take you in, bring drinks, bake cookies, cheer you on; it creates a positive dynamic like nowhere else.

Also, the parents of the students at Long Lots Elementary took on a starring role in regards to fundraising for The Sandy Ground Project. Led by PTA President Lauren Goodman—who was a driving force on many fronts of our Westport build—they were able to raise over $11,000 for our cause.

Dennis Monk of the Westport Kiwanis was also a huge asset when it came to fundraising and drumming up support throughout the community. And as I had never led such a widespread charitable effort as The Sandy Ground, I was beginning to see that these were the types of people I would have to identify and count on in town after town. The Dennis Monks and Lauren Goodmans of the world are invaluable—for this project, of course, and in their community all year around.

• • •

Dylan Hockley loved butterflies, chocolate, and the color purple. So his playground was designed with those things in mind—from the color scheme to the actual shape the playground structure was outlined in. We wanted to create a place that captured Dylan's spirit and, with the help of Ian and Nicole, we were able to come up with a design to accomplish just that.

In a Sandy Ground first, there was a significant amount of rain on the first day of construction. It was the first time we had ever had to pause to let the weather take its course, and I was frustrated by this. "This project is supposed to be blessed," I thought. "What is going on here?"

With the work stopped, I got to talking to Ian and he mentioned how—being from England—this was the sort of weather he had come to expect on an everyday basis. We laughed about it and chalked it up to the Angels wanting him to feel at home on Dylan's playground.

As the work finally got going again, that is when Jake took charge as foreman. Normally a very quiet and reserved kid, Jake jumped into his foreman duties with both feet (and a handful of his friends from school). He was involved in so many of the physical components of the build, his favorites being operating the Bobcat and tractor, and took great joy in it. The Hockleys were elated to see him flourish on the build. The Sandy Ground Project seems to have a way of not only bringing people together, but bringing individuals out of their shells.

. . .

As the building progressed, I was observing Jake's grandmother— Terry—proudly watching him come into his own. Until that time, it had never crossed my mind to get a grandparent's perspective on all that was going on. What did they make of our project? And, more importantly, how were *they* doing?

I spoke with Terry for a good while and the conversation really struck a chord with me. I was a fairly new grandparent at the time— my grandson Teddy was now about 2 ½ years old. Terry gave me the grandparent's-eye view of the Newtown tragedy, and how immensely painful it was.

Not only did Terry lose a grandchild that day—which is heart-breaking and devastating in and of itself, but she also had to see her own child suffer so greatly through such a loss. Having a child pass away is catastrophic, naturally. Seeing your own child go through something like that—to be in that amount of pain—must be just crushing.

I will never forget that conversation. She opened my eyes to something that I should have seen, but didn't. And ever since, at every ribbon-cutting, I have made a point to recognize the grandparents involved. They share and feel so closely with all that their children and grandchildren go through, both the good and the bad. And the playgrounds are for them as well. I thanked Terry for allowing me to see that.

More than a year later, Terry's sister passed away and left some money to her. Shortly thereafter, a check for $5,000 showed up at my house (now also known as the Where Angels Play Foundation Headquarters). A small note came with it. It said her sister would have been proud to know the money was going towards our mission. Keep up the good work.

. . .

As this was our second Connecticut playground build, I continued to marvel at the Angels Army and their dedication to the project.
Thanks to the Westport Fire Department, our Army from New Jersey
was able to stay the weekend at the firehouse dormitories. This saved
us hundreds of commuting miles, but more importantly it brought
our crew even closer together.

The Angels Army was becoming a band of brothers that did everything together. They worked like dogs, drank like fish, and slept like
logs. All of it with a joke, and a story, and a laugh. Weather conditions
meant little—they would toil through the rain and the cold, hell and
high-water. The worse the conditions, the more they thanked me for
allowing them to be part of it. When, really, they were the ones that
deserved all the thanks and credit for making it possible.

They were tireless in support of the cause. For the storm victims,
for the families of Newtown, and for each other. As time went on,
their faces became part of the landscape at every single playground.

One of those faces was that of Mark Virag.

. . .

Mark Virag is a retired Captain from the Carteret (NJ) Fire
Department and long-time Sergeant-at-Arms of the New Jersey State
FMBA. He is a massive, hulking man with a voice of gravel and a
handshake to rival any NFL lineman. He also has a heart of solid gold.

He was one of the original playground builders. As a veteran of
all three Mississippi builds, it was a no-brainer that Mark would have
a featured role in the physical efforts of The Sandy Ground Project.
His spirit, work-ethic, and leadership were as indispensable on the fire
grounds as they are today on the playgrounds.

. . .

Mark has been valiantly waging a war with cancer that has
spanned the past 12 years. It originally started in his throat and has
since moved into his jaw and cheekbones. He has endured grueling

cycles of chemotherapy. He has fought through the worst imaginable operations on his mouth, his jaw, cheekbone, face, and he has recovered from them time and time again.

None of this ever stopped him from being a part of The Sandy Ground Project. He would have it no other way. He would come to builds with fresh bandages on or straight out of a hospital bed after chemotherapy. Mark is probably the single toughest character I have ever had the pleasure in my life to know. And he would come back again and again, all in the name of making children happy.

In Westport he spent a long, hard day lugging cement bags and doing the artwork on our playgrounds. Totally unstoppable. As a joke at a later build, we'd given him a pink slip for not showing up the day before. He wasn't fired, of course. But it was our way of acknowledging that he had been missed. The build site just wasn't the same without him there.

That same night, after a full day building, the volunteers convened at the Black Duck—a famous Westport bar located on a barge. As we all raised toasts to Dylan, the project, and one another, Mark noticed a kid struggling to win a prize from one of those arcade machines with the drop-down claw.

He decided to assist the kid, but found that (of course) the deck was stacked against them. To even the playing field, Mark used all his strength to tip the machine over and allow the kid to put his hand in and pluck out a prize with ease. He delivered the toy—which was probably worth 10 cents, but in this scenario it was priceless. The two of them danced with joy.

Seeing this, every other child in the place rushed over and gathered around Mark. He was suddenly Santa Claus and it was claw-machine Christmas. He tilted the machine on its end again and again, all for the joy of the kids. He just shrugged his shoulders and gleefully celebrated one victory after another with the kids. The gentlest of giants, doing what he does best.

. . .

We cut the ribbon on Dylan's playground on June 15, 2013. It was a beautiful late-spring afternoon and we were glad to have wrapped up the entire build before school closed for the summer. The kids at Long Lots Elementary School were itching to try out the new playground and we were happy to present them with it on Dylan's behalf. Hundreds of the students—with their families—came to school for the ribbon-cutting even though it was a Saturday. A lot of the kids had made us cards and written us letters of appreciation for the new playground, which we gladly accepted and cherished.

Ian and Nicole both made beautiful speeches thanking everyone who had a hand in making Dylan's playground a success. They urged the schoolchildren to enjoy Dylan's gift to them to the fullest. Because that's what he would have wanted most. They unveiled the commemorative plaque featuring the Autism Awareness puzzle-piece logo and dedicated the playground to Dylan officially.

Also in attendance was Anne Marie Murphy's brother. He was there to represent her since she and Dylan had a very close, very special teacher-student relationship. She was holding him tight that fateful morning at Sandy Hook Elementary School. And now they each had their own playground. One more thing for them to share.

Another stroke of Angel luck occurred for the ribbon-cutting. We had a difficult time trying to figure out how to integrate Dylan's love of chocolate into the theme, but one of our people actually happened to be at Mohegan Sun and discovered some candies by a company called "Dylan's"… including a chocolate bar! So at the last minute we ordered hundreds of Dylan's Chocolate Bars and gave them out to all those at the ribbon-cutting ceremony.

• • •

The Sandy Ground Project is, at its core, guided by the Angels it honors. And they always seem to send us a very specific sign or message during our events and builds. Dylan was certainly no different and not to be outdone.

One of the themes in Westport was butterflies because Dylan loved them. During one of the speeches at the ribbon-cutting, I was standing next to my brother Bob when a butterfly randomly landed right on the bridge of his nose! I had never seen anything like it. This was something that would happen in a Winnie the Pooh cartoon— never in real life. But there it was, carefully balanced right smack in the middle of his face. It gave two quick flaps, took off, and floated away. It was a hilarious thing to have happen in the moment. But when you step back and really think about it, some things just go beyond the realm of coincidence.

.   .   .

Even after Dylan's playground was up and open for business at Long Lots Elementary School, the impact that the Hockleys have had on The Sandy Ground Project continued to be profound. They were the first family I'd had the pleasure of meeting and true advocates of the project. During that initial meeting, Ian came right out and said, "Let's go for 100%. Let's get all 26 families involved. I will help you."

He did exactly that and I'm not sure the whole thing would have come together without his help. He not only drummed up support for the project with many of the other families, but also vouched for me personally. He assured them that I could be trusted and, hopefully, I proved him correct on all counts. He made contacts and connections that I never could have made as an outsider.

Ian and I have become good friends. The build and ribbon-cutting cycle was not the life-span of our friendship and I hope to correspond with him and the Hockleys for years to come. Getting a text message like this one is particularly special:

"Hello Bill. We came to visit Dylan's playground today on his birthday. Thank you for giving us this to remember him by."

Ian Hockley, March 8, 2014

CHAPTER NINE

Playground Celebrating the Life of Victoria Soto

Stratford, Connecticut

As the summer of 2013 started to heat up, so too did the attention garnered by The Sandy Ground Project. With two playgrounds already completed in Connecticut—and another to follow shortly after—the story began to really get legs throughout the state. Obviously Connecticut took the Newtown tragedy very much to heart. Being such a small state, you get a sense that everyone was kind of in it together. Factor in the Superstorm Sandy angle and it was something that everybody could relate to and get behind.

I appeared on a local television show called "Better Connecticut" and spoke extensively about what we were doing. Between that, and some public service announcements we had produced in conjunction with MetLife, The Sandy Ground Project was starting to become known around Connecticut. There were a lot of radio and newspaper interviews, all geared towards raising the funds necessary for all these playgrounds. Even Lieutenant Governor Nancy Wyman had met with us and supported our efforts.

However, we were still struggling to get the ball rolling as far as bringing in substantial dollars. But I could sense a grassroots fundraising campaign forming in small pockets across the tri-state area and across the country in general. We started to see checks of all different amounts showing up from people who had been affected by our story. A car wash here, a bake sale there, a kindergarten class that pools together every penny they can find… it all was adding up and every single bit of it helped. And the momentum was only beginning to build.

• • •

As I have said, the amount of blessings and "signs" associated with The Sandy Ground Project goes far beyond any coincidence I've ever heard of. Sometimes it feels like I'm not even in control of what happens next. The angels seem to have an agenda, a specific plan, and we are all kind of following along as best as we can. Even the rainouts and setbacks always had a very definitive purpose in making the overall outcome the perfect one.

When I introduced the general concept of The Sandy Ground Project with the families of Newtown, Connecticut, there was one aspect that was striking a positive chord with them even though I didn't realize it. It was the number "26". That was the ultimate goal— 26 playgrounds to celebrate the lives of 26 individuals while helping in the recovery of 26 communities. That same number, again and again.

Little did I know, they really appreciated the fact that I had focused on that number—not 27 or 28. They were united in the think-ing that there were 26 angels of Sandy Hook Elementary School that fateful day. No more, no less. And those lives were the ones that shared a common ground and were worthy of celebrating—maybe even with a playground.

• • •

Victoria Soto was a beloved, young, energetic teacher at Sandy Hook Elementary School. She would be our inspiration for building our fifth playground.

• • •

One of the first parents I had heard from was Victoria's mom, Donna Soto. She expressed some interest in having a playground built in honor of Victoria and would like it to be in her hometown of Stratford. Just that fact alone made me realize how very different it was to build a playground for one of the teachers as opposed to one of the kids.

The students were all (obviously) from the same town, but the teachers were from different communities from around the state. And the impact was devastating to so many throughout Connecticut.

I initially met with Donna Soto along with her cousin Amy Wiltsie. As I laid out the project and its mission for them, Amy's husband Jim arrived. It didn't take long for me to pick up on the fact that Jim is a police officer. My brother Pat, as well as several other family members and good friends, are cops and I know their demeanor only too well. As I spoke, Jim kept that classic look of skepticism on his face. "Who is this guy? And what is he doing messing in my cousin's business?"

Although they gave me a very careful looking-over that first day, I can now safely say that Amy and Jim Wiltsie are my good friends. Jim and I can laugh about our first impressions of one another and the two of them form an amazing support system for Donna and the Sotos. The Wiltsies are kind of the spokespeople for their family and they perform that duty with strength and grace. Naturally, they played a critical part in getting a playground built for Victoria.

Donna was the key though and she was very specific about how she wanted the playground. And when that happens, when the parents or family have a definite vision and opinion, that is when the builds really turn out spectacularly. Having never met Victoria (or Catherine… or Dylan… or Anne Marie…) we really count on that direction and it only leads to good things.

• • •

To say that Victoria was beloved by her students at Sandy Hook would be an understatement. The name of "Miss Soto" was constantly brought up at the childrens' homes, on the weekends and at the dinner tables. They gravitated to her and looked up to her. She was young and vibrant and enthusiastic about the kids becoming good little students and people. She loved getting to know them and they adored her for it.

Victoria loved pink flamingos and Christmastime, which are two of the themes we would integrate into the playground design. The structure would have pink piping with green roofs, almost like flamingos walking through tall grass. And as part of the landscaping we planted several Christmas trees to stand guard around the perimeter of the playground.

Victoria's motto was simple: "Live. Laugh. Love." We would do all three of those throughout the build, inspired by the spirit of Miss Soto.

. . .

The choice of Stratford, CT, as a location for Victoria's playground was a no-brainer because that is where she grew up and where her mother wanted it to be. But ultimately it was made possible by Steve Lupinacci. Steve is the Director of the Connecticut Children's Burn Camp as well as a Stratford firefighter. He was able to arrange access to his department for us—the guys showed up with trucks both on and off duty to assist with every last element of the playground build.

In addition, Steve was instrumental in helping us to navigate the local politics in Stratford. As we well know, each town is its own little world with a plethora of moving parts. Steve was able to get those parts moving in unison and his personality and knowledge were invaluable to us.

Stratford is a very diverse, blue-collar town and—from the perspective of The Sandy Ground Project—we definitely felt the love there. Mayor John Harkins was an awesome supporter and basically gave us anything we might need for the build. In particular was Joe from the Department of Public Works. This guy was Johnny-On-The-Spot. No matter what issue or problem we would run into, or tool we would need… Joe was the man. The kind of guy who knows how to get things done. Donna's brother-in-law, Rob Cronk, also works for the town of Stratford and made it his personal mission to see that everything went right for his niece's park.

Also, it is always huge for us to have the support of the local business community. But in the case of Stratford, Connecticut, "Paradise

Pizza" was one that went above and beyond. In addition to holding multiple fundraisers, they couldn't do enough to keep our volunteers fed throughout the weekend. It's that kind of generosity that allowed us to build the entire playground in essentially one day.

• • •

The first day we showed up to build in Stratford, a Friday, it was pouring rain. We're talking buckets. So bad that no work could be done at all. It was our first completely washed-out day, and I was left looking up at the sky and thinking, "Hey, where's the blessing?"

With the day wasted, the Angels Army packed up and headed back to the fire department dormitories in Westport (our new home away from home). As we settled in, I went to check my e-mail and found one from a name I didn't recognize. It was from one of the teachers at Sandy Hook Elementary School.

It said: "I know you're probably upset that you were unable to start building today, but I want you to know that the rain was Victoria's doing. She postponed the build because her friends, the teachers of Sandy Hook, NEED to be there. And since today is Friday, a school day, we were unable to make it. Tomorrow will be sunny. We will be there ready to go…"

Tough to argue with that. We would build on Saturday, all day and all night if we had to. I was realizing then what good fortune could come from this rained-out day. And I realize now that this was also the day I met my sixth brother—a Puerto Rican brother.

• • •

Carlos Soto, Victoria's father, was hurting very badly in the wake of the tragedy at Sandy Hook. Normally a very funny, gregarious guy, he went into a shell that no one could seem to pull him out of. I had not met Carlos until that rain-soaked Friday morning, but I'd heard through Donna and the Wiltsies that he wanted to provide all the food and drinks for the volunteer workers. So, as promised, he walked up to the grounds loaded with coffee and donuts for everyone.

We got to talking and hit it off right away. Carlos is a crane-operator for the Connecticut Transit Authority, a union guy, so we didn't have any trouble finding some common ground. We became fast friends and he has played a huge role in The Sandy Ground Project ever since. He runs a lot of our fundraising operations and t-shirt sales. He is an ambassador for our Foundation. He even has stayed over at my house when there was a build or a ribbon-cutting down in New Jersey somewhere.

The Wiltsies marveled at what Victoria's playground had done for Carlos. In the aftermath of Newtown, he'd had ample opportunity to speak. Whether it was giving interviews, talking to the press, giving even a small quote here or there—but he seemed unable to communicate.

That all seemed to change the morning he showed up for the building of Victoria's playground. Pretty soon he would be doing regional and national news interviews. And here he was, in his element chatting up the Angels Army crew and being a part of the scene. He just fit. He smiled more and interacted with his kids more.

Victoria's siblings—Jillian, Carlee, and Carlos Jr.—were also vital to Playground #5. I got to know them well and they assisted mightily in the construction process. Carlos Jr. was hesitant at first to be involved, but after we gave him a tour of our other playgrounds he was all in. We could not have done it without them.

Since each of Victoria's siblings was too old for the "honorary foreman" role that was quickly becoming tradition, we figured that Playground #5 just wouldn't have one. But, lo and behold, one showed up.

• • •

Another blessing that stemmed from our Friday rain-out was that a little boy named Peter was able to make it on Saturday. He was a student at Sandy Hook Elementary School and he was especially lost and devastated after the tragedy. He had been very much attached to Miss Soto. He loved her. And the fact that she was gone left him barely able to speak.

When Peter heard about the playground build being planned to honor Miss Soto, he began to perk up. He asked his mother to drive him to Stratford to go and see it in person. Overjoyed to see him engaged in some way, she was more than happy to make the half-hour drive up Route 25 to get him there.

And on Saturday morning, our honorary foreman arrived. After hearing his story, we quickly got him a tool belt and all the necessary equipment. In no time he was out in the sun, smiling and building and getting his hands dirty. He had found a way to be close to Miss Soto again.

• • •

The construction effort on that Saturday was fierce. The Angels Army knew full well that we had lost a whole day due to weather, and they were more than willing to march double-time to make up for it. They worked fast and precise and adjusted on the fly. When the landscape proved to be too uneven, they changed over to a fiber-mulch surface. When the sun began to set, they set up the lights and picked up the pace.

And, as with any good team, the leaders come to the forefront when the pressure is on.

• • •

If the Angels Army is truly that—an army—then Herman Peters is a four-star general. A retired fire captain from the North Hudson Regional Fire & Rescue, Herman Peters could best be described as the missing link between man and bear. Just a monster of a man with a full, red beard and, when angered, eyes bugged out of his head like ping-pong balls. A true Viking. He was a long-time Northern District Vice-President at the New Jersey State FMBA, and I consider him to be one of the most loyal colleagues and friends I have ever known.

Herman was a veteran of all our playground builds down in Mississippi. Due to his background in masonry work, Herman has always led our cement team. This made him a critical piece of the building puzzle and, thankfully, he is also the hardest-working SOB of the bunch. He is the first to arrive and the last to leave, always pushing the other guys harder and reminding them why they're there. He leads by example.

When someone suggests taking a break or stopping for the night, Herman is right up in their face saying "Come on, ya [so-and-so], don't you quit on us now!" When the work is done and the troops are at rest, Herman is right up in their face again. This time saying, "I love you, man," and squeezing the life out of them.

And through all the bluster and gruffness and (sometimes colorful) language, Herman is the quintessential "big softy". After working his tail off by day—and toasting his tail off by night—Herman will be at that ribbon-cutting ceremony shedding as many tears as anyone else. He knows the reason for what we are doing and keeps it in his heart at all times. I'm pretty sure that's what drives him to work, and play, and laugh, and love, as hard as he does.

An entire playground gets built in a single day, and someone will ask how we got it done. All I have to do is point at Herman and say, "Because of guys like that."

• • •

Unlike Rome, Victoria's playground was, in fact, built in a day. So the ribbon opening Victoria's playground was cut that Sunday, June 23, 2013. Located at Penders Field, it stood adjacent to the same home softball and soccer fields of Stratford High School—where Victoria went to school. She had given us a beautiful sunny morning for the ceremony and it became Christmas in June.

We had all the Christmas trees on the grounds fully decorated and two of my brother firefighters from Elizabeth, NJ—Andy Rios and Danny Ramos—performed "Feliz Navidad". It was Victoria's favorite Christmas carol. Also in attendance to show their support were a couple of Connecticut dignitaries—U.S. Senator Richard Blumenthal and U.S. Congresswoman Rosa DeLauro.

A large crowd of people—from both Stratford and beyond—assembled amongst the Christmas trees and pink flamingos as the speeches commemorating the playground commenced. Above our heads, a plane was circling, carrying Victoria's simple and uplifting message: "TO STRATFORD… LIVE. LAUGH. LOVE… FROM, VICTORIA"

· · ·

In a move that took the rest of his family by total surprise, the suddenly-eloquent Carlos Soto chose to make a speech of his own that morning. I cannot recall many of the specifics, but he graciously thanked all the volunteers and the town of Stratford for honoring his daughter. He spoke about her amazing spirit and how much she would love the playground we were all about to open.

What I do recall specifically were the last eight words that Carlos left us all with. He was referencing Victoria's playground in particular, but it summed up everything The Sandy Ground Project was, and everything it was striving to be…

"Out of something horrible,
something beautiful has emerged."

Carlos Soto and Bob Brower

Storm Trooper down

CHAPTER TEN

Playground Celebrating the Life of Rachel D'Avino

Asbury Park, New Jersey

On a personal level, I will always remember Rachel D'Avino's playground as the point where I came to a crossroads. It is amazing how you come to certain realizations in life. And while planning—and eventually building—this particular playground on Asbury Park's shoreline, my own future seemed to crystallize in my own mind. I was becoming used to realizing certain things through apparent signs from our 26 angels. A rainbow here, a butterfly there. A happy accident or sudden change in the weather.

In this case, it would take a superhero.

• • •

One morning in Bethlehem, Connecticut, I sat down to coffee with Mary D'Avino and her two daughters. The meeting started off quite solemn, naturally. The main topic was the daughter and sister they had lost—Rachel—who was 29 years-old when she became an angel. She had recently been hired there and was teaching students with special needs. She was studying to get her Ph.D. in special education. Her passion in life was to make the world a better place for people with autism.

It was easy to see that the D'Avinos were struggling, and that Mary was the glue somehow holding them all together. Not only Mary and her daughters, but the extended family network as well. In the wake of the Newtown tragedy, the girls had struggled to consistently get back into the swing of things. It was a roller-coaster of emotions and who could blame them after suffering such a sudden loss of a loved one. Especially someone like Rachel.

Our meeting seemed to brighten once I started going into the particulars of The Sandy Ground Project. The D'Avino women perked up at the idea of having a playground dedicated to Rachel and have it constructed to reflect her spirit. There would certainly be no shortage of unique qualities to use for inspiration.

Mary and her daughters spoke lovingly of what made Rachel Rachel. She was a free spirit—very artistic and very caring. She loved superheroes, like Superman and Batman and Wonder Woman especially. They felt like she was the real-life version of Wonder Woman really. She was also very into Star Wars and her friends had actually started a petition directed at the Walt Disney Company requesting Rachel be named an honorary Jedi Knight. It has garnered thousands of signatures.

Also, Rachel's absolute favorite color was purple and there is a well-known picture of her wielding a purple Star Wars-inspired lightsaber. So it seemed as though we had our color-scheme for the playground as well.

Mary and her daughters didn't particularly care where the playground would be built, whether it was near or far. As long as it was needed they would support it being put up in Rachel's honor. Having gotten to know Rachel and her personality through the descriptions of those who loved and knew her best, I felt like I had just the place…

• • •

Asbury Park, New Jersey, is probably best-known nationwide as the breeding ground of the legendary Bruce Springsteen. In more recent years the town has come upon hard times, but its core values and its heart have always been intact. There are some Badlands parts for sure, but the romantic Thunder Road quality is still very much alive. A real slice of Americana, you know.

It's a very progressive community—artistic, musical—that's a little bit edgy and a little bit quirky. Not many towns can convey such personality, but Asbury Park is that distinctive mix of being on the cutting-edge… yet having an old soul.

Sounds sort of like Rachel D'Avino to me.

• • •

Matching up Asbury Park and Rachel D'Avino is easier said than done when it comes to getting a playground built, so I tapped into the vast (and growing) network of people I'd had the pleasure to work alongside throughout my life. This time it would be Dee Pellegrino, wife of PBA representative Mike Pellegrino, who would put the wheels into motion. She worked for THE country radio station in New Jersey—Thunder 106—and they had been great to the New Jersey State FMBA when we were doing various public relations campaigns.

Dee had floated the concept of The Sandy Ground Project to her boss, Rich Morena, who owns the radio station. He loved the idea and became a great friend to me, as well as a great ally to our cause. I did a presentation for him and his staff, and Rich said he would reach out to a friend of his who ran a philanthropic foundation. His name is Jules Plangere, former CEO of the Jersey Shore's largest newspaper chain—the Asbury Park Press.

The next time I met with Rich, he surprised me with a $75,000 check from Jules Plangere's foundation. Needless to say I was very touched. This was more than enough to cover all the costs associated with building a playground for Rachel D'Avino right there in Asbury Park, and our largest single donation to date. A check of this size also opened my eyes to the fact that this project was bigger than all of us. If we could get this kind of donation from one foundation, the sky was the limit. It was just a matter of spreading the word. And, for the first time, I could envision this project's completion from a financial standpoint.

Thanks to Dee Pellegrino, Rich Morena, and (most of all) Jules Plangere, the Angels Army was all set to storm the beach at Asbury Park.

• • •

It's amazing how so many of my experiences in life, and in my career, seem to have prepared me for this mission with The Sandy Ground Project. For the past 10 years, I have volunteered as a counselor at the Connecticut Children's Burn Camp. It is a life-altering experience to work with the kids summer after summer, and it's something I envision doing for the rest of my life. It is run by an incredibly dedicated group of firefighters, nurses, and healthcare professionals who manage and coordinate every aspect of the camp.

A wonderful side-effect of my work as a volunteer there has been the network of individuals—in Connecticut and beyond—who have assisted greatly in the success of The Sandy Ground Project. They are a huge asset, particularly on the Connecticut builds, and do everything from fundraising to allocating resources to navigating local politics.

The third week of July was upon us, and for me that means heading off to Burn Camp. With the ground-breaking, build days, and ribbon-cutting all planned for Rachel's Asbury Park playground, I drove off to camp in the Connecticut woods. And I didn't even realize the mess that I had left behind.

. . .

In an odd bit of Sandy Ground trivia, the ribbon-cutting for Playground #7 actually wound up taking place *before* the ribbon-cutting for #6. This was due to my own screw-up—a situation that was embarrassing for me personally and the project itself. However, it did put me on a path to making The Sandy Ground Project my top priority and kept me from ever making the same mistake again.

I had left for Burn Camp with the plans for the Asbury Park build in place. But a day or two after I arrived, I got a phone call from Rich Morena. Apparently he and Jules Plangere—the two men most responsible for making the whole thing happen, not to mention our project's most generous donor to date—were not able to make it on the date the ribbon-cutting was scheduled. I had thoughtlessly forgotten to consult with them when I was making all these plans. I just kept charging ahead and had overlooked them in the process. I felt terrible.

So here I was, scrambling through the forest somewhere in Connecticut, desperately trying to hold onto my cell phone's signal and apologize to Rich. It was almost comical that I'm conducting the business of a multi-million dollar charity while on break from camp counselor duties, but the humor was definitely lost on me in this moment. I was just plain mortified—like an ungrateful kid who had taken a gift and run off without a 'thank you'.

Ultimately, we would smooth things over. We would postpone the ribbon-cutting in Asbury Park, and rightfully so. But the slip-up with Rich and Jules opened my eyes to the fact that I was spread too thin. I was doing three jobs at once and it was clear that I needed to decide what my priorities were. It was also clear that The Sandy Ground Project—if it was going to be done right—needed to be at the top of my list.

I had floated the idea back in June of retiring as President of the New Jersey State FMBA. My heart was somewhere else, I couldn't stomach the politics anymore, and The Sandy Ground Project needed (and warranted) all of my attention. So while the snafu with the Asbury Park ribbon-cutting was a bit painful, it gave me all the motivation I needed to end my career as a union president. In the long run, this is what needed to happen to allow me to see this project all the way through. It freed up my mind going forward, and I consider that to be Rachel D'Avino's gift to me.

Speaking of being spread too thin, the point was further illustrated by the fact that I was unable to attend the first build-day for Rachel in Asbury Park. I had exhausted all my leave time at my primary job as Captain with the Elizabeth Fire Department and had mistakenly thought I'd arranged for someone to work for me that day. Ugh. This would be the first, and only, build-day I would ever miss throughout the entire process. But this too was not without its teachable moment. It allowed me to see that I was going to need someone dedicated to The Sandy Ground Project on a full-time basis. And I had a pretty good idea who that person was going to be…

• • •

Upon graduating from Rutgers University in 2009, my daughter MaryKate began a summer job as my secretary at the New Jersey State FMBA office. She soon became a vital piece of our puzzle and the summer job turned into a full-time gig going on five years. MaryKate has a knack for dealing with the plethora of personalities that the fire service can present you with. Yet, she's my youngest child and the only one whose entire life I have been a firefighter for. So maybe she's had the proper training just by being in close proximity to the cast of characters I have been surrounded by.

Throughout 2013, the tone around the State FMBA had certainly changed drastically. Instead of the yearly go-round of the same events, conventions, negotiations, rallies, and battles—there was a new-found excitement with our involvement in coordinating The Sandy Ground Project. It was just a different level of enthusiasm that the playgrounds brought out of people. And I certainly saw that happening with MaryKate.

That first build-day in Asbury Park, I needed to depend on MaryKate to be my eyes and ears on the beach as I sat in a firehouse 50 miles away. Along with my wife Kathy—who has been my ultimate partner in every success I've had in life—she was essentially coordinating the build and trouble-shooting on the fly. It was amazing to see her, at age 26 coincidentally (or not), stepping into a leadership role on such an expansive project.

As I was privately envisioning the end of my time with the New Jersey State FMBA, I was also envisioning MaryKate's as well. I knew I was going to need a full-time person to work for The Sandy Ground Project at some point. While I could certainly dedicate myself to all the meetings and ideas and plans and builds, I needed someone who could carry out the mission on a day-to-day basis, guiding the process. The Sandy Ground as an idea was a force and momentum was building, but it still needed a foundation. It needed a rock that the rest of the project could be built upon. And MaryKate was going to be that rock.

By November she had left her job with the State FMBA and began working for The Sandy Ground Project full-time. It has been a blessing, not only in regards to the playgrounds and the project, but for me personally as well. I get to see my daughter almost every day and the two of us have formed a great team. We are sharing in God's work, helping people who need it, and literally changing the landscape of the world together. You can't put a price on that type of experience.

• • •

The actual building of Rachel D'Avino's playground went relatively smoothly. The layout was very similar to our first playground in Sea Bright—right on the sand—so the Angels Army simply applied what had been learned and methodically knocked out the work. We also had tremendous support from the Asbury Park firefighters. As cut-and-dry as that sounds, their involvement was one of my proudest moments as President of the State FMBA.

Heading into Asbury Park posed a bit of a political dilemma from an FMBA standpoint. The Asbury Park firefighters' union was affiliated with the Professional Firefighters Association of New Jersey (PFANJ), not the FMBA. The relationship between the FMBA and PFANJ has always been tenuous at best throughout New Jersey, venomous at worst. Although we all were brothers in the same profession, there was a certain rivalry between the two organizations.

In the spirit of The Sandy Ground Project transcending all politics and differences, I reached out to their local president—Bob Fahnholz. I offered them the opportunity to get involved as much or as little as they wanted. He was actually a neighbor of one of our Angels Army guys, Bill Valentine, and through him Bob started to believe in what we were doing. Also, Chief Kevin Keddy was a good friend of mine and fellow bagpiper, so little by little the Asbury Park Fire Department was coming on board. What started off with strained conversations would wind up having beautiful results.

The Asbury Park firefighters stepped up in a big way, giving us 10 to 15 guys a day to work on the playground. They were with us every step of the way and were also able to garner support from the City Council and Department of Public Works. The guys working the tractors and machinery on the beach could not have been better. Couple all of that with picture-perfect weather, and Rachel D'Avino's playground turned out to be a homerun. Smooth sailing all the way.

When the playground was finished, the entire crew rendez-voused at a local place called Clancy's to celebrate our accomplishment together. I will never forget a conversation I had with Bob Fahnholz that night, which was particularly special with both of us about to retire as presidents of our respective unions.

He said he had heard a lot of negative things about me through the years… about how the FMBA operates and about me personally. He told me that his experience with The Sandy Ground Project had proved all of it completely untrue. He said the FMBA was a class act, and was glad to have realized this before he retired. As a statewide union president for 16 years, you get a kind of reputation one way or another. It never bothered me to be hated by those who didn't know me, because it's simply ignorance. It only really hurts when someone DOES know you, but hates you anyway.

The Sandy Ground Project was able to bridge that gap between the FMBA and PFANJ. I know Bob and I were both equally grateful to have worked together and both unions benefited in the end. The project knows no political divide. It is people working together to help others. Simple as that.

• • •

At long last, we cut the ribbon on Rachel's playground on August 24, 2013. It was a beautiful and festive evening on Asbury Park's shoreline—the iconic Convention Hall serving as the backdrop. The D'Avino family came out in full force, including Rachel's cousin John. He was instrumental in getting the D'Avino family involved and was a great leader from a fundraising standpoint. He had been with us going all the way back to the Sea Bright ribbon-cutting. He and the rest of the family were always there for us, and could be counted on to support all of our events or concerts or whatever else we would come up with.

Mary D'Avino made an amazing, heart-felt speech about her daughter that evening. She thanked everyone who had made the playground possible and spoke about Rachel as a real-life superhero who had left us much too early. She also pointed out the Autism Awareness theme that could be found throughout the playground, and urged everyone to be a champion for autistic children like Rachel was.

Since that day, Mary has made it to practically every other ribbon-cutting ceremony. She is an absolute sweetheart of a woman and she has traveled far and wide in support of our mission. I can't say enough about her as a friend and as a mother who has continuously held her family together through thick and thin.

• • •

Asbury Park was one of our most memorable ribbon-cutting events because of all the superheroes and characters who had come out in support of Rachel. There was Spider-Man, Wonder Woman, a bunch of Star Wars guys, and many others. It was sort of surreal to see all of them roaming the beach looking like they had just stepped out of a comic book or movie screen. But Rachel would have loved it.

At one point my grandson Teddy, not yet three years old, saw the new purple playground and ran straight towards it smiling, laughing, and pointing. Then he saw two Star Wars Storm Troopers—covered head to toe in white body armor—and turned right around screaming and crying. He ran away from the playground much faster than he had run to it.

A little later one of those same Storm Troopers fell off of the jungle gym and landed flat on his back. Because of all the equipment he was wearing, he was unable to get up, struggling on the sand like an overturned turtle. It looked like a painful fall but, man, we couldn't help but crack up at the sight of it. (He was fine.)

As the sun started to go down, we wrapped up our festivities on the beach and went to have dinner. We went on to celebrate that night—at Clancy's once again—the FMBA, PFANJ, the D'Avinos, the firefighters, the Angels Army, everyone breaking bread and raising a glass as family.

If Rachel D'Avino had taught me one thing throughout my time working on the Asbury Park playground, it was that The Sandy Ground Project is where I needed and wanted to be. I could not go on as union president. My heart was drawn someplace else. As much as it meant to me, and as much as I desperately wanted to advocate for firefighters, the angels seemed to be willing me in another direction.

There were still 20 playgrounds to be built and I knew it couldn't be done the right way without my ability to focus on the positive. Rachel's playground forced me to do that. My mind was finally free of all that had been holding me back. And I could go forth with a clear mission in my mind, knowing that the Force, and Rachel's spirit, was with me.

Bill Lavin thanks Bob Fahnholz

CHAPTER ELEVEN

Playground Celebrating the Life of Olivia Engel

Manasquan, New Jersey

While I was busy forgetting things and getting my priorities in order, The Sandy Ground Project was marching ever forward a few beaches south.

. . .

Olivia Engel was one week away from appearing as the Christmas Angel in her school's play. Even at such a young age, she loved the stage, loved to perform, and loved to dance. This is what her mother, Shannon, first told me when I initially met with her and her four-year-old son Braden. Now Olivia was one of the 26 real angels that were directing our Sandy Ground Project from above, and I presented Shannon with the idea of having her be the next to be celebrated with a playground.

The Engels were very much into the playground idea. I told them I would be back to meet with them again once we had a location picked out—not to mention the funds to build it. That day would come sooner than expected, thanks to a community group known as "Squan Strong".

. . .

Manasquan, New Jersey, is one of those towns that everyone knows of and has been to at some point or another. Every summer it is filled (ok, tightly packed) with vacationers—renting houses or staying in their own summer homes. Its vibrant bar scene and beautiful beaches keep people coming back year after year. So if you grew up in northern New Jersey, Manasquan should need no introduction. It's where working class America meets the Jersey Shore.

Geographically, Manasquan is almost completely surrounded by water—ocean to the east, inlet to the south, a lake to the north, and a network of creeks and lagoons to the west. So needless to say, this was one of those Jersey Shore towns that took it on the chin from Superstorm Sandy. The local businesses and famous bars were submerged. Sand was piled high in the streets. Cars and boats and houses were picked up and moved to God knows where. This small borough had gotten completely wrecked.

Led by the women of Manasquan, a community group called "Squan Strong" was formed shortly after the storm. Its focus was to provide relief within the town through fundraising and support the rebuilding process that would have to take place all throughout Manasquan. Our pipeline into "Squan Strong" was Mary Connors—wife of Union Township Fire Captain Dan Connors. She was a very active member of the Manasquan-based group, and felt that they had the wherewithal to be a great partner for The Sandy Ground Project.

Mary attended our second ribbon-cutting in Union Beach and brought along a woman named Dana Connelly—the leader of the "Squan Strong" effort. To put it mildly, Dana is a high-octane personality with an unstoppable will to get things done. She had spear-headed some incredible work that had helped to get the people of Manasquan back on their feet after Sandy. And now that she had seen what The Sandy Ground Project was all about, she was gung-ho for getting a new playground built in Manasquan as well.

Armed with her unlimited energy and imagination, Dana got to work on fundraising and drumming up support for a possible playground in Manasquan. She made up and sold chocolate shovels (to signify the building). She organized pub crawls and brought local businesses into the fold. She even got the approval of the mayor and had him designate the location on the beach where the playground would potentially be. Dana was a force to be reckoned with.

Once we knew we had the funding, I told Dana that we would be building our next playground for Olivia and the Engel family. I asked if Manasquan would be up for hosting it—with her leading the charge, of course. She burst into tears of joy, having worked so hard to bring The Sandy Ground Project to her still-suffering community. She could not wait to help add such a beautiful new piece to the landscape, and asked if she could come up to Newtown with me to meet the Engels in person. I was heading there to ask if Manasquan would work for them as well and see when we could get started. Dana wanted to go and learn more about the angel who would be taking up residence in her town.

On my second trip to the Engel home, Dana and I met with Shannon and her mother Suanne (Olivia's grandmother). When we spoke about Manasquan and what we were planning, Shannon and her mother seemed very familiar with it despite being from Connecticut. As it turns out, their family used to vacation every summer in the very same town. It sure seemed like Olivia and Manasquan were a perfect match, and would be sort of a homecoming for Shannon and Suanne.

The Engels told us a lot about Olivia that day. They showed us the picture of her in her Christmas angel costume and told us about her love of dance. I knew the picture of this angel would work for the playground's signage on many levels, but we struggled to think of a way that dancing could be conveyed in the playground's actual structure. Olivia's grandmother also mentioned her unique interest in dragonflies. She had loved to watch them and draw them.

As Dana and I wrapped up a very emotional meeting and got ready for the drive back to New Jersey, we all stopped on the front porch for a last hug good-bye. As the two of us stood on the steps looking at Shannon and her mother, a dragonfly swooped in and hovered over their heads. We didn't point it out at the time, but Dana and I gave each other a look as if to say, "Are you seeing that? Could that be what I think it is?" We got back into the car feeling like there could be no clearer sign.

Then I got in my car, turned on the ignition, and the Sirius satellite radio receiver lit up. A song entitled "Olivia's Song" was spelled out on the screen. Although the lyrics were in no way applicable to the situation, just seeing her name spelled out on the screen was jarring. I'd never heard of the song before or since. It certainly seemed like Olivia was letting us know that she approved.

• • •

Shortly thereafter, in the midst of planning our upcoming Manasquan build, I came home from the office one evening cranky and exhausted. My wife Kathy and daughter MaryKate were getting ready to head out to see a dance recital. My daughter Kelly is a dance teacher at Ocean County Vocational Technical School of the Performing Arts Academy and they were heading to her end-of-the-year show. Kelly has been a dancer since she could walk, studied dance at Rutgers University, and is now passing her gift on to high school students through her choreography and teaching.

I have probably seen more than a hundred of Kelly's shows throughout the years, but on this particular night I just was not in the mood. But I sucked it up and decided it was a more productive option than moping around the house alone. I was so glad I did.

Since my attendance at the show was last-minute, my seat was located across the theater from Kathy's and MaryKate's. As I sat down, I could see them from afar motioning for me to look at the program. I was thinking, "I don't know any of these dancers, what's there to see?" But as I opened the program, the title immediately caught my eye. The dance number was listed as: "Paying It Forward—*Inspired by The Sandy Ground Project*".

I was shocked. Kelly is the type of person who immerses herself in her work and her students during the school year—so I didn't even realize she was noticing what had been going on with the playgrounds. Let alone choreograph a dance about it.

The dance was unbelievable. Kelly's students, at her instruction, captured the essence of The Sandy Ground Project through movement like nothing I'd ever seen. They even integrated seesaws on stage, built by my son-in-law Billy Bourke. Just an amazing interpretation. As the dance went on, I was moved to tears. And I don't even mean "misty eyed" or "choked up"… more like "audibly weeping." I guess all the emotion of the project and my daughter's accomplishment on stage here had come gushing to the surface. I was seated there alone and sobbing. The couple seated next to me must have been thinking, "This guy is losing his mind."

I could not wait to see Kelly after the show. To thank her and hug her and congratulate her. It was only natural that I asked if she could put on the same performance when we cut the ribbon at Olivia's playground. It might be tough getting the dancers together in the middle of summer, but she would see what she could do.

• • •

The actual playground build in Manasquan got off to an inauspicious start. The morning we were set to break ground, one of the local residents (whose oceanfront home was directly in front of our construction site) began raising a fuss. She did not want the playground in front of her house, "obstructing her view", and was running up and down the street getting the other residents riled up. Although we had all the necessary approvals for the build—and the Mayor actually told us to go ahead and start building anyway—we did not want to begin putting Olivia's playground together under such negative circumstances.

In a snap decision, we moved ourselves up the beach—about 200 feet north. This wound up being an even better location for the playground. It was now right in front of the town's beachfront recreation center, which had more nearby parking than the original location. We always say the playgrounds are "built where they're supposed to be built", so that resident's protests turned out to be a blessing in disguise.

The volunteers began measuring and drilling the holes for our new location. And then the rains came…

• • •

Building Olivia's playground in Manasquan was one of the roughest in terms of weather. But if there is one thing I have learned about the Angels Army, and our volunteers in general, it's that they couldn't care less about the elements. The harder it rained, the harder they worked. And this was especially the case with our most unique and hearty group of soldiers. A regiment within the Angels Army affectionately known as the "Mud Ducks."

These playground builds, when done so fast and furious, are very labor intensive. Even more so at the beach builds, because moving people and equipment and supplies around on sand is that much more difficult. And when it comes to working with the cement on the beach, you've got a truly unenviable task on your hands.

But that is where the Mud Ducks come in. They are a band of brothers and sisters (females are "Mud Swans") who relish taking on the most difficult tasks available. If the Angels Army were a football team, the Mud Ducks would be the offensive line. They live in the trenches, love to get dirty, and are a cut above the rest when it comes to digging their heels in.

The Mud Ducks are led by Herman Peters, the hard-charging masonry man from North Hudson. He and his crew are tasked with moving 80-pound bags of cement, slicing them open in large wheelbarrows, and adding water. Then the cement is quickly mixed, a Mud Duck working a shovel or hoe on each side. Then, the wheelbarrow needs to be pushed (across sand in this case) quickly to the various holes that have been drilled throughout the job site. The wheelbarrows are then propped up into an inverted position and poured.

The Mud Ducks come in all shapes and sizes—and they deserve to be identified by name. You've got a petite blonde Mud Swan named Allison Dorko, a school teacher that moonlights as a cement mixer. Brian Dolaghan and Brian McGorty, the grizzled veterans from our Mississippi playground builds. Tommy Atwell and Kevin "Pops" Kennedy, the brute force of the crew. And my own real-life brothers: Butch, Bob, and Pat Lavin—who are all in their 60s (and 70s) but as relentless as anyone out there. Of course none of this cement work would be possible without the generosity of Old Castle and Sarah Melochrinos, who made sure we had all the cement required for each and every build.

Also on the beach that first morning, a young lady came up and asked me what she could do. I directed her to sorting out hardware with a group of women but she responded, "Hey! I can lift things." That was Laura Iden, and man she wasn't kidding. Laura carried, dragged, and pushed wheelbarrows and heavy equipment right alongside the strongest man. Another 'Mud Swan' in the making.

By the end of the day, a Mud Duck is completely coated. In cement dust, in sand, in sweat, and (naturally) in mud. Working with the cement, it gets everywhere. Your eyes, nose, mouth, hair. It sands down your skin, dries out your lips, and turns your whole body a hazy shade of gray.

Nevertheless, they relish it. They just take a drink from their exclusive 'Mud Ducks Only' cooler and keep on going. The grittier the better.

• • •

Another build-day MVP in Manasquan was actually Brian Engel, Olivia's dad. He got involved with nearly every aspect of the construction. Brian is an extremely hard worker and also very skilled. I can't recall a family member being more involved in the physical element of a playground build before or since.

Each build, it seemed, always provided us with incredible signs and this one proved to be no different. It seemed each day we worked on the beach there were always dragonflies hovering above us, keeping a watchful eye on the progress. That sign was not lost on any of us.

Seeing Brian throw himself so fully into the process definitely caused everyone around him to gain some perspective. Not only his fellow volunteers, but the people of Manasquan as well—who all seemed to be monitoring us and rooting us on from afar. The town was still very much in a rebuilding mode. You could see it on every single street. As we were building the playground, they were rebuilding their homes right along with us.

But it also made them realize that things weren't quite that bad. While losing your house is a devastating thing to have to go through in life, at the end of the day it's just wood and brick and plaster and vinyl. Material things. It cannot come close to comparing to the loss of a young life. So we were all there in Manasquan together, rebuilding *something*. And I think the storm victims took heart in realizing that they were the lucky ones. They really were honored to have the Engels putting roots down beside them.

Manasquan truly rolled out the red carpet and made us feel at home. There was a food truck called "Surf and Turf" that parked right next to the construction site and fed everyone the entire time we were there. They never asked for a dime. Several local restaurants sent over food and drinks—pizzas and sandwiches and Gatorades to fuel the build. And, of course, you had the women of "Squan Strong" who lived up to their name and then some. There was nothing they couldn't do and no problem they couldn't solve. Come rain or wind or cranky neighbors, they made our job as easy as possible.

As the build wrapped up, we decided to begin another tradition of The Sandy Ground Project—one that would continue at so many playgrounds to follow. It was the installation of flagpoles on the grounds. There would be three—the American flag, the flag of the State of Connecticut, and a specially designed flag for the child or teacher that playground is meant to celebrate. In Olivia's case, the flag would feature a dragonfly symbol.

The flagpole tradition, and the raising of the flags at the playground's completion, became a very special moment for everyone involved. It told people that The Sandy Ground Project was here. And, in Manasquan's case, Olivia still is.

• • •

On August 2, 2013, we cut the ribbon at Olivia's brand new playground at 1st Avenue's Seawatch Beach. So many folks from Manasquan (and beyond) attended on a bright, sunny afternoon as an airplane circled overhead with a message reading: "TO MANASQUAN... FROM OLIVIA... WITH LOVE".

Mary Connors, my original gateway to the town, had a connection with someone willing to provide this aerial signage extremely cheap. We had been paying top dollar before, but now we had the ability to create fly-overs for every subsequent build. The angels already had an Army of their own on the ground. Now, with Mary at the helm, they had an Air Force as well.

• • •

The Engel family expressed their appreciation and spoke beautifully about Olivia and how happy she would be to see such a sparkling playground. They had really been embraced by the people of Manasquan, and you could tell that a lasting connection had been made. Shannon Engel had vacationed here as a child and now her daughter would be bringing joy to the children who would be vacationing (and living) here for years to come. It all felt like family.

• • •

Even though it was the middle of summer, my daughter Kelly was able to round up all of her students to perform the "Paying It Forward" dance at the ribbon-cutting. They traveled to Manasquan from every corner of Ocean County to be there for us. It was no easy task either because they were used to dancing indoors on hard wooden floors. In this case, they would be performing on sand and outside in the mid-summer heat.

But as they say, the show must go on, and did it ever. The girls brought the house down, recreating the same incredible interpretation of The Sandy Ground Project that had brought me to tears a month prior. This time I wasn't alone as there was not a dry eye on the entire beach. I could not have been prouder of those kids and my daughter especially. They knocked it out of the park and helped make the day even more unforgettable.

• • •

Shortly after Olivia's playground was opened, I was contacted by People Magazine. They had gotten wind of The Sandy Ground Project and were going to do a story about it. The magazine wanted to send out some photographers for a photo shoot and Manasquan was their destination of choice.

Early one sunny summer morning, all of us converged on Seawatch Beach once again. Many of the Angels Army guys were there, their children, a lot of local kids from town, and many others who had been working so hard on the project with us.

The photographer took hundreds of pictures on and around Olivia's playground. But when it came time to publish the story in their upcoming issue, the picture and story was only about me. It had been earmarked for their "Heroes Among Us" section and the picture featured was just me sitting on a slide with some of the kids. There was nothing about the volunteers, nothing about the organizers or builders, just me. I was mortified.

I begged the magazine to change the story, to talk about all the amazing people that had come together to make the project possible. They refused. I was told that People Magazine has made its mark by focusing only on individuals, not groups. Always has, always will. I still struggle today with the perception that this project is somehow mine. That couldn't be further from the truth. In actuality, it is bigger than all of us. All I do is try and connect all the amazing people who can move mountains, and change the world for the better, all in the name of our 26 angels. I tried as best I could to convey this to People Magazine, but they stood pat.

As embarrassed as I was, there was no way The Sandy Ground Project could afford to NOT have the story run. People Magazine is everywhere you look. It's on every newsstand, in every dentist's office, on every coffee table, and in every line in every supermarket across the whole country. The publicity the story could bring to our cause was invaluable.

And that is exactly what happened. Just by putting our web address into that one-page feature, our fundraising effort went to the next level. The Sandy Ground Project was no longer a regional thing. It had made its way into the hearts and minds of people everywhere. It was a nationwide effort now and the donations that started to show up at our New Jersey office were all the proof we needed.

I didn't like being featured in that story. It made The Sandy Ground Project about me, which is not only uncomfortable personally but also untrue. However, the boost that People Magazine gave the project could not be denied. It gave us the momentum we would need to fund the next playground… and the next… and maybe get us all the way to #26 eventually. And, of course, I did enjoy the fact that the Connors' children (Dan and Mary's) were featured in the magazine as well—an honor that family richly deserved.

But one step at a time, right? Now it was time to focus on the job directly in front of us… which would be to continue our southward progress down the New Jersey coastline. We were set to storm the beach at Normandy.

As we wrapped up in Manasquan, we felt the Engel family was a part of ours. We felt we knew Olivia and vowed to honor her legacy and tell her story wherever and whenever we had the opportunity. To this day, the name Olivia is revered in our ranks and brings a smile to the faces of everyone who hears it.

Squan Strong meets Angels Army

CHAPTER TWELVE

Playground Celebrating the Life of Chase Kowalski

Normandy Beach, New Jersey

The Sandy Ground Project was quickly evolving into something of a juggernaut. While the fundraising for the playgrounds was still the linchpin to executing and continuing our builds, the tidal wave of love and support never seemed to be an issue. All the families, volunteers, news media, the general public, and maybe myself more than anybody—we were experiencing something of a high from it all. The positive energy at the builds and ribbon-cuttings was palpable. The signs from the angels above were very real and seemed to come with every single playground we built.

Yet, for those of us who were *not* those 26 families… for those of us who had not suffered the worst imaginable loss… it all came with an element of guilt. In the back of your mind you can't help but ask: Am I taking advantage of a tragedy here? Am I benefiting off of the loss of others?

While certainly no one was profiting financially from being a part of The Sandy Ground Project, there was no question that our lives were being significantly bettered. We were profiting spiritually. We were meeting amazing people. We were serving a higher purpose. And with all that, in the back of your mind you think about how it would not be possible without catastrophe.

Clearly none of us could have stopped what happened in Newtown, and we certainly can't change the past. The best thing we could do was to lift each other up and cherish the friendships and memories that have been made in the wake of a terrible tragedy. We can treat each family, playground, and legacy with the utmost reverence and respect.

This has been a feeling that all of us associated with The Sandy Ground Project have been dealing with from the very beginning. I mention it in this chapter specifically because of the great blessing and honor it is to call people like the Kowalskis our friends. And that would not have happened if the world didn't lose an incredible little boy named Chase.

I had heard of triathlons before. They are races that consist of swimming, biking, and running over long distances. It is an extremely tough sport to train for and even tougher to be good at.

What I had not heard of (until I met the Kowalskis) was a 7-year-old being a triathlete. But that is exactly what Chase Kowalski was. His high-energy personality and proclivity for any kind of sports-related activity had led him in that direction. It is difficult to imagine such a young kid being so dedicated to an endurance sport like that, but Chase had a spirit that went beyond his years. After having gotten to know Chase very well through the stories of his parents and sisters, a 7-year-old triathlete is not so hard to imagine after all. We feel like we know him very well.

. . .

On the way to meet with the Kowalskis for the first time, I got a call from Scott Zabelski of Blue Wave Printing. Scott had done some incredible work in the aftermath of Superstorm Sandy, raising funds with the sweatshirts and t-shirts printed in his Toms River shop. There was a point where you could not go anywhere in New Jersey without seeing one of his "Restore The Shore" logos attached to someone.

Scott had spent months donating the proceeds from his shirts up and down the Jersey Shore. At the New Jersey State FMBA, we had been helping Scott get the donations to the areas where they were needed most. Since we were the boots on the ground in a lot of places, we were best able to match the resource to the need. At our annual Valor Awards Dinner in the spring, Scott was honored with the prestigious "Civilian Award"—for someone outside the fire service who had gone above and beyond to serve their community. Since the onset of The Sandy Ground Project, Blue Wave Printing was supplying all of our shirts. They were all selling for $26 a piece (of course).

This particular phone call from Scott was purely playground-related though. He urged me to consider Normandy Beach as one of our locations. It was where he had grown up, and he was sorry to see that not a lot was being done there recovery-wise. I told him I'd consider it, and I would. Knowing Scott's ability to fundraise with his shirts, I figured a potential playground in Normandy Beach wouldn't be too hard to fund with his help.

. . .

When I arrived in Newtown for my initial meeting with the Kowalski family, I already had an in. Steve Kowalski's cousin was a good friend of Steve Lupinacci (from the Connecticut Burn Camp and Stratford Fire Department)—and he would be coming to the meeting as well. In addition to Chase's parents, Steve and Rebecca, a young lady named Michele Orzechowski was also at the meeting. She was sort of the de facto gatekeeper for the Kowalskis. With so many people looking to get something out of ALL of the Newtown victims' families at this point, Michele was there to prevent any kind of funny business. As one of Rebecca's best friends, she was trusted to protect the family as well as Chase's memory. As we all sat down at the kitchen table, it was clear that I would need to sell Michele on The Sandy Ground Project as much as I would the Kowalskis themselves. Her posture and demeanor told me she was very suspicious.

At first, I was very much struck by how at peace Rebecca seemed to be. Having met a handful of the families already, I was expecting her to be in a state of despair and turmoil to some degree. While she was obviously grieving, she had come to terms with what had happened to Chase. This was mostly due to the fact that he had come to her in a very real and vivid dream. He told his mother that he was okay, and that he was happy. Rebecca shared the details of the dream with her husband, and it had truly allowed them both to at least begin to heal.

Their focus had become the CMAK Foundation (for Chase Michael Anthony Kowalski)—a non-profit organization that focused on building family-friendly recreation centers. It was Rebecca and Steve's desire to create places in the community where children and their parents could go and be active together. Where they could bond through playing and exercising. They feel strongly that children are being left by themselves all too often these days, and end up immersed in video games, personal electronic devices, and things like that. (A situation that, possibly, could have even led to the tragedy at Sandy Hook.)

So the CMAK Foundation was created—not to establish more locations for kids to be dropped off at—but to foster a spirit of togetherness. For this reason, The Sandy Ground Project seemed to jive perfectly with that overall mission. It was active. It was outdoors. It was community. It was family. Rebecca and Steve loved the concept, and wanted to help us build a playground to celebrate Chase. And they ended up helping us well beyond that.

As we parted ways after that first meeting, the Kowalskis were enthusiastic and said they would get back to us. (I think Michele wanted to run a few background checks on The Sandy Ground to make sure we were legit.) Then Rebecca asked me if there was any way we would consider the town of Normandy Beach for Chase's playground. My jaw almost dropped. I had just gotten off the phone with Scott Zabelski about the very same town, and the chances anyone from Connecticut (or New Jersey for that matter) had even heard of Normandy Beach was miniscule. It was beyond coincidence.

It turns out that Steve's uncle, Michael Cunningham, lives in Normandy Beach and it is a location on the Jersey Shore that the Kowalskis are quite fond of. There was a playground there on the bay that had been destroyed during Superstorm Sandy. It was a playground that Chase had played on, and loved, mere weeks before Sandy made landfall on the New Jersey coast.

It was getting to the point where these types of signs from above were clear. And while I was learning to read them, they were never any less stunning or miraculous. I knew right then that Chase's playground would not only be built in Normandy Beach, but at the exact location where the old one had been.

. . .

Normandy Beach, New Jersey is a very small, very quiet town on the coast. It lies on a very narrow strip of land between the Barnegat Bay and Atlantic Ocean, and this strip of land got pummeled as bad as any area during Superstorm Sandy. Some of the most famous images from the storm came from this same peninsula: The bay meeting the ocean at the Mantoloking Bridge. Massive fires raging in the Brick Beach section. The Jet-Star roller coaster at the Seaside Heights boardwalk fallen into the ocean.

While it didn't have the same name recognition, Normandy Beach was right there in the thick of it. It was definitely an area in need of restoring, the most hard-hit part of Toms River Township. We were directed to deal with the "Normandy Beach Association" when exploring the possibility of building a playground there.

The President of the Association is a great guy named Joe Ferris. He could not have been a more accommodating or supportive host, and he really advocated for us when it came to dealing with the town and his fellow residents. I visited him in Normandy Beach for the first time around sunset and he showed me this idyllic bay-front location for the playground. Just a sleepy, peaceful little area where the tiny waves slide lightly onto the sand. It also had a clubhouse right next to it, which would serve as an excellent base-camp for the Angels Army. Because when you are doing all these outdoor builds, it's nice to know there is a little shelter nearby to eat in or use the bathroom. That wasn't always the case.

In addition to Joe, another local ally we had in Normandy Beach was the Toms River PBA. We never before had the local police department get involved, but through the leadership of Jesse Robertazzi we had exactly that. It is always a huge plus to have the cops in your corner and this project was no exception. Jesse and his fellow officers were a force when it came to fundraising and physically putting the playground together. They even helped out when the Kowalskis were ticketed in New Jersey by a State Trooper. Needless to say it was a great partnership and friendship.

. . .

There were a few months in between the time we'd decided to build Chase's playground in Normandy Beach and when we would actually build it. We were busy building all along the coast, from New Jersey to Connecticut and back again. But that time also allowed us to get to know the Kowalskis better and better. Rebecca and Steve—along with their daughters Brittany and Erin—were becoming fixtures at all the builds. They supported The Sandy Ground Project wholeheartedly and have become like family to not only me, but many of the Angels Army volunteers and our contractors Toni and Rich.

As we were working on Dylan Hockley's playground in Westport, I remember Rebecca asking me which playground, number-wise, Chase's would wind up being. With all the plans coming together in different towns, and some of those plans now overlapping, I told her it would be anywhere from #7 to #10. Erin, Chase's older sister, commented to me that it would be really cool if it could be #8. Eight was Chase's baseball number and Rebecca viewed it as a symbol for him. She would often talk about turning the number 8 on its side to make the symbol for infinity. This represented Chase's spirit living on forever.

Of course, two months later, we dug our shovels into the sand to break ground on Normandy Beach. Our eighth playground would be for Chase.

. . .

The build commenced with some concern about the high water table at the playground's site. After initially drilling the holes, we hit water each time. This caused us to alter the construction process a bit, but after doing so we were off and running. Chase's favorite colors were green and blue, and the playground structure reflected that. The special panel on the structure is a picture of Chase looking through a heart shape he had formed with his hands. It is an image that has sort of become his logo, and it's the first thing you see when arriving at his playground.

On the first day of building it became apparent that Steve Kowalski was not only a great friend and supporter of The Sandy Ground Project, but an asset on the construction site as well. Steve's background is in the heating/air-conditioning business, so he was obviously very saavy on a job site. He poured himself into the process for Chase's playground—as well as several other playgrounds to come.

The Kowalski family network also proved to be worth their weight in gold as they helped with every aspect of the build. Steve's uncle Mike Cunningham, in addition to being our gateway into Normandy Beach, had made a sizable donation to help fund the playground and provided all the food for the volunteers. His wife, Mary Lou, made an amazing flag for the playground that featured Chase's name and number ("CHASE 8"). And the Kowalskis family friend Charlie, who had flown up from Florida to be a part of the build, assisted us greatly with one of her ideas. She suggested that Rebecca, Steve, Erin, and Brittany place their handprints and a message to Chase into the flagstone on the playground. They loved the idea and so did we. So Mark Virag and Herman Peters, our two ace masons, set about creating a beautiful half-moon shaped stone for the dedication.

• • •

This build was at a time when Mark Virag was in the midst of one of his battles with cancer. His face was heavily bandaged from the treatments, but there was nothing that would stop him from fulfilling his duties as a member of the Angels Army. At one point, a friend of mine named Eugene Ambrosio pulled me aside on the job site. Gino is a fellow counselor at the Connecticut Children's Burn Camp who I've known for several years. He is also a nurse at Sloan Kettering Hospital and a key fundraiser, photographer, and social media expert for The Sandy Ground Project. He would go on to be the Chairman of our West Islip build a little further down the road.

On that first day in Normandy Beach, Gino said to me, "Bill, I know that guy," as he pointed towards Mark. "He probably doesn't know it, but I was his nurse." So Gino went up to Mark and asked if he remember him, which he did not. Mark was in particularly rough shape at the time. When Gino told Mark that he had taken care of him in the hospital, Mark lit up. He was shocked, but also seemed to have a light bulb go off. Gino's voice sort of came back to him. Mark gave Gino a big bear hug and thanked him. They became fast friends, another not-so-coincidental connection that the angels had arranged through The Sandy Ground Project.

Best of all, now we had an inside guy at the hospital when it came to Mark's cancer treatments. Gino would keep us all updated on Mark's future visits, and clue us in if anything was needed there.

. . .

Mark spent a lot of time that first day working with Rebecca Kowalski on the family flagstone. It was a key piece to the playground, one with such a personal touch, and Mark took great care in getting it exactly right. By late afternoon, it was time for the family to put their handprints into the cement and leave their message. There were about 15 to 20 of us who were gathered around, and had the honor of being present for what happened next.

There was total silence as each of the family members placed their handprints into the stone. Once it was completed, Rebecca unexpectedly pulled out an envelope. Inside the envelope were Chase's ashes.

As she sprinkled the ashes over the stone, Rebecca said, "Ok Chase. Now you can be with your friends forever."

Time just about stopped when she said that. Not a word was spoken, and not a sound could be heard except for the rhythmic beating of the small waves on the sand. It was almost like a drum. Tap... tap... tap... tap...

We all stood crying in silence for several minutes. We knew right away what an incredible and emotional moment this was—one none of us will forget as long as we live. Then, in a remarkable show of strength,

Rebecca turned to the rest of us and said: "C'mon, cheer up! This is supposed to be a celebration. Let's get back to work!" Her voice did crack ever so slightly, but the message was crystal clear.

We all marveled at Rebecca's resolve. Here was a woman who had lost her little boy, and she was the one cheering *us* up after such a heartfelt display. We all hugged each other, hugged the Kowalskis, and thanked them for letting us be a part of such a powerful moment.

And then we followed Rebecca's orders and got back to work.

· · ·

After a strenuous, emotional, and productive first day on the construction site, the Angels Army convened at the Crab's Claw Inn in nearby Lavallette. Everyone was unwinding with a drink or two and something to eat. After an hour or so, the guys began to trickle out—to go home and rest up for tomorrow's building duties. Mark Virag began making the rounds to say his goodbyes as well.

He shook my hand and said, "Thanks Bill, see you tomorrow," then reached over me and into a booth to say the same to Rebecca. Only she would not be satisfied with a simple handshake. She began to climb out of the booth and make her way around the table towards Mark.

Since Rebecca is barely five feet tall, and Mark is about 6-foot-4, she pulled up a chair next to him and climbed up on it. Rebecca gave Mark the biggest hug and kiss on the cheek you'd ever see. They had bonded throughout the day while working so carefully on that flag-stone, and this true display of friendship and love was the payoff. You could see Mark melting right before your eyes.

It was a simple gesture, but a remarkably cool moment. That Rebecca would give Mark—a man struggling so mightily through cancer to be there—such a gift was so special. She knew that a handshake wouldn't do justice to the day they'd shared.

· · ·

The following day we would wrap up the building of Chase Kowalski's playground in Normandy Beach. As the finishing touches were being taken care of, Joe Ferris—Normandy Beach Association President—came up to me and expressed his gratitude for being a part of such an effort.

Joe confided to me that he too had lost a child. A few years earlier, his 23-year-old daughter had been killed in a car accident. He was still having a very difficult time with it naturally, but he felt it gave him a special connection with the Kowalskis and the playground being built in his town. He strove to make this piece of The Sandy Ground Project the best it could possibly be, in honor of his daughter.

He shared this with me, not for sympathy or attention, but as a show of unity and friendship with our mission. "This is not about me at all, it's about Chase," he said. "I just wanted you to know how special it has been for me to be a part of this."

• • •

With the playground complete, Carlos Soto and I stood around on the beach that night smoking a couple of victory cigars. As we did, a young father and his mother walked by and asked us what was going on. We told them all about The Sandy Ground Project, Carlos talked about how much it had done for him, and the two of them were touched by how special it was to have one of these playgrounds in their small town.

The woman commented that she would like to do something really nice for us. A little while later, the two of them showed up with about 15 pizzas, a couple cases of beer and soda, and an impromptu beach party broke out. We had a great time with them. They had, in fact, done something really nice for us.

• • •

A few days before the ribbon-cutting, I was out to dinner with my daughter Kelly, her fiancé Billy, and her soon-to-be in-laws—Christine and Dennis Bourke. Dennis is a very talented singer/guitarist, sort of like James Taylor-style, and he was performing that night.

He played several favorites, but a rendition of one of his songs really struck me. It was "The Rainbow Connection", the song that

Kermit the Frog sings in the original Muppet Movie. For some reason the song really resonated with me considering all that had been going on with the playgrounds. The song seemed to capture something—to sum up something—that The Sandy Ground Project was trying to say.

I asked Dennis if he would play the song at the ribbon-cutting ceremony in Normandy Beach. He said he would be honored.

• • •

On August 21, 2013, a perfectly sunny and cool afternoon on the Jersey Shore, we cut the ribbon opening Chase Kowalski's playground. It was a sports-themed ceremony, so 26 One-World soccer balls were distributed to all the kids present. We had a huge balloon release—blue and green—and a plane circled overhead carrying Chase's message: "TO NORMANDY... WITH LOVE, CHASE... WHERE ANGELS PLAY"

Just before the official ceremony was to start, a young lady came up to me and introduced herself. She said that her mom and her husband had met us all the night before—the ones who had gotten us the pizzas and drinks. She said, "My mom wanted to do something nice for you guys, and wanted you to have this."

She handed me a check. This is not the first time this had happened, of course, and all donations are certainly very generous and very needed. But when I saw that this check was for $20,000... I couldn't believe it. I thanked her profusely, totally stunned by their gesture and the amount of money I was now holding in my hand. It was like The Sandy Ground Project always found a way to even itself out. While I had been counting on support from elsewhere to help fund the Normandy Beach build, this proved to be just another opportunity for a new angel to reveal herself.

I caught up with the woman later in the day and thanked her for her amazing gift. She said, "We have been lucky enough to have a great life, and we are honored to be able to help you." Her only request was to use the money in good health, and to keep the donation an anonymous one. Of course we would honor both requests.

• • •

Rebecca Kowalski made an amazing speech to thank all the volunteers who had built Chase's playground, and everyone responsible for making it possible. She said that, although we were all basically strangers just a few days prior, we were now standing with our newly-formed family. I thought that hit the nail on the head.

We continued our tradition of raising the flags. An American flag, a Connecticut flag, and the custom-made "CHASE 8" flag courtesy of Aunt Mary Lou Cunningham.

Dennis Bourke took the sand and performed his (now-famous) rendition of "The Rainbow Connection". I guess I was not alone in having that song strike a chord, because there wasn't a dry eye on the beach. As I looked up at the Kowalskis, I saw that Rebecca was full-on sobbing during the song. She glanced over at me and mouthed the words, "How did you know?"

I just shrugged. Know what?

Later on I would learn that "The Rainbow Connection" was Chase and Rebecca's favorite song—one they shared a bond over during his lifetime. And since his passing, Rebecca considered any rainbow as being a direct sign from Chase. A sign that told her he was there, and he was okay.

I was awestruck when she told this to me. I felt as though I was meant to be in that restaurant that night to hear Dennis play. And he was meant to play it for me so that he could be at the ribbon-cutting for the Kowalskis. Chase wanted it that way. When I told Dennis, he couldn't believe how special it was, to have Chase communicate that song to his mother through him. There are signs from the angels all around us, and then there are clear, concise messages. This was Chase's message to us and it was indisputably real.

· · ·

The Sandy Ground Project and the Kowalski family's relation-ship did not end after the ribbon-cutting ceremony that evening. Not even close. They have become great friends to me and to so many of the Angels Army volunteers. They have vacationed with many of our guys, spent quality time with our contractors (Toni and Rich), and have become our advisors and sounding-board for all things related to the project. Rebecca summed it up perfectly during her ribbon-cutting speech. We were all now part of a newly-formed (and huge) family.

We would even turn to the Kowalskis when tragedy struck in our own lives. One of our most loyal Angels Army members, Billy Valentine, lost his daughter Christina (21) to suicide nearly a year after the Normandy Beach build. In this immensely painful time, Rebecca and Steve were now there for him to lean on for love and support. The Sandy Ground Project kept expanding its network of friends and family—people who would be there for you when you need them the most.

• • •

That winter, around the one-year anniversary of the Newtown tragedy, Rebecca did an interview with NBC's David Ushery. They could have conducted the interview anywhere, but Rebecca chose to head to the Jersey Shore in December and do it in Normandy Beach. Chase's playground was where she felt him the most. Her and David spoke about Chase while strolling his beach and swinging on his swings.

Each playground built during The Sandy Ground Project sets itself apart in its own specific way. Some are defined by the end result. Some are defined by the community or school that hosts the playground. Some are defined by a rainbow, a butterfly, a speech from a parent, or a significant sign from above.

Chase Kowalski's playground was defined by the wonderful moments we experienced and the relationships that were formed because of him. And it is as simple as taking Chase's special number, 8, and turning it on its side—that will tell you how long those relationships, and those memories, will last.

Herman Peters and Bob Lavin the projects "heart and soul"

CHAPTER THIRTEEN

Fairfield, Connecticut

Fairfield—both the town and the University—turned out to have a great sense of community and, therefore, a great place for The Sandy Ground Project to have success. As I worked my angles through the fire service and Burn Camp contacts, we did the same through Fairfield University.

A great connection we made through the angels network was Anka Roberto, who took the lead as far as our relationship with Fairfield University. She is a nursing professor there, so she was able to drum up a good amount of support. This included events at the school, getting us volunteer workers through the school, as well as pulling off some big-time fundraising throughout the area. Anka's brother, who was a chef at a well-known restaurant in Greenwich, was able to arrange for us to hold an extremely successful fundraiser at his place. All told, we pulled in around $15,000 in a single night there. So Anka proved to be one of the biggest assets to carrying out our mission in Fairfield.

Meanwhile, I was picking up some key players for The Sandy Ground Project; some great guys who would wind up going the distance with us, well beyond Fairfield. Steve Lupinacci put me in touch with Bob Smith, the President of the Fairfield firefighters union. Bob is a very soft-spoken, humble, and genuine guy. He was able to mobilize the firefighters there to support and work for us whenever we needed them. Also, Joe Rainis and Pat Barry from Connecticut Tank Removal would come on board and become key players. Starting at Fairfield, they handled the majority of our excavation needs with their heavy machinery. The owner of Connecticut Tank Removal, Joe Palmieri, would become a great partner as well. So we had those guys leading the charge for our Fairfield playground.

. . .

A big player in local Fairfield politics is a group called the Fair Acres Association, and my new friends in town there clued me in that their approval would be necessary before moving any further. I did a presentation on The Sandy Ground Project at one of their meetings and, for the first time in a while, was met with a lot of naysayers.

They said it would be a distraction. That it would be too dangerous at this location. That it would attract too many kids and just wind up being a liability.

I told them it would be just the opposite. That the playground would be a safe place that kids could visit with their families, and be a symbol of a community living and working together for something good. With the help of the firefighters' advocacy and support from Fairfield University, we eventually won them over. They decided to accept the playground as a gift to the town.

From there, Sandy Ground Fever seemed to spread throughout Fairfield. Just about every business began selling these little clouds reading "I Believe In Angels" (similar to how Muscular Dystrophy uses shamrocks for people to put names on when they donate). So many stores, restaurants, and bars were soon covered in clouds. It really helped to not only raise money, but create a buzz in the town about what we were doing. The Old Post Tavern in particular came up strong for us, doing their own fundraising events and pulling in a lot of money. Overall the community was wonderful to us. A special shout-out needs to be given to the owners of the Old Post Tavern—they provided not only a fundraiser, but hosted any event we needed them to.

. . .

As we worked out the specifics, we decided that the colors would be blue, teal, pink, and white—a very nautical look with the playground being on the beach. Also, we knew that horses and orca whales would need to be included as well, and we would just have to figure out how.

Penfield Beach is a beautiful setting, a very peaceful spot right on the sound. As we broke ground to begin the build, we had U.S. Senator from Connecticut, Richard Blumenthal, on hand to make a speech and welcome everyone. As he spoke, he pointed out that Penfield Beach is the only beach in the entire state that permits horseback riding after a certain date. None of us had realized this, and now it was clear why the angels were pointing us in this direction. We decided right then and there to get some real-life horses on that beach for the ribbon-cutting ceremony.

So what about the orca whales? At this point I was half-expecting Shamu to jump out of the sound, do a massive belly-flop, and wave to everyone. That didn't happen, but as we all brainstormed how to get orcas involved in some way, a Fairfield firefighter named John Cieplinski spoke up. He said he'd never done it before, but he would like to try and make a sand sculpture of an orca whale on the beach. We told him to give it a try and acquired all the tools he would need.

What John produced was amazing. It was an extremely realistic and life-size orca whale, made to look like it was jumping right up out of the sand. It's no small miracle that not a professional artist, but a firefighter, could accomplish this on his rookie attempt. Now we had our horses, our orcas, and we were good to go…

· · ·

At one point in the middle of the build, it began pouring rain. We had to stop construction for a bit. That is always disappointing when it happens, but this rainstorm had a truly magnificent side-effect.

As the rain subsided, the sun came back out more powerful than before. The result was a beautiful rainbow—a full, vivid arc stretching from one side of the horizon to the other. It was so perfect, every color clearly seen, and it seemed to be framing the playground for us. Everyone rushed to grab their cameras and phones to capture the moment. But no rush was necessary. The rainbow stood there majestically over the water for more than an hour. Some of the greatest pictures of the entire project came out of that day.

We marveled at the rainbow, many of us thinking that the angels were trying to tell us they liked our work. And that work continued late into the night that night, more spirited than ever. The moment seemed to bring all of us even closer together.

• • •

One tradition that started on the Fairfield build was including a bell on each playground. There is a story behind this, very closely tied to the angels that the playgrounds are for.

Shortly before we started the Fairfield project, I had sent an e-mail to Amy Coyne, our friend from Bay St. Louis, Mississippi. I was telling her about how well The Sandy Ground Project had been going, that there were already eight playgrounds done, and that it all started with her daughter Karli's letter to us after Superstorm Sandy. I mentioned a quote from my favorite movie, *It's a Wonderful Life*, which was: "One man's life touches so many others." In this case, it was one little girl.

I mentioned this to my right-hand man Brian D'Antoni and he said that he loved that movie as well. But he had been thinking more about the quote: "Every time a bell rings, an angel gets its wings." I agreed that the line seemed appropriate with all the angels we had been hearing from lately. Then he suggested putting a bell on each playground and including the quote. I thought it was an excellent idea.

A retired Bridgeport firefighter, Bob Diaz, pointed us towards the Bevin Brothers Bell Company. They were located nearby in East Hampton, Connecticut, and he was sure they would be willing to donate the bells. As fate would have it, when Brian's close friend Paula told our story to the folks at Bevin, they told us that they were actually the company that made the bell for *It's a Wonderful Life* back in 1946. We couldn't believe it! They said of course they would donate the bells.

And so a shiny new bell was installed on the playground at Penfield Beach. It became sort of a phenomenon, as we began selling small replicas of the bells as Christmas ornaments. Pretty soon orders were coming in from all over the country. While it was a logistical nightmare for my wife and daughter (who were tying on all the ribbons and mailing them), it was a tremendous tool for fundraising.

. . .

On September 15, 2013, a bright, cool morning along the Long Island Sound, we cut the ribbon on the Fairfield playground. Penfield Beach was replete with horses walking the beach and kids running around on the sand, itching to play.

. . .

With the ribbon cut to open Playground #9, everyone went back (once again) to the Old Post Tavern for a celebratory lunch.

The community of Fairfield had embraced the Where Angels Play Foundation with open arms and allowed another community and family to heal if even just a little. The love and friendship we experienced there would carry us for months and years to come.

Chris Dorko & Anthony D'Esposito
digging the foundation for Caroline

CHAPTER FOURTEEN

Playground Celebrating the Life of Caroline Previdi

Island Park, New York

Superstorm Sandy was one of the worst—if not *the* worst—natural disaster to ever hit the New York metropolitan area. And in a time when information and images from the media, as well as private citizens, travel so quickly—the degree to which people were suffering and struggling was never any secret. It compelled people, whether the impact on them personally was large or small, to go out and do something. It seemed like the relief effort was everywhere you looked.

It was the relief effort, the selflessness of others that the storm victims counted on. The help from those lucky enough to be spared. And it's the spirit that best describes Caroline Previdi. She was always willing and eager to share her blessings with those less fortunate. She insisted on donating her toys to children who she felt needed them more, and gave up all her savings—a large jar of coins—to a priest who'd spoken about a children's charity called "Toy Chest". This from a girl only 6 years old.

Caroline, somehow, had an innate understanding that she was lucky and should do what she could to help out those who were not. But if ever her mom were to point out how lucky she was, she would quickly point out: "We're not lucky, we're blessed!"

The Sandy Ground Project, in addition to paying tribute to those who had lost their lives at Sandy Hook Elementary School, has the same primary objective that Caroline did. To pitch in and help those who were less fortunate in whatever way possible. We didn't really realize it until Playground #10 began to formulate in our minds and hearts, but we were merely following in Caroline's footsteps.

• • •

I met with Caroline's mother, Sandy Previdi (Sandy, of course!), on another cold Connecticut morning in the winter of 2013. This is where she first told me about Caroline's mature understanding of the needs of others. She was a giver, always giving away whatever she had (toys, coins, etc.) if she felt that someone else needed it more. And that is what ultimately won Sandy over to allow us to build a playground in Caroline's honor. Her thinking was, "Caroline was a giver, and what better gift to give than a playground for the victims of Superstorm Sandy!"

The Previdis are an extremely private family, led by Sandy who is a very sweet, strong, and religious woman. Very full of faith, particularly in the fact that Caroline was now in heaven along with the other angels. During our first meeting she expressed to me that, while they would love to be a part of building a playground to celebrate Caroline's life and spirit, she would prefer that it remain as under the radar as possible. No media, no fanfare, the less the family would be in the spotlight the better. We would definitely honor those wishes to the best of our ability. But whatever the circumstances, Sandy cherished the thought of other children playing in Caroline's name. Because it reflected her personality so perfectly.

On the flip-side was her son Walker—Caroline's big brother—who is a very outgoing and gregarious young man. He was all in on the playground project and his role as honorary foreman from the very start. He is good friends with Fred Hubbard (a veteran Sandy Ground foreman himself from Playground #3 in Ansonia) and the two of them excitedly traded notes on the job as Caroline's build approached. Walker Previdi was certainly going to be another great personality added to our team.

• • •

Caroline was known to be an avid little sports fan, especially of her beloved New York Yankees. They visited a Red Sox souvenir shop and Caroline would not enter unless she got the ok from her Dad. He had to be called at work to assure Caroline it was ok. As far as she was concerned, the only ballpark that existed—and the only one worth ever going inside—was in The Bronx.

But being a female sports fan does not necessarily make you a tom-boy. And especially not in Caroline Previdi's case. Her mother assured me that Caroline was nothing if not a "girly-girl". She was obsessed with all things pink. Pink clothes, pink room, pink shoes, and (naturally) a pink Yankees cap.

With such a personality, the look of Caroline's playground was easily coming into focus.

• • •

While there is obviously no shortage of Yankees fans in New Jersey and Connecticut, this felt like the perfect time for The Sandy Ground Project's first foray into New York. The Empire State had more than its fair share of communities battered by the winds and waters of Superstorm Sandy, so why not have the first Sandy Ground playground there inspired by the little girl with an "NY" on her cap? If only there was a New York town willing to have us…

• • •

The media coverage that The Sandy Ground Project received certainly had its benefits in the fundraising sense. Anything from a local Connecticut talk-show to People Magazine would bring us some sort of uptick in our fundraising returns. But sometimes the good press had different side-effects, like getting our name to those who could potentially benefit from *us*.

I received an email from a woman named Kathy Cleary, an elementary school teacher from Island Park, New York. The note was completely out of the blue—no one referred her, nor did she know anyone that I knew. No connection.

The email explained that she had seen what we were doing through the news. She'd visited our website and loved the whole concept of what we had been doing on the Connecticut and New Jersey coasts. She also explained the devastation that was experienced in her own town from Superstorm Sandy, and they were still trying mightily to dig themselves out.

Island Park had been absolutely crushed during Sandy, but it's not a town anyone would have ever heard of. Between nearby places like Long Beach and Breezy Point, who'd gotten much of the attention, Island Park had become somewhat lost in the shuffle. As a very small, working-class community, they had gotten every bit of the storm with only a fraction of the relief and publicity. Their town hall was destroyed and local government was now conducted from a trailer. The elementary school where Kathy taught was totally flooded. The people there were forced to come together in such a trying time and would persevere. She described Island Park as "the little town that could".

So where do I fit into this? Well, Kathy said that if we were looking for somewhere to build one of our amazing playgrounds, she would like to throw Island Park's hat in the ring. She assured me that, if somehow chosen, a playground was very much needed there. The people, and specifically the children, badly needed that kind of boost and sign of recovery. She said a town like Island Park would certainly not only maintain it, but collectively cherish a playground that was built there.

Our first attempt to bring The Sandy Ground Project to New York had fallen flat. Primarily because the proposed site was within the Five Boroughs (on Staten Island), and this meant dealing with the bureaucratic quagmire that is the New York City Parks and Recreation Department.

But Island Park was located just east of the city limits, on an actual island nestled within the channels and harbors near Long Island's south shore. As I read Kathy's email again, becoming more and more intrigued by "the little town that could", I started to think: This could actually work. Island Park was the sort of place that The Sandy Ground

Project was needed most. And also the sort of place that The Sandy Ground Project seemed to work best.

We could use Caroline Previdi's generosity of spirit to lift them up.

• • •

So I reached out to Kathy Cleary and told her The Sandy Ground Project was very interested in venturing onto New York soil and doing so in Island Park. It seemed to be the ideal place—a town that needed and wanted the playground, with a real underdog spirit to boot. In no time, Kathy had set up a town hall meeting at the local volunteer firehouse so that I could come and present The Sandy Ground Project in greater detail to the people of Island Park. As soon as I arrived, I knew I had the right place.

Word had somehow gotten out that Caroline Previdi was the potential namesake for our next playground, and the people of Island Park had done their homework. Every single person who attended my presentation that night was totally decked out in pink. It was quite moving to see such a show of support and unity. Clearly they wanted us there, wanted the playground desperately, and most importantly, they wanted to welcome Caroline Previdi into their hometown with open arms.

From there, my presentation was basically a formality. Island Park, New York was already home to a playground celebrating the life of Caroline Previdi. All we had to do now was build it.

• • •

As the ball got rolling in terms of planning and fundraising, Anthony D'Esposito quickly emerged as our point man in Island Park. Being a detective with the NYPD, as well as the Fire Chief of the Island Park Volunteer Fire Department, he was certainly a well-known and well-respected man in town. Someone who could get things done and someone you definitely want in your corner. We would become great friends during The Sandy Ground's stay in Island Park. The town was so welcoming and so enthusiastic, and Anthony was the ambassador leading the charge.

Not long after I received the email from Kathy Cleary introducing me to Island Park, I was hanging with friends and family at one of our Sandy Ground fundraisers. It was at Bar Anticipation in Lake Como, New Jersey—a famous Jersey Shore hot-spot that has always been extremely generous to us. This particular event was geared towards raising money for a potential upcoming build in Belmar. I wound up speaking with a man named Gene Hickey, who lives nearby and is my wife's best friend's brother-in-law. (How's that for "six degrees of separation"?)

Gene was particularly taken by the project, the outpouring of support it was garnering, and he wanted to get involved in some way. He mentioned that his company, Hallen Construction, would be interested in helping out should we ever wind up building a playground in New York. Hallen specializes in heavy construction—pipelines, bridges, utilities—so with all of their equipment and know-how, a playground would be a snap.

I said that would be great. We are always looking for more partners, more help, and (with fundraising a definite priority) more ways to get things done for free. I asked Gene if Hallen was based out of the city…

"No, we're actually in a little town near Long Beach… Island Park."

"No way!" I thought. I'm sure Gene assumed I had never heard of it, but I had just learned about Island Park from Kathy Cleary. The little town that could. I told Gene this looked to be another match made in heaven, and The Sandy Ground Project was all in to work with Hallen—most likely very soon in their own backyard. Caroline Previdi's playground, located in Masone Park, would wind up being only three blocks from their headquarters.

• • •

This turned out to be one of our most challenging builds, so we needed every last bit of the help Hallen Construction could provide. And they did turn out to be awesome—just loads of equipment and manpower at our disposal, and the beginning of a true friendship and partnership. They were able to fill just about any need. A cement mixer, guys to dig holes, an excavator, whatever the case may be. They would wind up helping us on future New York builds in East Rockaway, West Islip, and Roxbury as well. All in all, Gene Hickey wound up playing a huge part in helping us accomplish our ultimate mission.

Like I said though, this build was a tough one. Much like Chase's playground in Normandy Beach, the proximity to the water gave us trouble while drilling the holes. And even when we'd resolved that situation, a tool would break. Or there would be a problem with getting electricity. Or the weather would go sour. The Angels Army was no stranger to hiccups by this point, and pushed through every time.

While a bit frustrating at times, all of these challenges and obstacles to be overcome were not without a reward.

As a trying first day of work turned into a trying first night of work, the sun began to set. The effect on the sky all around Island Park, NY that evening was unbelievable. It turned the most brilliant shade of pink I've ever seen. It was so stark that everyone working just kind of slowed to a stopped, looked up, and looked at each other. Not an eye was dry, and not much needed to be said.

Much like the signs we'd seen in previous weeks and months, Caroline had sent us a clear thumbs-up. From the girl who loved pink, to the town that had worn pink for her… here was an amazing pink sight, taking over the skies.

• • •

Over the course of a few days, Caroline's playground began to take shape. It included the logo of her beloved New York Yankees, and was otherwise decked out completely in pink. This was also the second playground where we had installed the bell—something Sandy Previdi was very fond of because she always spoke of Caroline being an angel in heaven now. And with angels getting their wings in both Fairfield and Island Park, the bell was becoming part of the story, of the legacy, of The Sandy Ground Project.

• • •

When the construction on the playground was complete, the Island Park Fire Department hosted a dinner for all of the volunteers who had worked so hard on the project. As part of the ceremony, they swore me in as an honorary member of their department. Also, they swore in Rich Picerno as an honorary firefighter in their department and presented him with a full set of turnout gear. I have to say—honoring Rich in this way was as appropriate as it was deserved.

On the job-site, the buck stops with Rich Picerno. Through ten playgrounds now, his leadership of Giordano Construction was what ultimately got them all built. He is the man who knows where everything goes, how it's supposed to look, and how to execute everything quickly and correctly. He is the Xs and Os guy. He is also the only mainstay of The Angels Army without a background in the fire service. While he was becoming a brother to us, he was not a brother in the firefighting sense. Until now, that is.

When the Island Park F.D. made this presentation, both Rich and his wife Toni were in tears. Toni told me later that Rich had never received any kind of award or honor such as this, and it absolutely meant the world to him. Rich had been doing incredible things with us—and bonding with us all—by way of The Sandy Ground Project. And now he was our true brother in every sense of the word.

· · ·

On September 28, 2013—a bright, shiny day in Island Park—we cut the ribbon on a playground celebrating the life of Caroline Previdi. It was great to see so many of the other Newtown families come out in support of the Previdis and The Sandy Ground Project. Many of their loved ones had playgrounds already, and the others had playgrounds on the horizon.

The main thing I remember from that day was the speech that Sandy Previdi gave. To hear such a reserved, private person speak so eloquently to the crowd there was impressive—and even more impressive was the power of her message. I remember her thanking God for the precious gift that Caroline was, and thanked God for the six years of joy that she'd given to her and her family. After such a loss, here she was *thanking* God for what she had been given. If that isn't the epitome of faith, I don't know what is.

Originally this ribbon-cutting was planned to be an extremely quiet and private event, except that wasn't going to work for Caroline's brother Walker. Our honorary foreman was excited to open the playground and riled up by the prospect of it being on television somehow. After his mother's beautiful speech, Walker grabbed the clippers to cut the ribbon. He yelled out, "Who wants to get their playground on?!?" and all the kids excitedly streamed past him, yelling, taking over the sprawling pink structure.

The ribbon-cutting wound up getting some great coverage from the NBC Nightly News thanks to a producer named Michele Melnick and reporter Katy Tur. Michele had been observing throughout the build and really did an excellent job of telling the story thoroughly and in a sensitive way. There were interviews with the Kowalski family, as well as Carlos Soto, and the story wound up turning into a huge (and national) fundraising vehicle.

At one point, even Michele's cameraman pulled me aside and thanked us for providing him with the opportunity to film our build. He said he was so used to pointing his camera at negative stories, and this was the ultimate breath of fresh air. He was the one who described The Sandy Ground Project as "a triumph over darkness." I thought that was a great way to put it, and still quote him whenever it's necessary to boil our entire mission down to one simple phrase.

Michele and Katy's piece came out so well that when Brian Williams presented it to the nation, it struck a chord with him as well. And Mr. Williams would eventually come to one of our playgrounds personally later on. He wanted to see what was going on and report on it himself.

• • •

Less than 24 hours after a beautiful ribbon-cutting ceremony, I got a distressed phone call from Island Park. The bell that we had installed on Caroline's playground had been stolen. It was taken some time that first night. The people of the town were shocked, appalled, upset, and embarrassed that this had happened on their turf. They had welcomed the playground, welcomed Caroline, and now someone had gone and tarnished it. Or at least *tried* to...

There was some talk amongst the volunteers that there was an unhappy neighbor somewhere in the residential area adjacent to Masone Park. They had been grumbling something along the lines of "that bell will never last." Although the bell was never found, and nothing could be proven, many of the folks who attended that build have their theories. As far as taking action, we decided to take the high road and let the angels work their magic.

The media latched onto the story of the stolen bell—they love to focus on the negative and get people outraged. When they called me looking for a quote, looking for some anger and bitterness, I simply told them that Caroline had gotten her wings no matter what became of that particular bell. And the same could not be said for the party who had stolen it.

The story got tons of attention and that, in turn, turned something as negative as vandalizing a playground into a positive. Because as people heard about what had happened and became incensed that someone would do such a thing, they wanted to help fix it. They began sending us donations in droves.

They'd send us checks with a note that would say: Please use this money to replace the bell that was stolen from Island Park. All told, one stolen bell wound up bringing in enough money for us to buy 500 new ones. It was an amazing example of how there are so many more good people in this world than bad.

• • •

Shortly after, Caroline's bell was replaced and the playground built for the people of Island Park was whole again. Even as a young child, it was Caroline's way to reach out to those in need. To give them whatever she had, whenever she could.

She had begun her mission of charity with a jar filled with every coin she could find. She finished that mission with a beautiful pink playground in a place that desperately needed it. And that guarantees Caroline will be giving back for years and years to come.

Chapter Fifteen

Playground Celebrating the Life of Daniel Barden

Highlands, New Jersey

Daniel Barden always wanted to be a firefighter. He had two uncles on the job in New York City and Washington, D.C., and it was Daniel's hope to follow in their footsteps someday.

After the tragedy at Sandy Hook Elementary School, Daniel was actually given a full firefighters funeral. Hundreds of firefighters from so many departments throughout the region showed up to pay their respects, as they would for any one of their fallen brothers. All in dress uniforms, the firefighters lined the streets of Newtown, Connecticut, and gave Daniel Barden a final salute. It was a very emotional scene—a brotherhood saying farewell to a 7-year-old boy who was adopted as one of their own.

• • •

I had the privilege to meet the Barden family at their home in Newtown to present them with The Sandy Ground Project. Like many other sets of parents I had gotten to know, they were hurting but took a shine to building a playground in their child's name. For Jackie Barden, it had just been a matter of building up the strength to begin the process.

She told me how, for months, she had been telling her friends and family: "There is this guy that I know I need to call back and meet with. I can't bring myself to do it just yet, but I need to get back to

123

him." She was referring to me and her hesitancy in getting involved with our project. But I was glad to finally have heard from Jackie and her husband Mark. And now I was in their kitchen, getting to know Daniel and the Barden family.

Jackie and I had a unique bond right away, both of us having grown up in extraordinarily large Irish families. She is one of ten siblings, and I am one of eleven. The funny thing though, is that Jackie and I are both #9 in the pecking order. When you grow up in a family that large, you come to identify closely with your number. It becomes part of your identity in a way, much like an athlete would be closely linked with their jersey number. So it was cool that Jackie and I could both relate to wearing that number—9—our entire lives.

The more we got to talking, the more we realized that not only were our numbers the same, but our family dynamics too. She described to me how all her brothers and sisters would get together during the summer, down at the Jersey Shore, just staying up all night and partying. They'd be playing cards, telling stories, dancing, just cutting loose all together. It sounded exactly like the summer weekends and family parties I'd known all my life. The Giblins (her maiden name) seemed to me like the Connecticut version of the Lavins.

• • •

During that initial meeting, Mark Barden told me a very emotional and beautiful story about the last time he saw his son Daniel. On the morning of December 14, 2012, both he and Daniel were up uncharacteristically early in the morning. They had a great conversation about everything that was going on in their lives, at Daniel's school, just touching base with one another one-on-one. Then, they watched the sun rise together and talked about that as well. Soon it was time to start getting ready for their day, but they had shared a great, simple morning—just chatting as father and son.

The rest of that day would turn out to be the beginning of a prolonged nightmare for the Bardens, but in the aftermath Mark thought back on that last morning with Daniel. He felt that they were meant to be awake at that moment, at the same time, to touch base with one another and create that memory. It was a snapshot in time that Mark will always cherish, and sunrises would hold a special place in his heart from then on.

I also had the pleasure of meeting Daniel's older sister and brother—Natalie and James. They are two of the most polite kids you would ever want to meet. They came up to me, shook hands, answered "yes, sir", said please and thank you, wonderful manners all around. You could see right away that this was just a great, nice family.

And a very musical family too. Each member playing at least one instrument, and Mark being a professional guitarist in a band called 'Alternate Universe'. Even Daniel was a budding little drummer, and there is a really cool YouTube video of him playing the drums with his dad's band. I guess it was only appropriate then… that a benefit concert was already in the works for the Jersey Shore town that would eventually host Playground #11—the playground celebrating the life of Daniel Barden.

• • •

Much like its neighbors Union Beach and Sea Bright—who already had their playgrounds—Highlands, New Jersey, took an immense hit from Superstorm Sandy. Here we were, coming up on the one-year anniversary of the day the storm hit, and still many of the residents were not yet back in their homes. The recovery and rebuilding was a very slow and very painstaking work in progress. Highlands was in need of a playground as much as any town out there. And thanks to the efforts of Highlands residents Karen and Joe Burke, one would soon be on the way.

Karen Burke, who is a key player in The Sandy Ground Project and handles all of our finances, served as the accountant of the New Jersey State FMBA while I was President. She, along with her husband Joe, were hard-hit during Superstorm Sandy—to the point where they had lost their house and had to rebuild. They were big proponents of The Sandy Ground Project from the start, playing a major role on our first build in Sea Bright. Karen and Joe stayed intimately involved with the project ever since, and now it was time for their town to host a playground of its own.

Karen and Joe are kind of like the de facto mayors of Highlands, NJ. Between the two of them, they know everyone and everyone knows them. This includes the business owners, politicians, people at the schools, neighborhood groups, and everyone else in between. Although they didn't hold any official title within the town, they could collectively be described as the "straw that stirs the drink".

• • •

Daniel Barden and Highlands, NJ seemed to be a natural fit. Jackie and her family had made a lifetime of great memories on the Jersey Shore and the Bardens found it to be a perfect location. The bayshore of the Highlands, where Daniel's playground would eventually stand, is also an ideal spot for watching the sun rise over the Atlantic Ocean and Sandy Hook Bay.

Without further ado, we put together a groundbreaking ceremony that would be covered by the weekend edition of Good Morning America. It turned out to be a groundbreaking in name only, because it was not even at the exact location where Daniel's playground would end up. There was a lot of confusion within the town (due to local politics) as to where they would allow us to build. Also, A LOT of clean up needed to be done before we could begin. In some ways, it seemed as though Superstorm Sandy could have blown through just yesterday.

The Angels Army set about clearing the area. The boardwalk that would allow access to the playground area needed to be cleared, cleaned, and rebuilt. Debris of all types had to be removed from the area, including the remains of a playground that was destroyed in the storm. All in all, a ton of work was put in at the Highlands site before the building could even commence.

But the groundbreaking ceremony in and of itself was a great success in more ways than one. First, we gained more exposure for The Sandy Ground Project's fundraising efforts. We still were not in any kind of comfort zone money-wise (including for the playground we were about to begin building). The other great success of the day was more personal for me—relative to my mission as a firefighter and union president.

The politicians that came out for our groundbreaking event were there to acknowledge the great work being done by New Jersey's firefighters. They spoke about the sense of community and charity and togetherness. And The Angels Army—made up primarily of firefighters—was the group leading the charge. Our guests that morning included Lieutenant Governor Kim Guadagno, Senators Jennifer Beck and Joe Kyrillos, and Assemblyman Declan O'Scanlon.

Coincidentally, these were the very same politicians, closely aligned with Governor Christie, that were leading the charge *against* firefighters and all public workers. They were doing all they could, both in the media and in the legislature, to erode our salaries, pensions, and benefits (not to mention our reputations). Now here they were, on our turf, acknowledging our hard work and commitment to do something good for the community. The irony was not lost on anyone, particularly me.

I thought that maybe, just maybe, The Sandy Ground Project was actually helping people see firefighters for what we really are. Just regular men and women, there for their community, standing ready to try and save the day if needs be. We are not the greedy, self-serving scourge of society, motivated only by lining our own pockets, as described by certain politicians. If The Sandy Ground can allow people (and politicians too!) to see this more clearly, then that is a great side effect of the project as far as I'm concerned.

• • •

As I said though, we had no financial cushion and that included the upcoming playground in the Highlands. So Joe and Karen Burke sprang into action and utilized all the great people their town had to offer. The idea was to hold a benefit concert—what better way to help out a musical family like the Bardens?

So to plan and fund the event, the Burkes were able to get Bob Small and Rick Korn on board to make it happen. Bob, a local businessman and philanthropist, came up huge when it came to raising money and he was able to hook us up with Cablevision as well. Rick was instrumental in putting the pieces of the actual show together—the venue, the acts, and all that came with promoting a concert event. He is the resident mover and shaker in the area's music scene. Our concert could not have happened without him.

Simply put, the "Sandy Ground Concert" was a huge success. The Seastreak Ferry Corporation, our very gracious hosts for the evening, allowed us to pack 2,400 people into their parking lot for the event. Local radio icon "Big Joe" Henry donated his time and expertise as the emcee and several Jersey Shore legends showed up to perform. This included Bobby Bandiera, as well as Southside Johnny and the Asbury Jukes. Also, a woman named Linda Chorney asked to play and came all the way from Arizona to perform. She had heard about the event from all the way out west, made the trip, and was tremendous.

Perhaps greatest and most appropriate of them all was a performance by Mark Barden's band 'Alternate Universe'. They were tremendous musically, of course, but the fact that Mark could use his talents to raise money for his own son's playground was most moving of all. It really seemed meant to be… as if he were laying the foundation for Daniel's playground with his guitar.

• • •

With winter closing in, we decided to make the last week of October the most ambitious part of The Sandy Ground Project thusfar. Just as Daniel Barden's playground was starting to go up in the Highlands, we began building a second playground simultaneously. The other being about 20 miles down the coast in Belmar, NJ. The Angels Army was now fighting their joyous battle on two fronts, both in the wind and cold that late October always brings. Luckily our number of volunteers was continuing to grow and we had tremendous support from the Highlands community. While being back on the bay-shore was a reunion of sorts from the Sea Bright and Union Beach builds, the Angels Army was growing by leaps and bounds. More new faces seemed to show up every day.

The people throughout the town came out in droves, eager to celebrate something other than the one-year anniversary of Superstorm Sandy. They were so happy to welcome Daniel's spirit and Daniel's family to their town with open arms. The volunteer fire department in the Highlands was tremendous, assisting with every facet of the playground process—the ceremonies, the physical building, and the boosting of morale. Also, I was now starting to see The Sandy Ground Project get legs with our firefighters statewide. In this case, the Highlands build was sort of "adopted" by the guys from Paterson (which is over an hour's drive away). Much like our Locals had "adopted a town" in the aftermath of Sandy, they were now starting to adopt playgrounds.

• • •

There was one volunteer on the Highlands build that, for anyone who was there, will never be forgotten. Her name is Francesca Pippen— more affectionately known on the job site as "Mrs. Claus". She was an older woman, very motherly and sweet, and she worked every single second of that build. She continually cleaned up, made sure the workers had hot coffee or water, and just generally kept everyone upbeat with her positive energy. She seemed to float back and forth throughout the playground, sharing a pleasant smile and spirit. Almost like a Fairy Godmother or Mary Poppins-type character. And similar to those characters, she's never been seen before or since that playground build. But none of us will ever forget her—an angel of the Highlands.

• • •

Although it was right along the water, Daniel's playground was built on solid ground, not sand, and would have rubber surfacing as its floor. The themes were music, of course, and swimming—Daniel was a competitive swimmer for a team called the Torpedoes. Also, this would be the only playground (except for the 26th and final one) to feature a fire truck spring-toy, which was the showpiece of the playground. Daniel's dream was to be a firefighter and now every child who visited his playground could ride this fire truck and dream along with him. Natalie and James, his brother and sister, installed the fire truck during a special ceremony—knowing this was Daniel's favorite part of the playground.

Natalie and James also mounted the playground's special panel—which was a rendering of a drawing Daniel had done. It was a self-portrait, depicting him playing in the surf with arms outstretched. Amazingly, when we would unveil the official playground sign during the ribbon-cutting a few days later, it featured a photograph of the exact same scene! It was Daniel, in the waves, smiling with arms open wide. Almost as if he was saying "Welcome to my playground." There is no way the sign makers could have known about Daniel's drawing, so this was another one of the angels' not-so-coincidental coincidences.

• • •

The last part of a playground build like the one in the Highlands is when the rubber surfacing is poured. It is done by a company that specializes in this process, so no volunteers are really needed. But, in a true show of togetherness and family, the Bardens headed up to Belmar to help out with the playground build that was taking place up there. And this set the scene for one of the most memorable moments of the entire project.

Mark Barden was asked to speak at the school where the students had raised a lot of money for a playground in nearby Belmar. It was heart-breaking in a way to see him address all these kids, the same ages as his own children, but also a very cool moment. He spoke about the importance of cherishing their playground, cherishing each day, and how lucky they were to be a part of a project that is so special. While the circumstances leading Mark to this speech, at this school, were tragic and not to be wished on anyone—it was an unforgettable show of strength and grace on his part.

• • •

The Barden family, along with much of Jackie's family (the Giblins), had been loaned a beautiful oceanfront house for the duration of their time spent on the Jersey Shore for the build. Karen and Joe Burke had hooked them up with the accommodations—coming through yet again with one of their many connections.

On the night the building wrapped up in the Highlands, we all got together at the Bardens' shore house for an extended celebration. The Barden family, the Giblin family, myself and my wife, Carlos Soto, and many of the Angels Army—all of us partied late into the night. It was *exactly* like the family parties I had known my entire life. Brothers and sisters cutting loose and dancing together, reminiscing about the good times as well as the not-so-good. A lot of laughing and crying, raising glasses and making toasts. I felt truly at home, recognizing in the moment that this was a special night. I was lucky to be a part of it.

I was also very lucky to chat-up and hang out with Martin Giblin much of the night. The patriarch of the Giblin clan, age 90, was playing cards and holding court until the wee hours. We sat at the table together and had a blast playing hand after hand of poker for quarters. 10 PM turned into midnight in the blink of an eye. Midnight turned into 2 AM even faster. With the ribbon-cutting scheduled for the following morning (ok, this same morning) my wife wisely tried to get me to leave. But I was feeling right at home. And every time I started to get up, Martin offered up the same line: "Just deal the cards." How could you not listen?

So far as I could tell, this was just the Connecticut version of my own family—the Lavins. It was the definition of family as I'd always known it to be. A lot of love and togetherness... heavy, emotional moments followed by lighter ones. Mark took out his guitar, playing songs that everyone could sing along to. An especially stirring rendition of "American Pie" really brought the house down and seemed to sum up how everyone felt. Mark knew he could always make these people dance and, maybe, they'd be happy for a while...

A month or so later, I got a text message from Mark Barden—he and Jackie were out to dinner in New York City. The text said: "We were just talking about how strange it is that we feel we've known you our whole lives." I had never expressed it to the Bardens, but this was my feeling exactly. It was like we had been related in another life or something. It's a very difficult thing to describe, that kind of connection, but it was very clearly felt on both ends. The Sandy Ground Project does have its way of bonding people together, but I did feel like I had a history with the Bardens and Giblins that dated much further back. Something like déjà vu I guess.

• • •

On October 27, 2013, two days short of the one-year anniversary of Superstorm Sandy, we cut the ribbon on Daniel Barden's playground. Firefighters in dress uniform lined the grounds, stoically standing in tribute to Daniel once again. The kids of the Highlands lined the playground as well, all holding colorful signs to welcome Daniel and the Bardens to their hometown.

Mark was the spokesperson for the family that morning, thanking all of the volunteers and the members of the community who had made them feel so at home.

When asked if he had any message for the people of Highlands, Mark said the Bardens ARE the people of Highlands now. That is how they had been made to feel since day one, and it is perfectly appropriate that Daniel's playground is here. He talked about the residents of the Highlands understanding family, a fitting tribute and appropriate location for his son Daniel.

Mark spoke about Daniel's loving and compassionate spirit. He extended himself to anyone and everyone. If he saw someone sitting alone, he would go over just to keep them company. And this playground would be fostering that kind of togetherness and sense of community.

He also talked about how much good has come out of such a terrible tragedy, and insisted that captures Daniel's spirit perfectly. To be uplifting and turn any negative into a positive. Mark spoke about that spirit being alive in everyone in attendance that day. We presented Mark with a blue Sandy Ground jacket for being such a great friend and advocate of our mission.

• • •

Daniel's playground naturally featured its own custom bell, with our favorite saying from "It's a Wonderful Life". Even though the last one we put up had been stolen, there was not even a thought of discontinuing our latest tradition. We also had our patented fly-over welcoming everyone, as well as Dennis Bourke performing "The Rainbow Connection" as poignantly as always.

I also saw fit that morning to especially recognize some of the older members of our volunteer forces that play such an important role on the playground builds, and the project as a whole. Specifically, I mentioned Francesca Pippen, my mother-in-law Phyllis Middleton, and Daniel's grandfather Martin Giblin.

I just felt like the three of them exemplified the spirit of The Sandy Ground Project in the way that they give back in any way possible. Although they might not be pushing wheelbarrows and pouring concrete, they perform the necessary tasks and assist greatly in the process. Without them we would not be where we are today. Their contributions include, but are certainly not limited to, inspiring the younger generation to do the right thing, give back to the community, and create a sense of family as only they can.

• • •

When the ceremonies were through, the entire gang rendez-voused back at "Off the Hook" to prolong the celebration into the night. This was the same establishment that had been so good to us during the initial playground build in Sea Bright, hosting us so graciously yet again.

I could not help but see the irony in the crowd we had that day at "Off the Hook". Six months ago we'd had another big Irish family in the Murphys, and now we were back again with the Bardens and the Giblins. Only this time the families and the project were bigger. More members of our Angels Army family, our firefighting family, our Newtown family, the list goes on and on.

We were now eleven playgrounds into what I saw as a 26-step process. It was just awesome to be back at the scene of #1 and taking stock of how far we had come. And playground #12, which we had done simultaneously with Daniel's, would be opened in only a matter of days.

But first, we would have one last late-night blow-out with Daniel's extended family—the one we had only just met, but have somehow always known.

NJ Firefighters stand with the Bardens
in honor of their (our) Daniel

CHAPTER SIXTEEN

Playground Celebrating the Life of Avielle Richman

Belmar, New Jersey

I t doesn't matter if you are talking about a whale, or a mouse, or a human being. All mammals need to play. For their brains to develop properly and have emotional stability, mammals absolutely must have fun. They require playing, recreation, and down-time to express themselves. It is critical no matter how high or low the creature's level of intelligence happens to be.

A brilliant young scientist named Jennifer Hensel told me this, and I smiled at the very thought of it. At an almost molecular level, The Sandy Ground Project was bettering the well-being of anyone who would set foot on one of our playgrounds. I especially enjoyed hearing this information from Jennifer—who also happens to be the mother of Avielle Richman, the eventual namesake of Playground #12.

• • •

Avielle Richman was very much in tune with nature. This is what her parents—Jennifer Hensel and Jeremy Richman—spoke about the most when I first met them. They also were able to actually *show* me this unique quality in their daughter in the form of a photograph. It was Avielle, running through a field of dandelions, arms outstretched, with the sun on her face. It captured the sheer joy that a child can feel simply by being outside. Her smile, which was what her parents described to be her defining characteristic, made me feel like I knew her.

The Richmans consider that picture to be the perfect summary of Avielle's personality. She loved being outdoors. She loved animals. She had actually named all of the trees that lived throughout their property. They were like a part of the family to her. Every living thing, no matter what it was, held great importance to her. She loved and cherished nature, as it seemed to capture her imagination.

And that smile. Jennifer talked about Avielle's ability to light up whatever room she was in. Her spirit always seemed to cheer people up, and bring out the best in them. Her personality was very magnetic in a way, standing out in a crowd. She was without a doubt the light of her parents' lives, offering up a smile come what may. That smile was the last thing they saw when Avielle went off to Sandy Hook Elementary School that morning, and they seemed grateful to have that as a lasting image of her.

• • •

That first meeting with Jennifer took place at their home in Newtown. It is a big, beautiful house, surrounded by the trees that Avielle cared so much for and knew by name. It is a house that I have since driven past numerous times on my way to another Newtown destination or meeting with another family. And every time I think fondly of Avielle—how much she must have loved living there and how well it suited her.

Jennifer and Jeremy, a pair of published research scientists, are a couple of brilliant individuals. Even though they were very much grieving the loss of their daughter when I initially met them, this quality certainly came across. They are also two of the most sincere and open people you would ever want to meet. Because despite how very painful their loss was, they were still very open with me in sharing so many memories and impressions from Avielle's life. This is why I, and so many of us associated with The Sandy Ground Project and this build, feel like we know her so well.

Also, Avielle was an only child. This was a new set of circumstances as far as my experience in meeting these families from Newtown.

I could sense that this fact made it very difficult on the Richmans, because now this house—that suited Avielle so perfectly—was now without its child.

. . .

Jennifer and Jeremy, as I said, are scientists. So, naturally, they have a scientific way of thinking about things and solving problems. They were thrilled at the prospect of a playground being built in honor of Avielle because of a child's biological need to play. Jennifer in particular expressed to me her desire for children to use their imaginations more. They believed strongly in the idea that kids needed to be silly and express themselves in any crazy way they feel. Kids should be original and different; have fun and celebrate life. This is what the Richmans hoped children would do on Avielle's playground. Their little hearts and spirits desire that recreational outlet. And their brains actually require it.

In a similar vein, Jennifer and Jeremy had started "The Avielle Foundation" in honor of their daughter. The Foundation is geared towards bolstering research in examining the human brain. More specifically, the research would focus on figuring out what makes a person lash out in extremely violent behavior. Jeremy and Jennifer feel strongly that this is an area that doesn't get enough attention because "being violent" isn't exactly a disease and there is always a stigma when people seek help with mental health issues. The ultimate goal of the Foundation is to raise awareness, improve "brain health", and—in turn—prevent future tragedies.

. . .

While people across the nation have looked at the Newtown tragedy through the scope of politics, or society, or the culture of America—the Richmans were trying to cut through to the core of the problem. In their case, through science.

Between celebrating the life of their daughter, and the mental health benefits it would provide for children, the Richmans were all in for making Playground #12 Avielle's. It was their hope to have the playground built at a school that needed it, so that the nearby kids would have easy access and could have playing built into their education. When Jennifer shared with me her ultimate wish for what the playground would be, it was music to my ears. It was so good, in fact, that we quoted her on our "Where Angels Play Foundation" business cards.

She said: "When you and your children are on the playground dedicated to Avielle, look for fairies and their homes. Laugh openly. Climb a tree. Play tag. Blow dandelion seeds to the wind. Be a monkey on the bars. And see the beautiful polka dots, stripes, and squiggles that make up the landscape of a child's heart."

• • •

Belmar is one of the more popular tourist destinations at the Jersey Shore. It is known for its beautiful beaches, happening nightlife, but still with a small-town feel. Just about anyone who has grown up in New Jersey has been to a summer rental in Belmar, strolled the wide-open boardwalk, or partied at the sprawling "Bar Anticipation." Most New Jerseyans have probably done all of the above. It's the kind of town where the population quadruples between Memorial Day and Labor Day—and with good reason.

However, it was Belmar's prime location that made it such an easy target for Superstorm Sandy. The town is essentially bracketed by water with Shark River to the north and Lake Como to the south—not to mention the 20 or so blocks of some of the nicest beach in the entire state. Between the location itself, and Belmar's lack of any significant sand dunes, the entire oceanfront was ripe for the picking.

The boardwalk in Belmar was totally torn apart. Its remains—the boards that were still around anyway—laid strewn about Ocean Avenue. Only it wasn't much of an avenue anymore, just long strips of sand with asphalt buried somewhere underneath. Belmar's trademark pavilions were wrecked. The businesses along the shoreline were flooded, gutted, then boarded up. For a town whose landscape was so familiar to so many people, the images of Belmar in Sandy's aftermath were shocking.

So Belmar, which was definitely still working through the rebuilding process a full year after Superstorm Sandy, was an ideal landing spot for The Sandy Ground Project. And we had a good number of connections in town to get the ball rolling.

. . .

Lake Como is a very young little town—it had been "South Belmar" up until 2005 when it was renamed. The mayor there, Mike Ryan, has been a good friend of mine for years and he was able to point me in the right direction as far as getting things done in Belmar. He got me in touch with Belmar Mayor Matthew Doherty, as well as the Superintendent/Principal of Belmar Elementary School—David Hallman. The Belmar playground would also be special because my great friend David Fox and his wife Esther would be honoring their son Michael with their generous gift to Where Angels Play.

Mr. Hallman very much wanted a new playground for his school and it was very much needed. Since the Richmans were hoping to have Avielle's playground at a school of some kind, this seemed to be the perfect fit. I proposed the Belmar location to Jeremy and Jennifer and they loved it. All systems were a go and, with Daniel Barden's playground about to go up in the Highlands, we began planning The Sandy Ground's most ambitious project yet… Two playgrounds in one week!

. . .

Another great asset The Sandy Ground Project had in the immediate area turned out to be my niece, Jackie Adase. She had taken a great interest in our mission from the start and was working hard to raise money through grassroots channels. Jackie was running bake sales, selling lollipops, anything to pick up a few extra dollars to put towards our playgrounds. Jackie is a school teacher and most of her efforts were being done through her school and her students in Brielle, NJ—which is ten minutes from Belmar.

Because of her dedication and spirit, Jackie was named Chairperson of the Belmar build. In addition to bringing in the funds, she was instrumental in dealing with the Belmar Board of Education (whose cooperation was vital with the playground going up at one of their schools). She also set up an event at her school where I was able to address the students and thank them for all their generosity. It turned out to be an amazing experience all around. All the while, Jackie was teaching her students and prepping them to perform at the ribbon-cutting ceremony…

· · ·

With help from Avielle's parents, we were able to design a playground that reflected what she had always loved best—nature. There would be plenty of animals, flowers, trees, and bugs. In particular, ladybugs (because Avielle loved the color red as well) and fireflies were an overriding theme throughout the playground.

The build itself turned out to be very intense, what with the other one going on simultaneously in the Highlands. This was a true test of our Angels Army, our ability to allocate time and resources wisely, and the resolve we all had to keep going as the wind and cold strengthened with winter knocking on the door. Even with facing our biggest challenge yet, by now we had done enough builds for me to have ultimate faith in our crew. The Angels Army was battle tested and could overcome pretty much any obstacle. And those obstacles always seemed to show up.

Over the course of The Sandy Ground Project, we had been experiencing mounting problems with the playground manufacturer. The company is based in Georgia, so you can imagine the logistical challenges that come with getting a structure of that size, with all the right pieces included, up the entire east coast. The playgrounds would be driven—in many cases through the night—and planned for us to receive it and begin building at a set time. There had not been a complete disaster shipping-wise (yet), but the issues were enough for me to take notice.

A prime example of one of these problems came during the Belmar build. But it is also a prime example of how we were always able to work out a solution.

The railings on Avielle's playground were supposed to be yellow. When they showed up white, with the building process already in full-swing, we had to improvise on the fly. Our Angels Army network sprang into action, and we soon realized that we had a friend in the business of changing the color of playground railings. Sort of.

Union firefighter Danny Connors had a friend who owned a nearby auto body shop. Since the finish of these metal railings was similar to that of a car's exterior, Danny's friend was able to "powder coat" them to match the exact shade of yellow they needed to be.

This particular anecdote comes to mind, but scenarios like this took place throughout The Sandy Ground Project a hundred times over. If a particular part was missing, we found it at a local store. If we needed a specialized tool, somebody was able to locate one. If some of the hardware was omitted from the shipment, we manufactured it ourselves.

Like I said, our serendipitous ability to keep progressing was not a new phenomenon. But it comes to mind at this point in our story because of the two builds happening at once. Our sense of overcoming was heightened and every last bit of our network was utilized to make sure everything came out right. It also heightened our sense that, at the end of the day, our 26 angels were guiding the process. They were showing their support and approval again and again, and it was setting us up for success.

· · ·

One day during our week of building at Belmar Elementary School, Principal David Hallman came outside to talk to me during the late morning. He asked if we would be willing to take a break around 2 PM. The students, he said, would like to thank all the builders who were putting their new playground together. And they would like to do it right before the end of the school day. I said we would be happy to stop in for a break around 2. When the time came, I gathered up the crew and we headed inside to the auditorium.

Now, I've been to a good amount of sporting events in my day. Loud ones, wild, intense, some of the biggest celebrations and crowd noises anywhere. [Rutgers–Louisville in 2006 comes to mind.] Well, believe me when I tell you that the ovation we received at Belmar Elementary School was unmatched.

We were directed to head into the auditorium practically in single file from the back to the front. As soon as the kids saw us, they went absolutely nutso. Screaming, clapping, cheering, holding up huge signs on poster board. It was overwhelming. It was like we had just won the Super Bowl and this was the ticker-tape parade.

And the amazing part, the part that brought us all to tears, was that the cheering didn't stop. We were all in front of the auditorium, in front of the student body, and the ovation went on. Two minutes… five minutes… ten minutes… It was just an incredible amount of energy and love inside that school. Something that can't adequately be described. It was amazing just to be in the room to take it all in.

I spoke briefly to the kids, thanking them and their teachers and administration for hosting us. As did Mark Barden—Daniel's father—who had just completed a playground for his own son in the Highlands and was now helping us build Avielle's. It was a powerful moment that none of us would ever forget. We told the kids to be out on the playground after school on Friday, so they could be there for its official opening.

Even with the double-build happening, the work was remarkably harmonious. The week allowed us to maximize the resources and time of our Angels Army volunteers and our great friends at Giordano Construction. So many of our key people were pulling double-duty (two playgrounds in the same day!) and without that dedication there is no way we could have finished. The Belmar Board of Education, along with our Mayors Matt Doherty and Mike Ryan, were tremendous in pulling all the right strings. By the end of the week, Avielle Richman's playground was fully assembled without issue.

• • •

We were all set to cut the ribbon and open Avielle's playground during an after-school event on Friday, November 1, 2013. It was an extraordinarily windy day, even for mid-Fall at the Jersey Shore, and

Principal Hallman called me that morning to rearrange our plans of holding the ceremony outside on the playground. He suggested holding an indoor assembly of some sort, possibly in the school auditorium.

If I knew anything about The Sandy Ground Project by this point, it was that everything was going to work out as it should. Our angels would see to it that our ceremony was protected and go off without a hitch in good weather. And even if it didn't there would be a definitive reason why not. I told Mr. Hallman this. I told him to have a little faith. "You don't understand. It will be fine. You'll see." I'm sure he looked out his office window right then at 50 mph wind gusts blowing sheets of rain—and thought I was out of my mind.

At 4 PM that afternoon, outside of Belmar Elementary School, we cut the ribbon on their new playground under beautiful sunny skies. My niece Jackie had taught her students the popular song "Fireflies" by Owl City—which had become sort of a theme-song for Avielle and this build—and they did a really beautiful job with it. It captured the spirit of the moment perfectly.

We performed the ceremonial presenting of the bell, as well as raised the flags on Avielle's playground to signify the official opening. One of those flags, featuring a ladybug and emblazoned with "AVIELLE'S PLAYGROUND" almost didn't make it that day. Due to a snafu with the company that made the flag, my sister Joyce's friend Kathy Cehelsky drove all the way to Central Pennsylvania and back that day to pick it up. She made it *just* in time for us to raise it.

The ceremony also had a few speeches—from myself, the school principal, and the mayor—all thanking the volunteers and folks throughout Belmar who had made Avielle's playground a reality. Then, lastly, Jennifer summed up the proceedings as only she could. She addressed the schoolchildren directly in a short, but sweet, speech of her own: "Adults sure can talk a lot, huh? Let's get playing!!"

And the kids did just that, swarming the playground like the fireflies that Avielle loved so well. Our faith in holding the event outdoors was repaid. After all, how could you open a playground with no playground? As the crowd started to disperse and we parted ways, Principal Hallman came up to me and said, "No way I thought you'd be able to pull this off, but you were right." There wasn't a cloud in the sky. But I hadn't pulled anything off, Avielle had. I had nothing to do with it except believing everything would be okay.

. . .

I felt bad. I couldn't hang around for another one of The Sandy Ground Project's patented after-parties—in Belmar of all places. I had a family event that I needed to hustle off to that night, but I did get a chance to have one quick drink with Jeremy Richman. I apologized for having to run out, but it was clear that my (and all of our) friendships with Jennifer and Jeremy would extend well beyond one week of playground building.

The Richmans were, and continue to be, great advocates of The Sandy Ground Project and we remain in close touch with them. My daughter MaryKate and my niece Jackie stayed tight with Jennifer. Avielle's parents were the latest additions of our ever-growing Sandy Ground family.

Fast forward to May 2014. We are ready to cut the ribbon at Playground #22 in Ocean City, New Jersey, and the Richmans show up to show their support. They also made the drive down from Connecticut to show us, in person, that Jennifer was now four months pregnant! It was incredible to see this couple, this family, whose only child was an angel now to be so excited to welcome a newborn into the world. We were all thrilled. Like so many doting aunts and uncles, the Angels Army began sending Baby Richman all sorts of clothes and gifts.

. . .

Fast forward again. Five more months this time to Union Beach, New Jersey. I was sitting in the passenger seat of my son's car and we were conducting a tape-recorded interview—trying to capture all the information that would become this very book.

As I was speaking to him, answering a question about one of the earlier playgrounds, we pulled into the parking lot at Fireman's Park. This being the home of our second playground. He was dropping me off for an on-site interview with CBS's Connecticut affiliate. Just as he turned off the car, my cell phone rang out with this text:

> "The Richmans just welcomed a beautiful baby girl, Imogen Joy—born October 8, 2014 at 1:28 AM. 7 lbs., 3 oz.—19 ¾ in."

Obviously I was thrilled and honored to be included on such an announcement. And the significance of getting such joyous news, while arriving at such a joyous place, was not lost on me.

Billy Valentine and Mario DiPietro enjoying the choir

Goldfish welcome Allie's playground, even in the clouds

CHAPTER SEVENTEEN

Playground Celebrating the Life of Allison Wyatt

Norwalk, Connecticut

It had begun last winter at the Blue Colony Diner. I was sat across from Ian and Nicole Hockley, laying out the plan for The Sandy Ground Project. Now here I was, twelve amazing playgrounds and twelve amazing experiences later, sipping coffee at the very same diner. Only this time, I was seated across from Cheyanne Wyatt.

She politely listened as I talked about all we had been doing... with the families and playgrounds and communities throughout the region. I also spoke about our hope to build a playground in honor of her daughter Allison. Cheyanne was very reserved the first time we met. She and her husband, Ben, are very private people and were intent on keeping it that way. The two of them, along with Allison's younger sister Lauren, seemed to be hurting in silence. They just wanted their space, and I can't say I blame them.

Cheyanne told me a few things about Allison that first morning, but she didn't go into much detail. That would come later as Cheyanne would open up more and more throughout a series of phone conversations we had. I would learn about Allison's love of the ocean and beach. Cheyanne sent me a few pictures of Allison. It seemed as though our talks had built up a trust and rapport, and a potential playground for Allison was coming into focus.

· · ·

The coastal city of Norwalk, Connecticut lies on the Long Island Sound. Just like so many other communities in the surrounding area, Norwalk experienced extreme flooding during and after Superstorm Sandy struck. In many of the neighborhoods, people were forced out of their homes and into shelters. There was no electricity for an extended period of time. The amount of damage to peoples' homes was extensive and wide-spread.

Cheyanne Wyatt, although a resident of Newtown which is 45 minutes away, is very much connected to the City of Norwalk. She was a nurse at Norwalk Hospital—the same hospital where Allison was born. She has a lot of contacts and friends there; and the Maritime Aquarium at Norwalk was one of Allison's favorite places to visit. It seemed like the perfect spot, if I could get a few helpful contacts of my own there.

• • •

When I put out some feelers, looking for some direction with a potential playground build in Norwalk, all signs pointed firmly in the direction of Captain Jimmy Hines. Not only was he a great person to connect me with the mayor, union president, and local businesses throughout the city—but he is a builder in town, the perfect combination as far as I was concerned. And as a reference, all you had to do was check out the building where Norwalk Fire Department is head-quartered. It is an amazing structure, designed and built by Jimmy's construction company.

As I laid out our project for Jimmy, I could tell that he was all in right away. He has a couple kids of his own, loved the idea, and felt that Norwalk would be a perfect host for Allison Wyatt's playground. With Playground #13's go-to guy on board, we began searching throughout the city for the ideal location.

Jimmy brought me to a spot called "Oyster Shell Park". Given our ocean theme, the name sounded about right. It is also located right on the water and only blocks away from the Maritime Aquarium. I ran this location past Cheyanne and she gave it her seal of approval. With everything in place, now all we had to do was raise the funds.

. . .

Jimmy Hines made it his mission to drum up both money and support throughout Norwalk, and the city was more than willing to oblige. A great pub and restaurant in South Norwalk called O'Neill's did an awesome fundraiser. This establishment was very close to where Allison's playground was going to be built, so the folks there would be our new neighbors.

The biggest and most well-known business that calls Norwalk home is Pepperidge Farm. Jimmy was able to set up a meeting with them, so the two of us went and presented the entire concept of The Sandy Ground Project and how it was coming to town. Ruth Ann Walsh, a Vice-President who is heavily involved with marketing was our target audience. By the end of the presentation she was in tears and asking how Pepperidge Farm could get involved—particularly in the hometown Norwalk build.

Ruth Ann asked if it would be possible to incorporate a theme at the playground surrounding their Goldfish Crackers. Those Goldfish are a very popular (if not the *most* popular) snack food for kids to be eating on playgrounds all across America. It was their big seller, and a playful one at that.

I originally told her no. The playgrounds are designed to reflect the child's—in this case Allison Wyatt's—personality. And there was no way I was going to sell that out to a corporation. This project's mission is to help families and communities, not to be a commercial. So I politely dismissed the idea, but Ruth Ann insisted that Pepperidge Farm would love to be involved either way.

Then, later that same week, I came across a short bio of Allison. In the very first paragraph it described her as "a beautiful, shy child who loved to share her Goldfish crackers with a friend or a stranger on an airplane". I thought, wait a minute... There is actually a connection between Allison and these Goldfish?!? I checked with Cheyanne and she confirmed it. Yes, Goldfish were Allison's favorite, but it was really Allie's generous gesture to a complete stranger with those very goldfish that made Cheyanne and Ben so proud of her.

So I called Pepperidge Farm back and told them what I'd learned. They were thrilled and began to collaborate with us on how to integrate the Goldfish theme. They also made a sizable donation that practically covered the entire cost of Allison Wyatt's playground. Ultimately, Allison's generosity of spirit and willingness to share her favorite snack was what helped to get her playground built.

. . .

With that partnership in place, Cheyanne and Toni Giordano set about designing the playground itself. Between Allison's love of the beach, and Pepperidge Farm's backing of the project through the fish-shaped snack that Allison loved, we seemed to have a ready-made theme. As much as (if not more than) any parent or family member ever had, Cheyanne poured herself into the specifics of the playground structure. She knew best what Allison would like and made sure that every detail—the apparatus, a specific slide, the layout, everything— would be ideal for any kid who came to play.

Cheyanne was able to provide us with some of Allison's artwork that could be incorporated into the design, as well as a handprint from one of her projects. It is always a great personal touch to have pieces like this, because it illustrates the fact that the child has actually built a physical part of the playground. Cheyanne also chose the red, white, and blue color scheme. With Allison's sister serving as our little honorary forewoman and Ben doing a ton of work on the playground itself, the Wyatt family certainly had their fingerprints all over this build.

Pepperidge Farm lent us some of their creative people as well, who gave some great insight to the playground design process. The Goldfish actually spawned one of the coolest, and completely original, playground elements we had ever had. Since the playground would be built on solid ground, it would naturally get the rubber-surfacing poured once the construction was complete. But what made this surface different from all the others was we put small rubber Goldfish into the mixture. So amongst all the bits of color that make up the playground's floor, schools of tiny Goldfish are swimming towards the structure to play. They are built right in.

• • •

Physically speaking, this was probably the toughest playground build any of us had ever experienced. I don't know if it was the number '13' proving to be unlucky, or if we were just struggling to get over that hump to reach the project's halfway point. Whatever it was, nothing seemed to go right. The construction was off to an extremely slow start.

The land that was chosen for Allison's playground, as it turned out, was riddled with "ledge". Ledge is that tough, rocky layer of earth that lies not far below the surface and is an absolute terror to try and break through. And it seemed like every spot we went to dig a hole, boom!, we hit ledge. It would prove to be impenetrable or just flat-out break our tools. So we would rethink the layout and start drilling in a different spot. Of course, it would happen again in the next spot just the same. The Angels Army morale seemed to be at an all-time low.

There were two guys, however, who seemed totally immune to the frustrations of the job and rugged conditions.

• • •

The Conte brothers, Mark and Anthony, were on the job site working like total machines. They are the owners of Conte Construction Company, with Anthony mainly running the business, and they had done a lot of work with Jimmy Hines in the past. Mark is also a Captain with the Norwalk Fire Department. Between the two of them, they were doing the work of five men. As everyone else on the grounds seemed to languish, I remember commenting to Jimmy, "Who *are* these guys? Man, they're working like animals."

As the first full day came to a close, I went up to Mark Conte to thank him for his effort and hoping that we would see these two tomorrow. "Hey, you guys are amazing. I don't think we can get through this build without you. Thanks a lot." And then Mark thanked me. He said that this project was extraordinarily special to him—that he needed to be there—and he told me why.

About a year and a half prior, Mark had lost his 20-month-old son Jameson to a choking accident. It was a shocking tragedy for Mark and his wife Stephanie, as well as Jameson's Uncle Anthony and the entire family. Jimmy Hines later told me about how losing Jameson had rocked the whole Norwalk Fire Department and the whole town really, to its core. Everyone was understandably devastated.

With this playground going up in honor of Allison Wyatt and maybe providing a few days of joy for her grieving family, Mark made it his mission to pour his heart into the work and make a difference in honor of his little boy. When I offered my condolences, Mark thanked me but insisted that the project here in Norwalk was all about Allison, not him or his family. But he did say that the work was their therapy, and the energy that they poured into honoring Jameson could not be denied.

• • •

The Conte boys notwithstanding, the work was limping along pretty sluggishly. The weather didn't help matters as it was very chilly, wet, and just raw. It was the type of cold that cuts right through to your bones. And like I said, the issue with the ledge was killing our progress. Then, even when we seemed to overcome that problem, it would turn out the ground wasn't level. We couldn't win. We needed something to happen that would change momentum, to get us moving in the right direction.

Just when it seemed like the work was grinding to a halt, Cheyanne Wyatt grabbed a jack-hammer.

In the entire span of The Sandy Ground Project, I don't recall a mother that put in as much physical work as Cheyanne Wyatt did in Norwalk. She is a nurse, after all. Nurses are known primarily for their caring and compassion, and rightfully so. But they are also hands-on, hard-working people who are always ready and willing to get their hands dirty when duty calls. I had met her as a very quiet, reserved, woman. And here she was drilling holes in the earth with a 90-pound jack-hammer. The other volunteers couldn't help but take notice.

It was an inspiring sight. It was the type of scene that made you take stock of yourself and ask, "What's my problem?", because if she can get up the energy—the desire to work hard and help the cause—then why couldn't we?

Sort of like a turnover in a football game, Cheyanne's drilling caused a total momentum shift throughout the build sight. The Angels Army seemed re-energized and, lo and behold, things started to go right. The ledge became less of a problem. The ground seemed to level out just right. I feel like the temperature might have even jumped up a few degrees. It was amazing to see how Cheyanne's refusal to give up had caused this turnaround, and it seemed to permeate all aspects of the build.

With momentum firmly on our side now, we decided to work deep into that night. We ordered up some extra coffee, set up flood-lights all around, and pressed on in our mission to build a playground for Allison Wyatt. We clearly would not have been able to do all of that without the inspiring actions of her mother.

One "Angels Army" family that seemed to particularly hit their stride during this build was the Wetmores. Ron—a battalion chief from the Milford (CT) Fire Department—was becoming a vital cog in the growing Sandy Ground machine. Along with his wife Trish (a Stratford firefighter in her own right) and daughter Kylie (our climb-ing/jumping/swinging Sandy Ground mascot of sorts), Ron was now someone we would count on to be at each build and pouring his heart into it. I had known Ron through the Connecticut Burn Camp prior, so I knew of his commitment and dedication first-hand. He was one of the guys busting his butt in the rain there in Norwalk, even before Cheyanne's jolt of inspiration.

The Wetmores would eventually chair and sponsor a playground build in Milford the following spring.

• • •

In addition to Conte Construction, another Norwalk business really stepped up and put their beautiful stamp on their town's newest playground. It was Monet Landscaping and they did an incredible job of installing tons of plants and shrubbery all throughout the grounds. Their efforts pulled the project together so perfectly, and it had to be more than $10,000 worth of work they put in. The landscaping, in addition to the playground itself, had re-shaped the face of Oyster Shell Park.

After Cheyanne's work with the jack-hammer jolted us all into a more positive direction, the build was all sunshine and rainbows. Literally. It's crazy to say, but yet *another* rainbow showed up over *another* one of our playgrounds as the workers were putting it up. As many of us stood in awe, looking up at a now-approving sky, I said aloud, "Wow, geez, this is unbelievable." I happened to be standing next to Rebecca Kowalski when I said this, and she was quick to point out how believable this latest sign was.

She said, "This isn't unbelievable at all. It's totally believable. I actually expect to see these beautiful signs when I come to a playground now." She went on to talk about how very real the messages from our 26 angels were. It could no longer be called a coincidence, or fate, or unbelievable. This rainbow, like the other blessings we had seen and felt along the way, was there as a thumbs-up. It was from Allison, to us. There was no two ways about it.

Rebecca has had an uncanny way of describing the moment so poignantly throughout the life of The Sandy Ground Project, but this is one I'll never forget. She was right. I realized that these angels—some still with us, some not—had taught me enough to expect the unbelievable to happen. I'd had a brush with that sort of faith when I told the Principal of Belmar Elementary that the weather would change. And this moved me even more in that direction.

So with the clear blessing and approval of its namesake, and underneath the rainbow she had sent down to us, the building of Allison Wyatt's Playground was completed without issue.

• • •

November 10, 2013, was a sunny Sunday morning on the Norwalk waterfront. The playground celebrating the life of Allison Wyatt was up, decked out, and ready to be played on. Allison had sent us a clear blue sky that day, but a lot of wind as well. I guess she wanted to put the Angels Air Force to the test.

Following our Sandy Ground tradition, a fly-over was scheduled that morning to carry Allison's message overhead during the ribbon-cutting. But due to the extreme wind, it was suggested that the airman not fly that morning. Basically defying orders, he took off into a stiff wind anyway, having ultimate faith that he would be protected. At times it seemed like the plane was standing still, flying headlong into a driving wind.

The pilot, daring as he was, made it up and down safe and sound. He delivered the most important message of the morning: "KINDNESS MATTERS... PLEASE SHARE YOUR GOLD-FISH... LOVE, ALLISON"

• • •

At the Wyatts' request, the ribbon-cutting was a relatively private affair. No press or media coverage, just an intimate gathering of family and all those throughout Norwalk who had pitched in and were so happy to be hosting Allison's playground. Although we didn't advertise it, the turn-out was huge. Norwalk is such a close-knit community that people came out in droves based solely on word-of-mouth.

As people arrived that morning, they were greeted with (what else?) a small bag of Goldfish to snack on. We were sharing them upon Allison's request. Several speeches and presentations were made, as always, from myself and Jimmy Hines and representatives of the City of Norwalk.

We presented Cheyanne with Allison's bell—another one of our angels surely getting her wings. Today, Cheyanne is not only a great supporter of Where Angels Play, her presence at our events and subsequent builds is a morale boost for me personally and to everyone involved.

There was one more angel that I felt should be recognized at this particular build, and that was little Jameson Conte.

The Conte brothers had given so much of their heart and soul to Allison's playground. To make sure that they knew of our appreciation, that their efforts would never be forgotten, we felt it was important to present them with a bell in honor of Jameson. He was Norwalk's angel, and now he was ours as well. In a very emotional addition to the ribbon-cutting ceremony, Jameson's Uncle Anthony accepted the bell on behalf of his parents—Mark and Stephanie.

A month later we received a beautiful letter from Stephanie (who I had never met in person), wishing us a happy holiday season and expressing her family's appreciation for the bell and remembering Jameson. We were glad to have him as a special part of The Sandy Ground Project. The Conte family was recovering, Stephanie said, and the playground played a significant role in that always-ongoing process.

• • •

With the ribbon-cutting ceremony finished, the Wyatts and Angels Army families rendezvoused at our Norwalk headquarters—O'Neill's Pub and Restaurant. This post-build celebration was one out of many, of course, but it took on a special meaning to the Angels Army crew in particular. Allison's playground in Norwalk marked 13 playgrounds in the books—half way to the ultimate goal of 26.

Somehow, the accomplishment of getting half way done removed all doubt as to whether we would get to the end. We were getting to 26 one way or another. At the beginning I thought, "Hey, however many we can get done, that's great." But now it was feeling more and more like 26 or bust.

Part of the equation was that, with each playground built, our team of advocates was growing. I thought that there could be a family here and there that just wasn't interested or willing to get involved. But one by one, our Sandy Ground family was growing and the Newtown families were talking. What started out with support from the Hockleys, and Bardens, and Kowalskis... had now ballooned to include 13 families willing to vouch for us. With these amazingly strong people on our side, not to mention our 26 angels, what could possibly stop us? The always quotable Rebecca Kowalski commented, "I want all the families to experience this," and we all certainly hoped they would.

I think the volunteers felt similar. The benefits they were getting personally from the work—it was something they wanted everyone else to feel. That long afternoon at O'Neill's, many of the volunteers spoke of this hard-to-describe feeling in a barroom exercise we had come to call "Open Mic". While everyone had their unique (and sometimes colorful) spin on the project and their relationship to it, there was one overriding theme. At the center of it was togetherness.

There were many times throughout the project when we were cold, or wet, or tired, or just plain overwhelmed with the magnitude of the task at hand. But at the end of the day, we were in it together, building towards our goal of healing these families and communities as a community all our own. It was something that none of us ever wanted to end, and some of the guys were even starting to worry—"What happens after #26?" At this point, it was just time to focus on #14 and make each one a special experience.

• • •

In the fire service, we are always training. Always learning and preparing and staying ahead of the curve to be as ready as possible when duty calls. With that credo in mind, The Sandy Ground Project and Angels Army had to always be training as well. Not so much in the physical sense, but more in the social sense.

Firefighters are a unique breed, sometimes with a language and sense of humor all its own. We had to always keep in mind that the playground build sites were not firehouses. While we were absolutely feeling exuberant and enthusiastic about each and every project, it was important to be reverent as well. These playgrounds were sacred land as far as we are concerned, and need to be treated as such.

The banter on the build site was something we always had to be mindful of. After ten or twelve hours of work, it could be easy for anyone to take the joking or language or chop-busting a little too far. But we always stressed to the crew that you never know who is within earshot. It could be a parent who had lost a child, or a resident from nearby who lost their home. We had to remember that the builds were about them, not us. And when it comes down to it, they are living with their loss every single day. The playground is just a snap-shot of joy and peace for them.

• • •

And the training I mention goes for me as an organizer of the project as well. It could never be assumed that one family would want the same as the last (or the next), so every aspect of the build had to be cleared with them. Every song, or poem, or the presence of media, or flyover, or bell, or playground apparatus. All of it needed to be double-checked, with both parents, every single time. The old saying of "when you assume, you make an 'ass' out of 'u' and 'me'" was something we had to keep in mind. We had to learn the hard way a time or two, but we were definitely improving with time.

So with streamlined organization and our well-trained crew, striking the right balance of joy and reverence and straight-up hard work, we were ready to tackle the second half of The Sandy Ground Project. And we were progressing faster than any of us thought possible.

CHAPTER EIGHTEEN

Playground Celebrating the Life of Emilie Parker

New London, Connecticut

In regards to Sandy Hook Elementary School, one of the last things that Emilie Parker ever discussed with her mother was recess. Alissa, Emilie's mom, told me about this when we first spoke. Emilie was a very fair-haired little girl, very averse to the sun. The Parker family had lived in Arizona prior to relocating to Connecticut, so you could imagine what a relief the move must have been for Emilie.

Alissa said that Emilie told her about a special "shady spot" that she'd found to hang out in during recess. It was a hidden little nook, trees shielding any sun bearing down overhead. Emilie was happy to have found this little space of her own. Somewhere she could be comfortable.

• • •

I got to know Emilie's parents Robbie and Alissa, and her sisters Samantha and Madeline. A very sweet, caring, and spiritual family who were going through an extremely rough time. Of course there was the tragedy at Sandy Hook Elementary, which is more than any parents or siblings should ever have to bear. But their sorrow was being compounded by a faction of people called "Truthers" who were harassing them on the internet. Actually, to call them people is really a stretch…

These cruel, heartless individuals who call themselves "Truthers" are obsessed with the belief that the tragedy at Sandy Hook Elementary was somehow a staged government plot. There is no sense or reason to any of their conspiracy theories, and I hesitate to even get into it any further. Lest it seem I am somehow giving any credence to these ridiculous fools. But they are out there and, with the anonymous protection of existing exclusively through the internet, they have pestered, upset, and downright harassed numerous Sandy Hook families. Not just the Parkers. The fact that people like this even exist in the world is enough to almost make you lose faith in humanity.

The Parkers, however, have more conviction than probably any family I had ever met. Even as the stalking and harassment from the "Truthers" got to the point where Emilie's fundraising web page had to be taken down, the Parkers remained composed. Not only composed, but forgiving. Being of the Mormon faith, this is how they strove to be. They were certainly practicing what had been preached.

. . .

After all they had been through, I could not blame the Parkers if they were to decline having a playground built for Emilie. But they wound up feeling just the opposite. Robbie and Alissa were completely on board with the project, mostly because it was another way to prove that love and compassion will triumph over evil and ignorance.

When the conversation turned to the specifics of the playground, Alissa told me about Emilie's desire for shade. Classically, all of our playgrounds are in big open spaces. On beaches, in open fields, in a cleared area where a playground had once stood, that kind of thing. None of those locales, and no playground we had built to this point really, offer any kind of cover. So now we had to find a place to build that could be "Emilie's Shady Spot". It was just a matter of figuring out where that would be.

. . .

The seaport city of New London, Connecticut had been on my short-list of "potential playground hosts" for a few months by this point. It is a very blue-collar town; just salt of the earth New England people who you'd love to have a beer with, tailgating out in the cold, stuff like that. As far as Connecticut goes, in New London you've got the Boston feel much more than New York. It's where Red Sox caps start to outnumber the Yankees caps—I guess that's the easiest way to describe it.

New London had been on our radar for a while, mostly because of a Fire Department Lieutenant by the name of Victor Spinato. He served along with me as a counselor at the Connecticut Burn Camp, and is a like-minded individual who had been supporting The Sandy Ground Project in any way he could. He had been working—on potential plans and on me—trying to bring a playground to his hometown.

• • •

Being a port of entry on the Connecticut coast, New London is obviously very much surrounded by water. Therefore, New Londoners took on some serious damage during Superstorm Sandy. It lies right on the Long Island Sound (to the south) and is at the mouth of the Thames River which runs north and south within the city. While it is true Sandy's effects in New London were significant, there was a park there that needed saving—and had been saved—for reasons unrelated to the storm.

Along the riverfront sits Coast Guard Station New London. And adjacent to it is what locals call Riverside Park. For the past few years, the waterfront property that houses Riverside Park had become a point of contention. It was about to be purchased by the Federal Government and added to the Coast Guard Station, but many local residents took issue with that transfer. It is a beautiful park that many of them had grown up visiting, so New Londoners were hesitant to give it up. So hesitant, in fact, that they formed the Committee to Save Riverside Park. The group was led by Corina Vendetto.

When it became known that the Coast Guard Station was set to absorb Riverside Park, Corina and her Committee made it their mission to take the park back. It had fallen into disrepair so they set about sprucing it up, planting flowers and landscaping the grounds on their own personal time. They restored the park and made it a place the people of New London would love and cherish again. At the end of the day, they blocked the government's purchasing of Riverside Park. It would remain a part of the fabric of New London by a very close vote.

When the idea of a playground in New London started to crystallize, Victor Spinato introduced me to Corina and I gave her the Sandy Ground presentation. She loved it. And summed up her feelings by saying, "I knew there was a reason we saved this park."

Corina became our greatest champion in New London—the true MVP of the build. She would wind up coordinating everything. From a house for the Parkers to stay in, to spaghetti dinner fundraisers. She got the local schools involved, got support from the VFW, and coordinated hotel rooms for all of our volunteers. She was everywhere, doing everything, and there is no way a playground gets built in that park without her.

. . .

With the wheels steadily in motion, I went along with Corina and Victor to tour the park. They had two locations in mind, the first one being up on the hillside. It was nestled up high, amongst the trees, with an amazing view of the river. The second location was down along the water, but I didn't even need to see it. Nowhere else could have been more perfect—up above the water, but underneath the trees. I could feel it in my bones that this was "Emilie's Shady Spot".

While all of our playgrounds are beautiful, this one just might be the best—geographically and from a scenery standpoint. Just a very peaceful, bucolic setting—hidden away a little bit, but definitely a reflection of the playground's namesake.

Shortly after my visit to the park, I called Alissa Parker. I told her to let her family know that we had found a location for Playground #14 and it was right up Emilie's alley. They were thrilled. It wasn't too far from where they lived (although they would eventually relocate) and they loved the set-up, location, and story of the park. Clearly the new playground would be in good hands in New London.

So along with Alissa and Robbie Parker, we began putting together the designs. Emilie's preferred color scheme was always pink, black, and blue, so the playground structure itself would be a mixture of those colors. She also loved to draw, and the Parker's contributed a lot of her artwork. We could then recreate it and have Emilie personally decorate the playground.

• • •

Having Pepperidge Farm come aboard as a corporate sponsor on our previous build was a blessing—not to mention a huge factor in getting the playground completed. For New London, another corporation came completely out of the blue and handed us a huge donation. They had been watching us.

The Founder and CEO of the "5-hour Energy" drinks, Manoj Bhargava, is not only a tremendous businessman, but a philanthropist as well. His company makes it their business to monitor charities and assess them, then dole out up to $50,000 for their cause.

I had never met the man, but one day an associate of Mr. Bhargava showed up and handed over a check. She said it was compliments of "5-hour Energy". I opened it up and, sure enough, it was made out to our foundation in the amount of $50,000. The maximum amount they give. We were overjoyed; I was holding about half of a playground in my hand.

And it seemed like whatever else we needed in regards to financing the New London build was raised by retired Battalion Chief Ed Halisey. He turned out to be a fundraising dynamo all throughout town. He knew everybody and put out the good word. Ed was also instrumental in getting us tons of local media coverage. Local newspapers, television shows, radio spots, you name it.

Between Battalion Chief Halisey and Manoj Bhargava, we had all the energy we needed and plenty of money in the bank. From my perspective, at least, there was now finally a little bit of breathing room funding-wise. No longer were we piecing each playground together on a shoestring budget. It felt like the sky was the limit, and our biggest sponsor of all was still on the horizon...

. . .

As far as building Emilie's playground, we had more volunteers than we could have ever hoped for. The weather was really turning cold now and the icy winds were howling off the river, but it didn't matter to anyone. The Angels Army, now on the "back nine" of the 26-playground mission, were chomping at the bit—working harder, faster, and more efficiently than ever. It was like an assembly line operating at top speed. All of the specialized technicians doing what they do best, with an expanding support staff to boot.

Our workforce was coming in from all angles now, first and foremost from right there in New London. They gave us everything we needed—volunteers, food, drink, lodging—they could not have been better to us. Especially an Italian restaurant called Tony D's, which was located across town. They basically gave us carte blanche, anything we could ever need or want, for the duration of our stay.

The New London High School football team would show up in busloads after their school day had ended so they could help out. Numerous teachers and students from the schools across the city would come by just to show their support. We felt more than welcome there and had more help than we knew what to do with.

At one point during a busy build day, a couple of the Angels Army guys were pointing out two female volunteers. "You have to go meet them," they said. I assumed they were a couple of locals, nothing out of the ordinary, and figured I'd get over to say hi eventually.

When I finally introduced myself, they seemed star struck by me—which is obviously as unwarranted as it is funny. But it was because they were from Iowa and had only heard about The Sandy Ground Project through People Magazine. They recognized me from the picture. What had brought them from a small suburb of Des Moines all the way here?

Simply put, they said, the project moved them. So they decided to take a few vacation days from work, hop a flight to the east coast, and help us out. I was shocked and, honestly, humbled by this. They believed enough in what we were doing and had made a pilgrimage of sorts just to lend a hand.

I found it amazing how much the project was touching people and expanding throughout the country. The two ladies, Becky and Kim, enjoyed their experience with us in New London so much that they returned to volunteer again in Mystic, CT and Watertown, CT the following year. We were always thrilled to have them.

We were also thrilled to have our friends at NAGE come out in strong support of The Sandy Ground Project. The Boston-based "National Association of Government Employees" has always been a great friend to the fire service. And through David Holway, their President, NAGE came a little ways down the road to New London and came up strong.

With the abundance of help and spirits high, the build went off without a hitch. This was another "surface mount" build, which meant a concrete slab base with rubber surfacing poured on top of it. This format was really becoming our bread and butter. And all the while, the builders enjoyed an amazing view high atop the Thames River. Every once in a while a submarine heading to (or from) the Coast Guard Station would float by. A real slice of Americana.

• • •

One person who I probably haven't given enough credit to thus far in telling the story of The Sandy Ground Project is Brian D'Antoni. He was one of the original believers—in the project itself and in my ability to piece it together. He was the one who insisted on going to meet with the families up in Newtown and telling them about the playground idea face-to-face. He was a big catalyst during the project's inception, and continues to be.

Through the life of The Sandy Ground Project, and at the builds themselves, Brian has stepped into the role of documentarian and media specialist. He, along with his girlfriend Gina Aiello, have done an amazing job marketing the project.

Brian is an ace with the video camera, and he has been tremendous in capturing the look and feel of all of our Sandy Ground events. The ground-breakings and ribbon-cuttings and the general atmosphere around the job site as the playground comes together. He talks to the volunteers, onlookers, and the families of the angels—getting all of their perspectives.

Sometimes it works out that the general public sees what we're up to through a short clip on the local news or a one-page profile in People Magazine. But for anyone that followed The Sandy Ground Project on a more regular basis, it was through Brian. He is diligent in promoting us on our website (www.whereangelsplayfoundation.org) and on just about every form of social media. He gives people a window into our world, and that is so important for so many reasons.

And I feel like Brian's presence behind the camera was never as important as it was on November 17, 2013. The day we cut the ribbon on Emilie Parker's playground.

• • •

November 17th in Riverside Park was sunny, a bit breezy, and had all the traditional pomp and circumstance that Sandy Ground dedications were becoming known for. But that morning was a turning point because of Emilie's parents, Robbie and Alissa. They made two of the most remarkable speeches I have ever heard—and I mean *ever*. In person... on television... anywhere.

The first speech, by Mr. Parker, was incredibly eloquent and insightful in its analysis of the Newtown tragedy, its aftermath, our society, and the human spirit. The latter, by Mrs. Parker, was perfectly simple and immensely powerful. It boiled down everything The Sandy Ground Project was striving for into a handful of concise phrases.

I wish I could place a video clip into this book, Robbie and Alissa were *that* good. They are ideas and feelings that should be shared with anyone and everyone—the subject of national notoriety, really. So I will transcribe their beautiful messages in full. I'm honored to share their words here...

Robbie Parker:

"It's an amazing experience to see all of you here. There are a lot of people that we know, and so many people that we don't know.

And to see everybody from this town… and from across the state of Connecticut… and from across the country… To come and support us, and to support this project, is probably the one of the most touching things I've ever been a part of.

When we were first approached with the idea of a playground for Emilie, I can't tell you how immediately that struck a chord with us and how perfect it sounded. Because playgrounds were where Emilie spent so much of her time.

I was one of the weird people that actually was trying to make my way through school while at the same time building a family. And so we lived on very very meager budgets. And while I was gone for most of the day, Alissa had to spend a lot of time trying to find free things to do with the kids—so playgrounds were perfect. It was also a great place for her to practice her photography skills and hone the talents that she has. And what better way to do that than at a playground, photographing children expressing the purest form of joy?

As we moved around for my medical schooling, and the different rotations we had to go through, there was a section of time where we had to move every six weeks. And as we moved away from a place, and talked about the places we'd visited, the names of the towns wouldn't make much sense to Emilie. But we could explain the place we were talking about by the playground that she would go to. We'd say, 'Do you remember the playground with all the trees? That was by the lake.' Or, 'Remember the playground that had the big steeple?' And that's how she was able to connect her history and her past. Through playgrounds.

Everybody knows that Emilie's favorite color is pink. But a lot of people don't realize that she had a favorite color combination, which is expressed beautifully here: pink, black, and blue. She saw the world in color. She was a bright, beautiful, loving girl. And that's how she expressed herself. To see that symbolized here so wonderfully is the perfect way to embody her spirit at this park.

It was so touching when I showed up here the other morning. It was just a little after 7:30, it was probably about 30 degrees outside.

And there was already about 150 volunteers here, eager and ready to get going on building the playground. That sacrifice, and that love expressed here, touched me so deeply.

After December 14th, there have been a lot of labels placed on Emilie. And on us as a family. And on the community of Newtown and the families that were directly affected. We get labeled with "victims". We get labeled with numbers—"one of the twenty", "one of the twenty-six", "one of the families".

While all the labels—in essence—are correct, they don't capture the full story. They're adjectives—one word adjectives—to try and help you understand the significance of something. But labels do a very poor job of that.

After December 14th it was amazing for us to see how that evil event sponsored so much love, and unity, and renewal across the country. And there were so many people that felt that. And it's a project like this that highlights the love and unity that came out of that tragedy.

Shortly after the tragedy, however, I was terrified to see how those feelings of unity and renewal and love quickly metastasized into an angrier and more divided posture. People started to focus on the things that differentiate us from each other, instead of what unifies us together.

We started to put labels on ourselves. We started to use adjectives to describe ourselves as "pro-gun", "anti-gun", "liberal", "red", "blue". And by doing so, we took the focus away from what drew us together, and the epicenter of what united all of us together throughout this world. And spread it out to areas that took away from that love.

Labels do nothing more than build walls, segregate us from one another, and drive wedges between us. That is NOT why these people died. That is NOT the remembrance they need to have. And that is NOT what embodies Emilie.

We need to be brave enough to stand up and practice what we preach. And to let people follow our example with our words, with our actions, and with our art. To stand up and show people who we really are, what we really stand for, and focus on the commonalities that we all share.

My hope is that we'll stop looking at each other and seeing the differences that we have. And start looking at each other and just realize we're all people. We can look at each other as citizens of New London… or citizens of Connecticut… or Americans… or just people… all here together, sharing our experiences. So why not lift each other up?

This project does that in the purest form. And that is what happened when I came here Thursday morning. There were people from all different economic statuses, representing different nationalities, different ages, in every color. They are all here with one mind, one heart, and one purpose.

I challenge all of us, when we leave here today, to go home and break your mirrors. Stop focusing on yourself. Start looking towards other people. It is charity which binds us together.

This effort, from so many people, is an exemplary form of charity. Which, in itself, is the purest demonstration of love.

I want all of us to insist on heroes… then become one.

Thank you for being here. God bless."

Alissa Parker:

"For me, I look forward to days when I can feel close to Emilie. And I have looked forward to this day for a long time. I feel very privileged to have so much of my family here, and my new family as well, and all of you.

I hope all of you can feel that sweet spirit. And be able to see that light in the childrens' eyes as they play. For me that's the greatest gift, and to be here to share it with all of you is amazing.

It's a good day!!! And I'm really, really excited to be here to enjoy it with all of you. Thank you."

• • •

At its core, that is all The Sandy Ground Project was designed to do. Give these families one good day. One good weekend. One safe place to go and feel their loved one's presence and spirit. One location where they can find some solace in a tribute to how their loved one had lived. And, in the case of Emilie Parker, one shady spot.

After experiencing Robbie and Alissa's speeches in person, it's almost hard to recall anything else that happened that morning. We did have some children there to sing for the family, a dove release, and our presentation of the bell as we always do.

The Angels Army, the Parkers, and all family and friends got together after the ceremony at Tony D's Italian Restaurant for a final celebration. Since the Parkers are Mormons and don't drink, we joked about today's party having the lowest bar bill of the entire Sandy Ground Project.

On her way out, Alissa gave me a gift basket with a beautiful note attached to it. I read it and it brought me immediately to tears. I realized I had been in the zone with all of the organizing and building. And now Alissa's words had brought me back in touch with the emotional side of what The Sandy Ground is about. She simply thanked me and said that her and her family couldn't have made it through without the project. Many of us remain very close to the Parkers... still comfortable enough to check in and see how the kids are and let them know we're thinking about them.

• • •

After wrapping up in New London, Brian D'Antoni's footage of Robbie's and Alissa's speeches became the centerpiece of our presentations about The Sandy Ground Project. They have such incredible impact. I have shown the video no less than 150 times and I've gotten a lump in my throat every single time. Even though the Parkers have since moved to the west coast, Robbie has offered to fly anywhere to speak on behalf of the project should we need him.

Just recently I was doing a presentation for the family of Martin Richard. We will soon be building a playground for Martin, who was lost at age 8 in the Boston Marathon bombing. (Spoiler alert: The Sandy Ground Project ends at Playground #26, but the Where Angels Play Foundation carries the torch well beyond that.) As the presentation came to Robbie's speech, I watched the Richards react.

They had brought their priest along that day, an Irish Catholic from Boston. I watched as he took notes, hanging on Robbie Parker's every word, and welling up with tears himself. He told me he would be passing Robbie's message along during his sermon that coming Sunday.

I called Robbie and told him this. We marveled at the fact that a parish full of Irish Catholics in Boston was going to hear the message of a Mormon thousands of miles away. And this cuts to the core of his message that we really are all the same, beyond labels, looking out for one another. "That is the reason," Robbie said, "this project should never come to an end."

Pat, Butch and Tim Lavin mixing it up

CHAPTER NINETEEN

Playground Celebrating the Life of Josephine Gay

Bridgeport, Connecticut

R ight around the halfway point of The Sandy Ground Project, I heard from the largest corporation yet. They knew about what we had been doing, had monitored our progress for quite a while, and were excited to support us. They also happened to be bringing their ultimate highlight event—probably the *world's* highlight event—to our part of the country.

In its almost 50-year history, the Super Bowl has been played outdoors in a cold weather city once. One single time. And as far as I can tell, Super Bowl XLVIII (48) will be the only one played under those circumstances for quite a while. But that is fine by me, because the one time the National Football League staged America's biggest sporting event out in the cold… it happened right here in New Jersey, the year we were in the thick of The Sandy Ground Project.

• • •

Not long after wrapping up Playground #13, MaryKate was contacted by Rich Petriccione from an organization called the Snowflake Foundation. They had been working with the Super Bowl Host Committee, looking for local charities worth supporting and sponsoring.

Super Bowl XLVIII was scheduled for February 2, 2014 in East Rutherford, New Jersey. Although the game would technically take place on Jersey soil, the game was billed as the "New York Super Bowl" and was really hosted by the entire tri-state area. Every year, the NFL looks to impact the local community that hosts the Super Bowl in a positive way. We certainly felt like we could help them do that.

After some introductions, our conversations with Rich turned towards the finances of how The Sandy Ground Project builds its playgrounds. I let him know that, all told, each playground winds up costing $100,000. Sometimes more, sometimes less; but that is the nice, round ballpark figure we use as a benchmark. He said that sounds great… The NFL would like to build three.

Of course this sounded too good to be true. Three?!? That would be amazing, but why three? So Rich explained that the NFL is focused on positively impacting the *entire* tri-state area—not just New York City. Therefore, they would like to sponsor a playground in all three of the states we have been building in—one in New York, one in New Jersey, and one in Connecticut. He assured me that a check for $300,000 would soon be on its way. But there was a catch…

The NFL wanted to have all three of the playgrounds completed by the time the Super Bowl kicked off on February 2nd. I first heard from Rich in probably mid-November, so that didn't give us much time to pull it all together. And even if you assume that we can find three locations, plan out the builds, and assemble manpower… How could I go to a family and propose that their loved one's playground be built in December or January?

We'd had such great experiences, starting in April, throughout the spring, summer, and fall. But winter was uncharted and potentially unpleasant territory. What if it snowed? What if we couldn't dig into the frozen ground? How could we do a ribbon-cutting in 20-degree temperatures? Or in an ice storm?

Clearly there were a lot of questions, but by this point in the process I'd learned to trust the signs. It's not every day the NFL (or anyone) cold-calls you, ready to put a check in the mail for three hundred grand. So I told Rich we would gratefully and proudly partner with the NFL's Super Bowl Host Committee. Challenge accepted.

Within three weeks, there was a check in my mailbox for $300,000.00.

The Rainbow Connection

The Angels Army after a Hard Days Work in Manasquan

Catherine's Rope Swing gets its First Test

Overcoming the Elements for Allie

Daniel's Gift to the Highlands

Fairfield Visited by Orca Whale courtesy of Firefighter John Cieplinski

The Spirit of Christmas

Scarlett Lewis and the Lavin brothers

The Future of Where Angels Play

Dennis Bourke gives the Project it's Melody

Mark Virag Our Foundation's Foundation

Charlotte's Playground ready for Play

Where Angels Play Responding into Generations to Come

Angels to Watch Over Angels!

The Sandy Ground Project complete,
perhaps just the beginning of an ever growing Angels Army

Blessed to have a Beautiful Support Team

. . .

By the time I met with Michele Gay, her and her family had relocated to the Boston metropolitan area. Her daughter Josephine, known affectionately and almost exclusively as "Joey", was lost in the tragedy at Sandy Hook Elementary School. Joey was an autistic child who expressed herself primarily through sign language and the use of her iPad. She was seven years old.

Michele graciously agreed to meet with me to hear more about The Sandy Ground Project. By now she had heard some good things about the project from the other Newtown parents she'd been in contact with. And that was enough to give her the faith and trust to meet up with me, sight-unseen, at a roadside Cracker Barrel near the Massachusetts/Connecticut border. If she was willing to hear me out, I could certainly meet her halfway.

As I explained my own history, the project's history, and laid out the plan—I could see Michele's eyes light up whenever I mentioned the actual playground. It was clear that the essence of the project struck a chord with her and she was immediately asking where and when we could get started.

Michele told me about her family and their lives being rocked by the Newtown tragedy. Her husband Bob and two daughters, Maria and Sophie, had relocated shortly after Joey's passing. They were reeling from their loss of course, yet thankful for the seven years they'd had with her.

Michele seemed very eager to get things started on Joey's playground. I told her to sit tight, and I would get her more details as soon as I could.

. . .

The largest city in the state of Connecticut is Bridgeport. And with a significant portion of the city sitting directly on or near the Long Island Sound and Pequonnock River, large areas of it were ravaged during Superstorm Sandy. Several neighborhoods were underwater. All sorts of trees and wires were left mangled, leaving the citizens without power for days and weeks in some places. It was like a warzone.

Through Steve Lupinacci's involvement with The Sandy Ground Project, I had become very familiar with the layout in Bridgeport. Many of their firefighters helped us out during the build in Fairfield, which is the next town over. We'd held fundraisers at places in Bridgeport, at Sound Tigers hockey games, stuff like that.

With this newfound money from the NFL, and time being of the essence, it seemed logical to turn towards Bridgeport for our Connecticut "Super Bowl" playground. Through Steve and a firefighter named "Zolli", we already had troops on the ground there. We also had amazing support from Bridgeport Mayor Bill Finch.

Mayor Finch, I have to say, is the real deal. For a mayor and fire department to get along so well, in a city of that size, is nothing short of miraculous. Trust me, I would know. But the fire guys insisted that Mayor Finch was solid and he definitely proved to be. He not only gave us access to his ace Parks & Rec man Thomas Carroll (a Newtown resident) and greased the wheels on all approvals for the playground; he also donated $10,000 of his own money to the project. With the money already there from the NFL for his city, he insisted on making the contribution to the overall mission anyway. He is easily one of the top handful of politicians I've ever dealt with.

We wound up settling on the beachfront area known as Seaside Park for the location of Playground #15. That was half the battle. The other half would be convincing a family to allow us to build their loved one's playground on the oceanfront... in December... in New England. And also ask them to come out and support us. I felt bad even asking honestly, but here was our chance with the NFL's funding. I decided to give the Gays a call first.

• • •

I got in touch with Michele Gay and explained the situation. With Bridgeport, with the NFL, with the need to build as soon as possible, the whole story. I was practically apologizing when I asked if they would be up for making Playground #15 in Bridgeport Joey's. I should have expected the answer that came next...

Michele was thrilled. She said she had been meaning to call me because Joey's birthday was coming up. It's on December 11th. (Her seventh birthday party was actually scheduled to take place one day after the Newtown tragedy.) She wanted to see if there was any way to possibly build the playground around that time. And now here I was, asking if that very thing would be okay.

It was another one of the great miracles that took place throughout The Sandy Ground Project. Pieces somehow come together—the town, the birthday, the Super Bowl—and you're just along for the amazing ride. We were all set, time to begin designing Joey Gay's playground. And I guess this is where I learned exactly *how* perfectly this all worked out.

• • •

Joey was in love with all things purple. She was obsessed with wearing purple in some capacity every single day. Any shade of the color was fine, but what Joey really favored was the deep, darkish, "royal purple" worn by the Baltimore Ravens.

Bob Gay is a die-hard Ravens fan, making Joey one by proxy. She watched practically every single game, tucked onto Bob's lap in their favorite chair. She was obsessed with wearing this one Ravens shirt constantly, a solid purple shirt with the team's logo sitting front and center. Joey loved this t-shirt so much that she'd try and put it on almost every day. Keeping it clean became an impossible task. So they wound up getting three of that same shirt so there was always a clean one ready to go. Less than two months after the Newtown tragedy, the Baltimore Ravens won the Super Bowl. They were still the defending champs of the league that was now helping us build her playground.

Needless to say, Joey's playground would be as purple as we could get it. We would also build in the Autism Awareness theme as well as Joey's artwork. One of her drawings even said "Come and Play—Love, Joey", which we featured on the main sign. But the purple color was the key, Joey's absolute favorite. We assured the Gays that, with the build taking place on the beach in December, some of our volunteers would be turning purple too.

• • •

The first week of December at Seaside Park in Bridgeport was viciously windy and cold. No surprise there. As we began the actual machinations of erecting the playground, it became clear that the cold was just too much. Not for our workers, of course. The Angels Army is plenty tough and hearty enough to build through the worst of conditions. But it became a matter of whether the equipment and materials could function in sub-freezing temperatures.

In order to build a playground like Joey's would be, you need to first put down a cement slab. Then, you would have the rubber surfacing put down on top of that slab to serve as the cushioned playground floor. The thing is, the rubber surfacing material needed to be kept above 40-degrees in order to settle properly. During that week in Bridgeport, we'd be lucky to get up to 40-degrees at all.

So we decided to erect a giant tent on the beach… kind of like one you would hold an outdoor wedding in (like my own daughter's actually). This way we could essentially build "indoors" and have the tent heated to our desired temperature. So while the icy wind pounded on the tent's walls day after day, our volunteers pounded away at the playground. This included our honorary forewomen, Marie and Sophie Gay, who worked happily and comfortably beside us at (precisely) 72.6-degrees.

• • •

With a cement pad already installed on the beach, the Angels Army set their sights on building the playground structure directly on top of it. This is where our team of technicians were really shining and making these builds fly. Guys like Joe Rainis, Alan Ballester, Ron Wetmore, Dan Gurrera, Jim Stelman, Ricky Testa, and Mario DiPietro. These are the individuals responsible for all of the playground-to-cement connections. It is a complicated job that takes precision, and our guys operate like a well-oiled machine.

We also have Danny Conners and Bruce Pollock, who actually created all of the models and braces and templates to facilitate a quick build. Their handiwork is almost like a giant erector set. And then there is Billy Valentine, our quality control specialist. He checks and double-checks every element of the playground to ensure its safety. He tightens up every last screw, makes sure all connections are completely set. To this very day, Bill continues to maintain and inspect the playgrounds periodically. Of course our skilled guys would be lost without Marty and Pilar Sanzari who make sure all of our tools are charged, in good order and ready to go.

It is because of all these guys that we began to strongly encourage the towns who were getting playgrounds to put cement down first. Our slop-loving Mud Duck crew was none too happy about the lack of dirty dusty cement work to be done, but this was clearly the way to go. With our specialists, the work would get done quicker and easier.

All of this speaks to the expansive "skill set" that the fire service has within its ranks. It is something I first noticed in Mississippi and continues to amaze me. If there's a job that needs doing, no matter what it is, you can find a firefighter with expertise. Anything from painting a house to sand-sculpting a whale. From specialized masonry work to water heater maintenance to comic relief—there is a firefighter who can provide it. And we seemed to utilize every bit of that repertoire throughout the life of The Sandy Ground Project.

• • •

As the Angels Army cranked out work like an assembly line at GM, the spiritual aspect of the group, the camaraderie, was rocking as well. You had some pretty sizable characters coming out of the woodwork, making every build, and creating the little traditions and quirks of the project. During breaks in the work on Joey's playground, we would all go out in the cold and make bonfires and bond.

Guys like Tommy Atwell and Pops Kennedy would practically emcee little exercises like mock "court"—where they would charge the other volunteers with slacking off or drinking on the job. Or they would call people out to do "open mic", prompting anyone and everyone to speak what was on their mind. The results ranged from the sublime to the ridiculous.

In Bridgeport, Tommy and Pops invited along a handful of Toronto firefighters. These were guys who they'd played hockey with and gotten interested in The Sandy Ground Project. The Toronto guys, clearly thriving in the cold, spent the week building alongside the Angels Army and became part of the scene. We were now an international force. Guys like Mark Goode, Bucky Hasslefelt, Joe Stone, Steve Robb, Paul O'Brien and Wally, proving brotherhood truly has no borders.

· · ·

As we were building Joey Gay's playground in Bridgeport, I got a call from ESPN. The Baltimore Ravens were playing on Monday Night Football the following week and Rick Reilly was looking to do a special piece on Joey for the broadcast. It would be about her family, her playground, and the connection between the Gays and the Ravens in the wake of the Newtown tragedy.

The ESPN crew (based in Connecticut of course) made the trip from Bristol down to Bridgeport to check out the build. They filmed the construction going on inside the tent, conducted numerous interviews, and even stuck around for the ribbon-cutting on Joey's birthday. They were total pros and the piece came out amazing.

On December 16, 2013, the Baltimore Ravens defeated the Detroit Lions 18–16. But none of us from The Sandy Ground Project were tuned in to watch the actual game—we just wanted to see Joey and the Gays on the pre-game show. It was perfect. It told Joey's inspirational story, showed her decked out in her trademark purple, and did an incredible job of portraying what our project was all about.

The reaction was immediate for us. I don't need to explain the insane number of people nationwide that watch Monday Night Football (or the NFL in general for that matter). If The Sandy Ground Project wasn't mainstream before, it certainly was now. Michele summed it up during the interview by commenting how this little girl, who couldn't speak, was now speaking to millions of people with her spirit.

One segment of the interview really jumped out at me personally though. It was when Rick Reilly asked Michele, "What did you think when someone comes to you and says 'We want to build a playground in your daughter's honor?'" She answered, "It was like a breath of fresh air. Somebody gets it."

I can't express how much those three words meant in that moment. Somebody gets it. It was awesome to hear that the feeling we were getting by executing the actual work of the project was mutual. That we were in tune with these families. Somebody gets it. Those three words from Michele were true validation of what The Sandy Ground Project represented now.

• • •

For her 8th birthday Josephine Gay got a playground. Actually… no. For her 8th birthday Josephine Gay *gave* a playground. And it ensured that the children of Bridgeport would be playing for her for years and years to come. It was December 11, 2013. The airplane circling overhead carried her message: "A GIFT TO BRIDGEPORT ON MY BIRTHDAY… LOVE, JOEY"

• • •

We left up our big building tent, but held the evening ribbon-cutting ceremony just outside of it. Mayor Bill Finch made a great speech on behalf of the people of Bridgeport, welcoming the Gay family and thanking them for bringing Joey's spirit to them. Bob Gay made a beautiful speech as well and led the crowd in a singing of "Happy Birthday" to Joey.

All of the ribbon-cutting ceremonies we have are moving, but this one took on an overwhelming tone of happiness. It was a birthday party after all, and not even Disney could have created a more magical setting…

As the sun began to set, the sky turned a very distinct color common to winters in the northeast. It's that pale purple, the classic look of an overcast night where it might snow or it might not. Between the playground structure, the signs and balloons, and the sky itself—we were all enveloped in Joey's favorite color. One big purple hug.

Since it was an evening ceremony, we put on a fireworks show and set it to Stevie Wonder's upbeat rendition of "Happy Birthday". Then, all the kids were able to head inside the tent to be the first ones to play on Playground #15 and celebrate the life of Josephine Gay.

. . .

After the ribbon-cutting, Bob Gay and I joked about how this process had all started. With Michele telling him that she was going to meet up with some fireman at a highway rest stop 100 miles away. He was skeptical, naturally, but we were laughing and hugging now, thrilled about how beautifully the project had turned out for Joey.

Since building the Bridgeport playground, the Gay family has continued to work with us through our Where Angels Play Foundation. Living in the Boston area now, Bob and Michele are our chairpersons for the upcoming playground build in honor of Sean Collier—the MIT police officer who lost his life in the aftermath of the Boston Marathon bombing. Through their foundation, Michele will also be traveling to Moore, Oklahoma to explore the possibility of building a playground there. The two of them will be representing the Sandy Ground families as they "pay it forward" in the years to come.

. . .

But all of it was kick-started by Joey. The NFL coming up with the money, her birthday, Monday Night Football—clearly it's beyond coincidence. At this point you'd have a hard time convincing me that the Ravens winning the Super Bowl six weeks after the Newtown tragedy wasn't Joey trying to put a smile on her dad's face.

And now there was a shiny, new, and—above all—purple(!) playground on the shore of Bridgeport. As Michele said on ESPN: "It's her birthday. It was just meant to be. Without a doubt."

CHAPTER TWENTY

Playground Celebrating the Life of
Mary Sherlach

Roxbury, New York

At the ribbon-cutting ceremony in Bridgeport, everyone was on a high. There were fireworks and singing; it was Joey Gay's birthday party on a bright purple Wednesday evening. Only three days later, the following Saturday, was a much more somber event. It was December 14, 2013. The one-year anniversary of the tragedy at Sandy Hook Elementary School.

Being in such close contact with so many of the families who'd been directly affected by the tragedy, we knew that they wanted absolutely no part of acknowledging any kind of anniversary. December 14, 2012 was an unmitigated nightmare that they had no interest in reliving. The wounds were still so fresh and the media was gearing up to descend upon Newtown for the obligatory "one-year later" story. It was all well and good to show up and do a story on a certain date, to commemorate it and pay respect. But from the families' perspective, this was their everyday struggle. This was their reality and their pain that was being dealt with every single second since it happened. December 14th being the date was immaterial. It was heartbreak that lived in perpetuity.

For all of these reasons the families, for the most part, made it a priority to get themselves out of town. Some went to Hawaii, some visited family in other states, others went to Florida or Disney World to put some distance—physically and mentally—between themselves and Newtown. One parent, Victoria Soto's father Carlos, even trekked down to my own personal condo in South Carolina to get away.

Unfortunately, as I was still an active Captain with the Elizabeth Fire Department, I was unable to make the trip with him. But one of our most dedicated Angels Army guys, Ron Wetmore, escorted Carlos down south and the two of them enjoyed the warmer weather and a cocktail or two. We didn't want Carlos to be alone at a time like this, and Ron has continually proven to be wonderfully generous with his time and energy for the Sandy Ground cause. The two of them had a ball, I'm sure.

Knowing what we knew about how the families felt, we completely stayed away from commemorating the anniversary in any way. It was our job, I felt, to help them navigate this difficult weekend in the most sensitive way possible. We prayed for the victims, our angels. We prayed along with their families in many cases. But otherwise, we just focused on the upcoming task at hand. Which was Playground #16.

· · ·

Bill Sherlach and I hit it off immediately. He reminded me so much of my own brothers. An easy going, down-to-earth guy you can just hang out and enjoy a cold beer with. That sort of kinship shone through when we first met, despite the fact that the subject we were speaking about was a tough one. The loss of his wife, the school psychologist at Sandy Hook Elementary, Mary Sherlach.

Mary loved her job at Sandy Hook. As an 18-year veteran at the school, she was the senior member of the staff. She treated the children with love and attention as if they were her own. That is why, when the ultimate emergency struck that fateful morning at *her* school, she was running towards the trouble rather than away from it.

As a firefighter, I—and the majority of the Angels Army—can identify with having that instinct and desire to protect. It is that sense of duty that compels you to run into the fray when reason and caution compel you to do just the opposite. Mary is woven from the same cloth as we are. And that is why building a playground in her honor would be all the more special.

Mary left behind her husband Bill and two brilliant, beautiful daughters. Maura, an amazing singer and music teacher, and Katy, a chemist who was in the process of getting her Ph.D. from Georgetown. Bill spoke about his girls with pride, clearly the products of a wonderful mother. And when I asked about a playground being built in honor of Mary, Bill assured me that the three of them would support it and cherish it wholeheartedly. It didn't matter where it was or when it was built; as long as it was needed and necessary they were grateful to be involved. Bill's feeling was that the playground was all about the kids, so do whatever we need to do. As the organizer of the build, I was certainly very grateful for the Sherlach family being so flexible. Particularly because it was almost Christmas and getting colder by the day.

As we began to chat about the specifics of Mary's playground, Bill told me more and more about her. They lived in Trumbull, Connecticut, but had many ties to upstate New York. They had met and fell in love in college up there—at SUNY Cortland—and kept a lake house in the Finger Lakes region that Mary loved to visit whenever she could.

Mary loved red roses, so the playground's color scheme would be predominantly red with green support poles to look like stems. This would create the impression that giant roses had sprouted up from the ground, only these were the type of flowers you can climb and play on. We would also incorporate the message of "Mary's Fund", a foundation started in Mary's honor to support mental health services for children in need.

When I mentioned to Bill that Mary's playground would be the second to be sponsored by the NFL's Super Bowl Host Committee, he told me that she was also a big football fan. Specifically, she loved the Miami Dolphins. I had to laugh about the irony of this. I am a lifelong fan (for better or worse) of the New York Jets. And if there's one team a Jets fan hates, it's the Dolphins. But this twist had nothing to do with me, really. The true irony is that we were about to build

Mary's playground in a town with possibly the highest concentration of Jets fans anywhere in New York...

. . .

From September 11, 2001 until now, you would be hard-pressed to find a town that has endured more suffering than Breezy Point, New York. A very blue-collar, coastal section of Queens, Breezy Point is a throwback sort of neighborhood. A lot of Irish and Italians, cops and firefighters, very much a family atmosphere throughout the town. And that family is probably all the more close-knit because of what they have endured together.

Start with 9/11. Between the FDNY and NYPD, this small town lost a total of 29 of its residents in the attacks on the World Trade Center. Then, two months later, an American Airlines flight leaving JFK Airport headed to the Dominican Republic crashes down into their town. All 260 passengers were killed, as well as five more people on the ground, and ten homes were completely wiped out.

Then there's Superstorm Sandy and the massive Breezy Point Fire. Extreme flooding in the town ignited an electrical fire and the high winds associated with the storm caused it to spread rapidly. Given the limited access the Fire Department had to the area due to the high water, the fire just burned and burned. All told, 130 homes in Breezy Point burned to the ground. Another 50 were damaged.

Needless to say, Breezy Point was a town that could use a ray of sunshine. And given that it is *technically* not governed by New York City although it is considered to be a part of Queens, this made the planning and organizing much easier from our perspective. We would get to build a New York playground (an area where we were lacking to this point), plus we could circumvent the tangle of red tape that comes with dealing with the City's Parks and Recreation people.

So being able to deal directly with Theresa Flanagan of the Breezy Point Cooperative, we were able to fast-track a build that would take place the week of Christmas. Our 16th Playground, in honor of Mary Sherlach, was coming to the Roxbury section of Breezy Point, New York.

• • •

As the Events Coordinator of the Breezy Point Co-Op, Theresa Flanagan was the go-to person for anything and everything we needed to facilitate a Roxbury build. She deftly cleared the way as far as politics within the town, set up all the catering and meals needed for our volunteers, and provided any logistical support we could possibly need there.

My other main ally in building the Roxbury playground was Gene Hickey. If you recall, Gene (a family friend) and his company Hallen Construction came up huge at our first New York build in Island Park. Well, it turns out that Gene has even more connections in the Breezy Point area. In addition, the Breezy Point Mayor—who'd lost her own home in the Superstorm Sandy Fire—had put together a core group of supporters to make sure our volunteers had everything they needed at all times.

Between the funding from the NFL, the construction power and prowess of Hallen, and the old school New York neighborhood love we were getting from the townspeople—this build was a guaranteed piece of cake. A breeze at Breezy Point. In a day or two, there would be a brand new playground on the beach with a breathtaking view of New York City. What could possibly go wrong?

• • •

Out on the ice-cold sand, the morning of December 20, 2013, about 100 of us stood ready to begin building Mary Sherlach's playground. Hallen Construction, the Angels Army mainstays, and a lot of new friends and family from Roxbury and throughout Breezy Point were all in attendance. The only guest that didn't show up to the party? The playground.

The physical structures, the playgrounds themselves, are trucked up to our area from Georgia each time around. When the truck wasn't on time that morning, I made a couple phone calls and was told it was about an hour away. Which would have been fine, really. I can keep everyone waiting another hour to start, I figured. But in truth, the truck—and the playground sitting inside of it—was broken down somewhere in the Carolinas. It had suffered a broken brake-line and would be en route shortly.

So here I was with all these volunteers, all the good vibes, and absolutely nothing for them to do. Most people milled around, chatting each other up, warming their hands over some burning wood barrels and wondering when we'd start. As the morning's coffee and donuts wore off and it got on towards lunchtime, it was apparent that there'd be no work to do anytime soon.

I was aggravated. The day was a bust and it wasn't a weather-related act of God bust. It was a bust in the sense that the trucking company hadn't fulfilled its obligation and was giving me bad information to boot. When it was clear that the troops needed to be fed, we gathered everyone up for a two-block walk to the local Catholic Club in town. It was in this small white building that Theresa had arranged a good, hot meal for all of the volunteers. What happened over the next couple of hours turned out to be the genesis of this very book.

• • •

As everyone convened for lunch, I felt like something needed to be said. These people had given their time and had a right to know exactly what was going on. So I apologized for the lost morning, gave them the updated plan of attack, and thanked them once again for their time and effort.

But somehow this two-minute briefing turned into a 90-minute open forum, the topic being all things Sandy Ground. As I began to tell a story from one playground… then another… then another… I began to realize that these were great events and anecdotes that not everyone was totally filled in on. Even the Angels Army—you had some guys that were at most builds, some that were at a handful. You had people who'd been to one or two, and for some it was their first time volunteering. But practically no one knew the ENTIRE story. They knew some stories, but not others. So as we talked (mostly I talked, I guess), everyone was getting completely filled in. They were just now grasping the full scope of what, exactly, they were a part of.

Even my own brothers—Butch, Bob, Pat, Tim—all four of whom happened to be there that afternoon, didn't know all that had happened. Every rainbow, or butterfly, or purple sky, or orca whale… every "god-incidence" as our special strain of coincidences were coming to be known. Two of my nephews—Danny Beirne and Rob Jordan—were there eating lunch and had heard barely any of this. They were shocked. The more stories that came out, the more everyone wanted to hear. People I didn't even know were listening intently, in tears. Someone even said, "You should write a book." Yeah, sure.

Carlos Soto was at the Catholic Club that afternoon as well, and he stood up and spoke about how much the project meant in his life. And the volunteers were wowed by his words, his pouring his heart out. It was proof that they had done something great for somebody else, and were standing ready to do it again. Suddenly a wasted day didn't seem so wasted after all. It was The Sandy Ground Project's most memorable State of the Union Address/Press Conference/Group Therapy Session to date. We built something together that afternoon, for sure, but for once it wasn't a playground.

Little by little, the volunteers made their way back to the beach where they would wait some more. Then, finally, well after dark, the truck showed up with the playground around 8 PM. The drivers, you could tell, felt awful and you could practically smell the brake-line burning as they pulled in. They had spent the last 10 hours driving no more than 30 mph, but were finally here.

It was too dark to build and bitterly cold, but many volunteers were still there ready to unload the truck. So we cranked up the forklifts and laid everything out with an eye toward hitting the ground running the following day. Since this was a beach build there was no rubber-surfacing to be poured, and therefore no reason to panic about letting the playground settle for two days. We all parted ways that night feeling ready to rock for tomorrow.

• • •

With everyone having a full understanding of The Sandy Ground Project and their spiritual batteries fully charged, we returned to the build site the next day and crushed it. Hallen Construction made the build soar with all of their resources and heavy machinery (one behemoth piece cranking and smoking like something out of Willy Wonka's factory).

A great, and somewhat comical, illustration of how diametrically opposed these two build days in Roxbury were, was a time-lapse video done by Brian D'Antoni. On December 20th, he set up a camera, up on a crane, to film an overhead view of the playground coming together. But, as I said, that was the day the truck didn't show. So the video was just—the sun rises, people walk back and forth, the sun sets. Nothing happens. But on Day #2, December 21st, the playground sprouts up in an instant. The sun rises, a swarm of hyperdriven doozers invades the beach, the sun sets with Mary's bed of playground-shaped roses having bloomed in a snap.

For all they had been through, the Roxbury Fire Department could not have treated us better. That night they put on a huge pizza party for all the volunteers, and even housed a lot of the guys right there in the firehouse so they wouldn't have to commute back and forth again for the ribbon-cutting. For a Fire Department that was so decimated, and beaten-down, and overwhelmed—those guys are a true testament to the fire service. They know better than most what it means to stick together, and what brotherhood is all about.

So it turned out to be the easy Breezy Point build I had expected in the first place, only performed in half the time. Maybe we all needed that day to take stock of the project, simply spend time together talking and gaining perspective. As the build was just about to wrap up that night, another one of our memorable Sandy Ground skies appeared at twilight. I'm not sure who noticed it first, but suddenly all of us were staring up at the most brilliantly teal sky we'd ever seen. It was like nothing I'd witnessed before or since, that color. I'd seen water that color before, in the Caribbean maybe, but never the sky. It was a clear thumbs-up from Mary Sherlach. That Miami Dolphin teal.

Speaking of Miami...

. . .

Breezy Point is the self-proclaimed coldest part of New York City. So scheduling a ribbon-cutting in Roxbury for December 22nd, outdoors, was by all accounts a bold stroke. It was guaranteed to not only be windy, but frigid as well. But The Sandy Ground Project had defied the odds for 15 playgrounds in a row, and Mary was not going to allow #16 to be the exception.

At 11 AM, three days before Christmas, it was 72 degrees on the beach in Breezy Point, NY. The previous record high for that date, set in 1923, was 62 degrees—so the morning of Mary's ribbon-cutting was a record-smashing anomaly if there ever was one. Not only that, it was actually warmer in New York that day than it was in Miami! It was almost as if Mary had flip-flopped the weather for a day in honor of her Dolphins. I'm sure they were shivering in 60-degree temperatures down in South Beach while we were opening up Mary's new playground in short sleeves.

With Christmas right around the corner, we had our chief merry-maker Tommy Atwell dressed up like Santa Claus for the occasion. He gleefully distributed gifts and Christmas cheer to everyone present. (I received a make-up kit—a jab at all my time spent in "hair and makeup" prior to doing appearances and interviews about the project).

We also had the children from the nearby elementary school come and perform Christmas carols in their little Santa hats. They had made the "ribbon" for the day's event—which was actually an interlocking chain of red roses that we would cut to open the playground. We were worried that the kids were going to come and help us with the ceremony and it would be too cold for them to enjoy the playground. But with the warmest day on record, the kids were itching to get swinging and sliding. It was like an oasis of a day amidst a long, cold winter.

Bill Sherlach and his daughters were in attendance, and Bill gave a wonderful speech about his wife, the volunteers, and the town that would hold Mary's playground dear. He expressed his faith in their ability to cherish what had been built and enjoy it together through thick and thin. Bill would join us on many future builds and become a part of the Angels Army himself, paying it forward.

Mary Sherlach's life and spirit had certainly changed the landscape of Roxbury, NY and changed the world in general. To illustrate this, we had 26 hard-core local New York Jets fans (myself included) wear Miami Dolphins jerseys for her ceremony. This was unheard of on any other day, particularly in this town. Around here, wearing those colors would give any Jets fan a good reason to pour a beer on your head. But, alas, Mary was uniting us all. She was changing the world, the weather, and us. We were all on the same team now.

When the ribbon-cutting ceremony wrapped up, we rendezvoused back at a little neighborhood joint called Pebbles Pub on Breezy Point Boulevard. We hung out with the Sherlachs, made toasts, and celebrated the final playground of 2013. But we couldn't help but gravitate back to the beach, to the playground, and bask in the miraculously beautiful weather that Mary had sent us. This Miami-like winter warmth was too great of a gift to waste sitting inside. So we wound up enjoying some refreshments out there on the beach until well after sundown.

By Christmas Eve, the biting winds and sub-freezing temperatures were back home on the shores of Roxbury. The residents expected it, just business as usual. But that one late-December day when the sun burned brighter here than in South Florida—that day won't soon be forgotten in Breezy Point, New York. And neither will Mary Sherlach.

• • •

With two out of three "Super Bowl Playgrounds" done in Connecticut and New York, we had one left to go in New Jersey. Next on the docket in Jersey was Long Beach Island, and it would have to be done in January to be ready for Super Sunday. Clearly that was a difficult task between the winter weather and the time-crunch, but the Angels Army was now making difficult tasks its specialty. And Mary Sherlach had blessed us tremendously with that Miami weather in Breezy Point, but what if our next playground namesake was a Green Bay Packers fan? We'd be up for the challenge either way.

All in all, the January build on Long Beach Island was nixed by the NFL because of proximity. They felt it was too far from MetLife

Stadium (in East Rutherford) to be relevant to the Super Bowl Host Committee's mission. Therefore, we collectively decided to retroactively assign Playground #12 in Belmar, Avielle's playground, to the NFL. It was our most recent Jersey Shore build and had no major sponsor attached to it, so that seemed to be the logical move. The NFL agreed to pay their donation money forward to our next build, Playground #17, which would be coming soon in Milford, Connecticut. The NFL proved to be an outstanding partner for The Sandy Ground Project, and their generosity allowed us to schedule and build more aggressively heading into the New Year.

• • •

As the calendar flipped from 2013 to 2014, everyone associated with The Sandy Ground Project was coming to grips with the fact that there would be no building for three solid months. In the interim, we decided to get everyone together for a night of appreciation and reflection on all that we had done thusfar. It was a night to acknowledge the volunteers for all of their hard work and dedication. To thank the families of Newtown for having the faith and trust in us and the project's mission. And to serve as another opportunity to strengthen that bond that had been forged between us all throughout 2013.

Thanks to Rich and Toni from Giordano Construction, we organized a "Wintermission" event on January 24th at The Valley Regency in Clifton, New Jersey. They had family who ran this beautiful banquet facility and they treated us to a spectacular soup-to-nuts affair. It was like a wedding with about 350 of our newest and closest friends.

We invited all 26 of the families from Newtown, and the ones that came were mostly those who had gone through the playground process and felt comfortable with us. We put on a slideshow that highlighted all of our builds. It really gave us all some perspective on exactly how much we'd accomplished in such a short time. And how much our lives had changed in that timespan as well.

Perhaps my favorite touch of the event was the way we organized the tables. While most formal seated events simply use numbers to identify the tables, we decided to use symbols from each of our 16 completed playgrounds. If your table had a rainbow, that was in honor of Chase. If it was a flamingo, that was for Victoria. A red rose for Mary, a Ravens logo for Joey, a dog for Anne Marie, a fire truck for Daniel.

Only if you were there that night, the symbols needed no explanation. It just took you right back to that certain playground or snapshot in time. Who you worked with or took a lunch break with during the build. Who you laughed with or cried with when we cut the ribbon. And mostly you thought about the angels who had lifted us up and carried us to this point.

And the point where we were at was a winter break, but with a chance to set the stage for an extremely ambitious spring of building. Starting in mid-March, we would be looking to crank out roughly one playground a week over the course of a few months. It was an ambitious plan for sure but, with 16 playgrounds complete and 10 more to go, the excitement was building. We could see that light at the end of the tunnel, and miracles were happening every day.

Ron Silbernagel, Herman Peters and Greg Meyer
staying warm on the beach

CHAPTER TWENTY-ONE

Milford, Connecticut

The long winter wore on without any building to do, but the Angels Army was more than ready by the time we settled on some dates in March to start up again. It was going to be an ambitious spring, but it wasn't feeling very spring-like outside just yet. Either way, we were ready to roll on ten more playgrounds. And I was really happy to be starting 2014 at a location where we were long overdue.

Milford enjoys lots of coastline on the Long Island Sound and is also bordered by the Housatonic River to the west, separating it from Stratford. A lot of that coastline, like in the neighboring towns we had gotten to know, is very developed. Many waterfront neighborhoods and businesses—including Jesse Lewis's grandmother's shop—and those areas were decimated when Superstorm Sandy rolled through. The floodwaters were extremely high, and the city's low-lying areas were quickly filled up and destroyed.

Clearly Milford had all the on-paper qualifications for a Sandy Ground playground. But the one intangible factor, and probably most important one, was the quality of people there.

The city of Milford had stood by and watched The Sandy Ground Project swoop in and build playgrounds for all its neighbors. Actually, "stood by" is a bad phrase because so many people from Milford were intimately involved in the project for almost a year now. But by March 2014, they had to be thinking "How about us?" First there was Ansonia (#3), then Westport (#4), then Stratford (#5), then Norwalk (#13), and finally Bridgeport (#15) right before the holidays. That's five of our 16 playgrounds, all of which were within about a 20-minute drive of Milford. Considering all the work they were doing and funds they were raising, I can't say I blame them if they were getting a complex. This is the main reason they were at the top of our list for the New Year, and the main reason I was so happy to finally get building there.

As far as The Sandy Ground Project, the Milford Fire Department was clearly the driving force in the city. Led by Ron Wetmore, who is a Hall of Famer as far as our project is concerned, and a group of retired firefighters called the "Dinosaurs" were with us every step of the way. And this wasn't just a handful of guys joking around, calling themselves old. This was a legitimate club of seasoned veterans—both of the fire service and the art of tailgating—who organized events, held meetings, and stayed extremely close even after leaving the job. Brothers for life.

The active Milford Firefighters, and their Union President Mike Dunn, teamed up with the Dinosaurs and raised an unbelievable amount of money for The Sandy Ground Project. Far and away the most of any fire department or community in our project's history. And they did this through tireless effort. They organized and hosted every kind of fundraising event you could ever think of. A golf outing, pub nights, a 5K race, dinners, 50/50 raffles, the list goes on and on.

They just kept bringing in money for the project as a whole. But to give you an idea how prepared—and anxious, really—Milford was to get their playground, the location was chosen and cement foundation laid down back in October. A good five months before the build would actually take place. I'm sure there were guys at union meetings thinking (or perhaps shouting), "We raised all this money and still no playground?! What the heck?!"

So, personally, I was relieved when we finally pulled the trucks into Milford on March 14th. I was also excited knowing how special their fire department, their Dinosaurs, and the whole town were going to make this build.

• • •

As all the volunteers arrived to get working that first morning in Milford, it was clear that the Dinosaurs had already been there for hours. March may bring spring to the Northeast, but it clearly hadn't brought it yet. The Dinosaurs didn't mind the cold though. They had been cooking up an amazing spread, and you could smell it as soon as you opened the car door.

Bacon, egg, and cheese sandwiches were ready for everyone as they arrived. A side of beef was roasting on the rotisserie, as lunch was already in the works. The amount of food, and the aromas and flavors, was like nothing we had ever smelled or tasted. They really rolled out the red carpet. We had not even finished our breakfast—or done any work for that matter—and we were already salivating thinking about lunch. And lunch, believe me, did not disappoint. There are not enough synonyms for delicious to describe the roast beef sandwiches, so I'll just go with "succulent". It was impossible to eat less than three.

It was time to take off the feedbag and get cracking.

· · ·

As in so many other locations, Connecticut Tank Removal was once again our ace in the hole. Like with the other builds in the area, the time and work they put in made our job a hundred times easier than it would have been otherwise. Their dedication really speaks to the overall outpouring of support that we were feeling up and down the Connecticut coast—and in Milford in particular. Sometimes I would feel like, "Geez, there are so many volunteers showing up. How I am going to keep them all busy?"

Luckily, in most cases, nobody was waiting around to be given direct orders. They would just follow their hearts and do what suited them best. At the Milford Playground, we had a landscaping company just randomly show up and start planting trees and bushes. They did outstanding work and created a great environment surrounding the playground that we hadn't even planned.

Another group of firefighters restored an old, beat-up picnic table. They basically rebuilt it and painted it our trademark Sandy Ground royal blue color. They also painted on our logo—the number "26" topped with a halo. It really was a work of art, and it is touches like these that make the project so special. When there are so many people willing to help—adding their energy and talents to the mix—it really augments the process greatly. In this way, the builds take on a life of their own… and not even the designers know exactly what the final product will look like.

That's how the angels guide the process.

• • •

As an Irishman, the timing of us building a playground in Milford, CT could not have been better. We broke ground on March 14th, a Friday, and the very next day was the city's St. Patrick's Day Parade. And this is a city that takes its parades very seriously.

Each year, numerous groups get involved in a city-wide competition to see who can create the best parade float. You've got the police, different schools, a bunch of community organizations, and—naturally—the firefighters as well. It is a pretty big deal. Bragging rights are on the line. With The Sandy Ground Project coming to town the very same weekend, the Milford Fire Department made our playgrounds the theme for their float.

I'm still not sure how they did it, but the Milford Firefighters essentially put together a playground on wheels and entered it into the parade. It was fully equipped with a slide, working swings, and featured our colors and logo prominently throughout. It was awesome. So for the afternoon, a large group from the Angels Army took a break and headed off to march in the parade.

As we took turns alternating between walking the route and riding the float, we were treated like conquering heroes. There were literally thousands of people lining the streets of Milford that day, and all of them seemed to be screaming at the top of their lungs as we rolled by. We tossed out candies and beads and they went even crazier. It was like a ticker-tape parade in New York after a World Series win. It felt like the Canyon of Heroes. We even had one Milford firefighter dressed up like a crazy leprechaun, riling the people up even more. It was like a traveling Sandy Ground pep rally, and our guys loved it. We really felt right at home there.

Lo and behold, as the parade route ended, The Sandy Ground Project float was awarded first place in the contest. Best in show. It was the perfect capper to a great day; we were officially introduced and welcomed into their city.

Later that evening, as the fanfare and revelry of the parade finally died down, I arrived back at the build site to find that so many of the Angels Army soldiers had beaten me there. They were already fully involved in mixing cement, raising the roofs, assembling benches, attaching slides, you name it. Almost as if the parade had never happened. While there is a lot of satisfaction and we enjoyed being together on these builds, at the end of the day, everyone is clear on why we're there. The playground project is our top priority.

• • •

When the building wrapped up the following day, stood sprawling across this park in a patriotic red, white, and blue was a magnificent playground. We finished in plenty of time for the rubber-surfacing to be poured, and that process went off without a hitch.

With the ribbon-cutting scheduled for the following weekend, the Angels Army and the fire departments from the surrounding area (Milford, Stamford, Fairfield, etc.) congregated at the local VFW to celebrate a job well done. In true Milford fashion, the amount of food and drink was out of this world.

It turned out to be a very intense and emotional night for all of us. Once again, the toasts and conversations were flowing, and the atmosphere took on a very reflective tone. My own daughter, MaryKate, made an emotional speech about what the project had meant to her. A lot of it had to do with how miserable I had been before The Sandy Ground Project had found me. She'll get no argument from me on that one.

More importantly, we recognized our brother—Mark Virag—who was now having more and more trouble making the Sandy Ground builds due to his battles with cancer. Even in his absence, he was the heart and soul of the Angels Army, and his comrades spoke about him time and time again.

There were so many faces there—both new and old—crying and laughing simultaneous as only this project can make them. Amidst it all, I saw that Rebecca Kowalski was there. She was now in a very unique, sort-of dual role when it comes to our project. She is first and foremost Chase's mom, a Newtown parent who had gone through the process with all of us nine playgrounds ago. But by now she was also a full member of the Angels Army, dedicated to The Sandy Ground Project's mission of bringing all 26 playgrounds to life. I couldn't help but feel for her even more so than usual in this moment. That it must be difficult to hear that such a horrible tragedy in her life had created an opportunity for others to find themselves by trying to heal others. I can only hope that, being there with us for so many of these events, she knows all of our hearts are in the right place.

. . .

Mike Dunn spoke on behalf of the remarkable firefighters from Milford. Then, he and Ron Wetmore presented me with a check made out to the amount of money they'd raised for The Sandy Ground Project. It was a whopping $95,000! This was far and away the greatest fundraising effort by a single town we had seen (and still is)—and that is a testament to the dedication of Mike Dunn and Ron and Trish Wetmore. The city was now paying it forward. It was enough to cover an entire playground further on up the road.

As the flags were raised on the new playground, a class of local first-graders sang "Angels Watching Over Me."

The efforts of the Milford Firefighters really was without reservation. Led by Ron Wetmore, they had formed an unbreakable bond with the rest of the Angels Army. Ron and Trish and Mike Dunn and Jason Dombroski along with many others would form an entire new wing of our army of volunteers and continue to be invaluable.

CHAPTER TWENTY-TWO

Playground Celebrating the Life of Ana Grace Marquez-Greene

Hartford, Connecticut

As Playground #17 was being erected in Milford, the ball was already rolling on our next mission. In between shifts, the guys from Connecticut Tank Removal and I were shuttling the 45 minutes up to Hartford. Everything had to be coordinated there, which is no easy task in a city of that size.

If our spring building season was going to be as successful as we thought it could be, we were going to have to hit the ground running in each and every town. The builds were going to be coming fast and furious—just about every week—and there was no time to waste. So as Playground #17 was going up, the planning and the cement pad for #18 were going down.

• • •

A lot had changed since I first heard from Nelba Marquez-Greene. Her initial email, in January 2013, was the first correspondence of any kind we had gotten from any of the families in Newtown. The timing of her message had been perfect. I was standing in front of a conference room full of people—the eventual core of the Angels Army—and we were trying to hash out the particulars of The Sandy Ground Project. Could we do it? Should we do it? And, if so, how?

And then my phone chimed and I read everyone her note. It was simple. She had gotten my letter and would like to know more. This inspired all of us in that moment. It gave us the belief we needed to get started.

A full year later, I still had not met Nelba. Through a third-party I was told that she and her husband Jimmy were just not ready to engage us yet. They chose to keep their distance and I could certainly understand and respect that. But I did receive a brief note from Nelba sometime in the Fall. She wanted to let me know that she was watching what we were doing from afar.

Over time, Nelba and Jimmy became more and more comfortable with the thought of getting involved with The Sandy Ground Project and building a playground in honor of Ana Grace. This is thanks in no small part to Mark Barden, with whom we'd had such an amazing experience building a playground for Daniel. Mark and Nelba had been working together on advocating for making schools safer. Mark ensured Nelba and Jimmy that working with us was a positive experience and urged them to give me a call. Heading into our second year, the project was gaining tremendous momentum—spiritually, emotionally, and financially. And that is mostly due to the parent advocates, like Mark for instance, who were out there in the world vouching for us.

So, in January 2014, a full year after Nelba had lit our fire with that first email, I finally met the family of Ana Grace Marquez-Greene. I walked into their home on a snowy afternoon and they were actually apologizing to me for having taken so long to set up this meeting. I was taken aback by this and told them no apology was necessary at all. They could have never met with me, never even responded, and I would have understood completely. But here I was, meeting this amazing family and planning a playground for little Ana Grace, and I was certainly glad to do it.

Nelba and Jimmy are a fascinating pair. She is a tiny, pretty, proud Puerto Rican woman who is very intense and passionate and, in our case, very dedicated to overseeing the process. She wanted everything to be perfect for Ana. Jimmy Greene, who stands about 6-foot-6, is a gentle giant and a world-renowned jazz saxophonist and composer. He is also a professor of music at Western Connecticut State University. Just a cool, laid back dude—as you would expect a saxophone player to be I guess.

I would also come to know Nelba's mother Elba who, like me, is one of 11 children in her family. That is not something you hear every day, so we had a unique bond over that. Once I was able to visit the Newtown area, I was honored to stop in for some of Elba's wonderful cooking. "Arroz con Pollo", naturally. Elba's cooking was delicious.

But the member of the Marquez-Greene family I really hit it off with was Isaiah, Ana Grace's older brother. Isaiah is a hockey player (a goalie) and the two of us share a favorite team—the New York Rangers (actually, one of Isaiah's three favorite teams). The Rangers were in the midst of a great season, gaining momentum heading towards the playoffs, and the two of us went back and forth, through Nelba, on their chances to win the Stanley Cup. Isaiah is a really bright and talented kid—both athletically and musically—who we all enjoyed getting to know. He would serve as the honorary foreman in building a playground for his sister.

Upon arriving at the Marquez-Greene household for the first time, I picked up on a theme they had adopted in Ana Grace's memory. It was the slogan "Love Wins" written inside of a purple heart. This, as it turns out, was their way of dealing with and responding to what had happened to their daughter—with love. And that love, at the end of the day, would overcome. The purple heart was for Ana Grace, her favorite color. Their home was actually decorated in purple Christmas lights when I came for that first meeting, and I knew before walking in the door what color Ana Grace's playground would be.

After we all had gotten to know each other, hitting it off right away, Nelba and Jimmy spoke more and more about Ana. How she loved singing and music and dancing and food. Nelba told a funny story about how it had been proposed that a road race—a 10K or something—be run in Ana's honor. Nelba had to laugh about this because, as she said, running and Ana did not go together. She would much rather dance through a race like that, she wasn't much for athletics. Ana Grace was just a free spirit like that, dancing wherever she went. Eating her grandma's cooking was more Ana's idea of fun.

As we wrapped up that first day, I told Jimmy and Nelba about the high-energy spring building season The Sandy Ground Project had coming up. I said I would begin figuring out a location for Ana's playground, and Nelba suggested New Britain where she worked as a family counselor. I would do my best to make that happen but, ultimately, we would wind up in an even more appropriate location.

• • •

Obviously, the Newtown tragedy and The Sandy Ground Project are very Connecticut-centric things. We've built playgrounds in New York and New Jersey as part of the Superstorm Sandy relief effort, but in Connecticut it is much more personal. It was one of *their* towns, one of *their* schools, and above all *their* children. What happened at Sandy Hook Elementary School was no doubt a national tragedy, but when something that terrible happens in your own state (and a small state at that) it cuts right to your core.

That being said, there was a prevailing thought amongst us that a playground should be built in the state's capital—Hartford. Even though the city didn't take the brunt of Superstorm Sandy's wrath like, say, a Sea Bright or a Breezy Point—this is where the storm after the storm was ongoing. Being the focal point of state government, Hartford is where all the legislation and political wrangling in the wake of the Newtown tragedy was taking place. Lawmakers and lobbyists, parents and teachers, all of them trying to come up with some kind of answers or solutions. Why did this happen? How do we keep it from happening again?

And believe me when I tell you, Robbie Parker was right. The labels put on the families of the Newtown victims do not do them justice. You cannot paint them with a broad brush. They are 26 different sets of people with 26 different backgrounds and opinions. Some were pro-this, or anti-that, or felt strongly one way or another about the how and why of the Newtown tragedy.

But as far as I could tell, all 26 were pro-playground. And that is why we felt it was important to bring a movement like The Sandy Ground Project to Connecticut's capital city. To prove that everyone could get behind something independent of politics. We clearly had no other agenda than to celebrate the individual, not to lump them all together as victims. They were all our angels, and each of them special in their own way. I think that is at the heart of why all 26 families got behind us. The Sandy Ground Project was about nothing more than highlighting how each of them lived, and using those highlights for the benefit of other children and communities.

Being the seat of state government, we had a lot of built-in allies when it came to a potential Hartford build. The Lieutenant Governor, Nancy Wyman, was a big supporter and had attended ribbon-cuttings in the past. Also, we had a big supporter in Joe Gaetano from the Connecticut State Judicial Marshals, as well as Andy Matthews and the Connecticut State Troopers and SEIU (State Workers Union). All of them are based in Hartford and eager to have us come to town.

While I definitely felt like we had the support of Hartford Mayor Pedro Segarra, that didn't necessarily resonate with other departments. But, you have to remember, Hartford is a large city with a lot going on. The Sandy Ground Project just didn't seem to be a high priority like it had been in other places. We were just another park in a city full of them. Not a rallying point as far as they were concerned. Therefore, a build that should have come together quite easily got bogged down with a lot of red-tape and technicalities. As I said, it could simply be that we were a big fish in a little pond in so many other places. And here it was the other way around. The Mayor, thankfully, was sincere and enthusiastic and helped to negotiate most challenges.

All things considered, Hartford was a go. Now I just had to find a family that would like a playground there, and this was around the time I'd begun to correspond more and more frequently with the Marquez-Greenes. I knew that Nelba had wanted New Britain, but since Hartford was just about on-deck I figured I would mention it.

Jimmy and Nelba were thrilled. Hartford is actually where both of them had grown up. It is where they met, fell in love, and where both Isaiah and Ana Grace were born. Having her playground there would be a homecoming for her, as it would be for so many of their friends and family. When I described the playground's location—a very diverse, eclectic neighborhood on the edge of West Hartford—it turned out to be a spot they knew very well.

. . .

Shortly before we were to break ground in Hartford, I was on the train headed to Madison Square Garden with my nephew Danny Beirne. We were on our way to the Rangers game, the only one I'd attend that year. As the train rolled towards Penn Station, Danny got an alert on his phone—Ryan Callahan, the Rangers captain and fan favorite had been traded. He was sent to the Tampa Bay Lightning in exchange for Martin St. Louis. I loved Callahan, a long-time Ranger, who is a hard-nosed New York guy. I'd barely heard of St. Louis, so Danny (the biggest hockey fan I know and expert on the NHL) gave me the lowdown and pulled up a picture on his phone. My mood quickly changed when I saw St. Louis's jersey number. Number 26.

"It's a sign!" I thought. The number had been popping up every-where, and now Martin St. Louis was going to lead the Rangers to the Stanley Cup. (He literally almost did. They made it to the Finals.) I looked forward to getting Isaiah's thoughts on the trade, thinking maybe it was a good sign for his pee-wee hockey team as well—also the Rangers. Danny and I got to the stadium and took our seats in Section 226.

. . .

Exactly a week after we'd dedicated Playground #17, we broke ground on Playground #18 for Ana Grace Marquez-Greene. It was March 29th, and the build could not have gotten off to a better start. Isaiah graced us all with a beautiful performance—playing a song on the keyboard for his sister. Jimmy Greene's musical gifts are clearly present in his son. He is a chip off the old block. It was a moving tribute for such a young kid, and it really inspired everyone there to get building.

Even though the City of Hartford had altered our original layout for the playground, which caused us to make adjustments on the fly, Ana Grace's playground was still basically built over the course of one day. We were able to accomplish this mostly because of the overwhelming amount of volunteers. Even though the calendar said it was Spring, it was still bitterly cold. It didn't keep anyone away.

So many family and friends of the Marquez-Greenes had come out to work and support them. All of them decked out in custom-made wool hats as a show of solidarity. I remember Nelba standing off to the side, bundled up as could be, just marveling at the process. I also remember Jimmy—the biggest man in the entire park—sporting a Hello Kitty winter hat… a piece of Ana Grace keeping him warm with her presence.

With us already having so many state-related contacts in Hartford, I think there was a bit of a communication breakdown between The Sandy Ground Project and the Hartford Fire Department. To our understanding, their feeling about the project was only lukewarm. I was glad to find, on that build day, that this impression was incorrect.

As we were getting started that morning, two rigs pulled up and all the guys came onto the site. They told me they loved the project, were all in, and would get right to work. Many of them had friends and relatives from Newtown who had lost loved ones and been affected by the tragedy there. Led by Firefighter Mario Oquendo, the Hartford FD quickly became a huge part of making Ana Grace's playground a beloved part of their city.

Overall, the build went great. Our biggest challenge was actually figuring out how to utilize all the volunteers who had come to help. There were so many, in fact, that we needed to set up a system where each person would get a small piece of the playground—a railing, a panel, a chain, or pole. Then, they would basically stand off to the side and wait to be called, sometimes as long as an hour or more. And when they did get called, when their piece was ready for them to install it, they would let out a cheer and run right up.

It was pretty funny, like people at a crowded cold-cut counter at the supermarket just waiting and hoping for their number to come up. While it was amusing, as well as a logistical challenge, it really illustrated how the project spoke to people. They would do anything to perform their task and get a piece of the action. A lot of people won't wait an hour to go on a ride at Disney World. But in this case they would wait as long as it took, in 30-degree temperatures, to work for Ana Grace. To contribute. To be able to say they built her playground. And every last one of them helped to make it special.

After literally hundreds of people built the playground for Ana Grace, Herman Peters led a ceremony with her family to dedicate a custom-made flagstone. It would feature the handprints of Jimmy, Nelba, and Isaiah. The message, *their* message, was simply: "To Hartford, Love Wins. Isaiah+Ana"

There was nothing left to do now but let the temperatures rise a few more degrees and pour the rubber surfacing. And have a well-deserved post-build celebration, of course.

Our guys were all unwinding post-build, as they are known to do, at a local restaurant called the Half Door. At least 20 or 30 of us, having a few beers and burgers and appetizers, that sort of thing. At one point during our meal two middle-aged women, who had lived in the neighborhood all their lives, came over to me to talk about The Sandy Ground Project. They were saying how honored and excited they were to have one of the playgrounds near their home, and they promised to help take good care of it after it was completed.

I thanked the two women and they were on their way. About an hour or two later, I went to pay the tab. Only there wasn't one. The bartender said that two ladies had paid for everything for our entire group. I was stunned, as it had to be close to a thousand dollars. I looked around to thank them, but they were long gone. I never got their names or saw them again. Just two anonymous angels doing a random act of kindness and helping us on our way—really capturing the spirit of Where Angels Play.

• • •

The forecast for April 4, 2014, in Hartford, Connecticut called for rain. Around 90 to100% chance, so it was coming one way or another. Our ribbon-cutting was scheduled for 5:00 PM and, if our past experiences meant anything, I knew our angel would make sure we had enough clear sky to dedicate her playground. So when city officials talked about rescheduling, I told them it wouldn't be necessary.

Despite the forecast, we had a huge turnout that night. Connecticut Governor Dan Malloy and Lieutenant Governor Nancy Wyman came out for the festivities. As did Hartford Mayor Pedro Segarra, who we put to work commandeering a truckload of porta-johns when it became clear that the crowd in attendance would be much larger than expected. The ceremony kicked off with all of Isaiah's hockey teammates, in full uniform, leading everyone in the Pledge of Allegiance.

Thanks to Ana, the ceremony was rain-free and beautiful. The entire playground was decked out in purple and white balloons. They danced in the wind as Isaiah performed once again for his sister and Mario Oquendo's wife and daughter sang for her. The Marquez-Greene family's pastor gave a stirring blessing, pronouncing this—Playground #18 celebrating Ana Grace—as holy ground.

After an intense search, I was able to locate three #26 New York Rangers jerseys for Jimmy, Nelba, and Isaiah. They were extremely hard to find since Martin St. Louis had just been added to the team, but The Sandy Ground Project always has a way of finding things. I reached out to my nephew Danny. Not only was he able to quickly locate three jerseys, but he picked up the tab as well.

I presented the family with the jerseys at the ribbon-cutting and they loved them—especially Isaiah. A couple weeks later I would get an awesome picture of Jimmy and Isaiah wearing them at Madison Square Garden, part of a great 'Pay-It-Forward' story.

Nelba addressed the large crowd in attendance that evening and thanked everyone for all of their efforts in making Ana Grace's playground exactly as she had imagined. She spoke about this build being a homecoming for her and her family, and she was even able to point out the section of the park where her and Jimmy had gone to make out as teenagers. This got a great reaction from the crowd, but the comment seriously spoke to how this is where Ana's playground was meant to be. It brought them full circle somehow. It was still home.

Then Jimmy Greene took the microphone. In his (now famous) Hello Kitty wool cap, he delivered an unforgettable message on behalf of his daughter. He spoke about the importance of the project, and how all of us—black, white, Puerto Rican—had come together to do something great and prove that the world is still beautiful. He and his wife were so moved that there were people out there willing to do this for their daughter.

Jimmy assured us that Ana Grace's life is continuing through us when we show one another compassion and understanding. That she is looking down on us today and smiling. You could physically feel the pain in his voice—everyone was in tears. He said that maybe Ana had not died in vain if the kind of love present today can continue to grow and change the world. He thanked our team, the Angels Army, and implored us to keep on going.

Ana Grace had ensured that we were able to conduct the ceremony free of rain. It was that classic case of the Sandy Ground umbrella of the angels giving us just enough time. Even against the forces of nature, love wins.

But as Jimmy Greene's inspirational and moving speech was wrapping up, you could begin to feel the lightest of drizzles. A drop here… then another… one more a few seconds later. My first thought was, "Wow, it's like these are tears from heaven." They were blending with the tears that Jimmy was bringing out of us all with his words. And after talking to so many people at the reception that followed, I was not the only one who had that same exact feeling.

When Jimmy finished his stirring speech we cut the ribbon. Ana's playground was open for business, a gift to the City of Hartford. We all began making our way to a local hall where a Puerto Rican feast awaited. Five minutes later it was raining cats and dogs.

Luckily the reception following the ribbon-cutting was inside, and we had a great time and great food prepared mostly by the

Marquez-Greene's friends and family. There were some custom-made bottles of grape soda (Ana's favorite) with "Love Wins" inscribed on the label. We also enjoyed a concert put on by one of the most accomplished jazz musicians in the world—none other than Mr. Jimmy Greene and his hand-picked trio. Easily the best act The Sandy Ground Project could ever have hoped to book for such an event. Nelba had insisted this be a celebration and it surely was. She had us all doing salsa dancing. It was a riot watching the Governor, Lieutenant Governor, and U.S. Senator trying to dance.

. . .

After sharing the amazing experience of celebrating Ana Grace with a playground in Hartford, we have remained tight with the Marquez-Greenes. We still keep tabs on how Isaiah's hockey team is doing, go back and forth about the Rangers' chances, and now we are working together on another exciting project.

I had the pleasure of traveling down to the coastal town of Maunabo, Puerto Rico last year to explore the possibility of building a playground there. A gift from Ana Grace to the island. Maunabo is the hometown of Elba, Nelba's mother, and I was happy to visit with her and her husband while I was there.

Nelba had spoken to me so fondly of her step-father—a man she described as being such a wonderful and needed addition to her family. He is a builder in Maunabo, so I was able to speak with him in detail about the potential construction of a playground there. His name, I should mention, is Angel.

Based on that, it is safe to say that Ana Grace Marquez-Greene will be the driving force behind at least one more playground. And so love—undefeated to this very day—wins again.

Artwork by Ana Grace

Chapter twenty-three

Mystic, Connecticut

The Sandy Ground Project has been such a positive experience for me. My network of family and friends has grown by leaps and bounds. I've seen incredible sunsets, skies change color in an instant, and weather shift at the drop of a hat. I've seen the best come out in people time and time again. I feel like I've been in touch with angels and have tried to follow their lead as best I could.

So why was I—at 11 PM in the back of a tractor-trailer in Mystic, Connecticut—yelling at the top of my lungs, alone, unleashing a torrent of frustration? I guess our project, like life, can't always be sunshine and rainbows. And I still needed to learn how to keep things in perspective.

Mystic, CT was chosen for sentimental value and its historic significance in the State of Connecticut. We thought it only proper to build one of the Angels playgrounds in perhaps the most famous waterfront community in the State.

A beach build, of course, located right on the Connecticut Sound on the property of the local YMCA, which was sure to guarantee a steady supply of children to make great use of it and take care of it for generations.

Mystic, Connecticut, would be home to Playground #19. It would prove to be a bit of a challenge because of its location. It's one of our northernmost playgrounds, so getting the majority of the people up there was going to take time and coordination. They were also going to need places to stay, literally hundreds of volunteers. Luckily, we had some great friends in the area. We just didn't know it yet.

Williams Park Beach is also home to the Ocean Community YMCA, which served as a great little staging ground/headquarters for The Sandy Ground Project during our time there. Dan Reeve, the man at the YMCA, could not have been more helpful or supportive. Dan, by the way, had lived and worked in New Jersey and spoke our language so to speak, he soon became part of the family.

Also, as luck would have it, Gina Aiello (Brian D'Antoni's girlfriend) had a cousin who owned a bagel store in Mystic. When I heard this I thought, "Cool, we'll get some bagels and coffee outta the deal." But little did I know, Gina's cousin Nicole Lapolla was basically the de facto Mayor of Mystic—and "Wide World of Bagels" was City Hall.

Just about everything in town ran through "Wide World of Bagels". It was the hub of local politics, where the "meetings of the minds" in town takes place (including many of ours), and Nicole seemed to know every single person in Mystic. So I underestimated our connection there, big time.

Not only did Nicole supply us with breakfasts, she was also able to hook us up with the folks at the Engine Room Restaurant. Whatever Nicole couldn't get us food-wise herself, she arranged for it to come from somewhere in town. Nicole was also able to get hotel rooms for so many of the volunteers, and made sure that everyone was comfortable and accounted for. Nicole and her husband Dan (everyone in that town seemed to be named Dan) were the key cogs in coordinating a Sandy Ground build in Mystic, CT.

• • •

Now it's 7 AM on Thursday, April 24, 2014. Build day for the 19th playground of The Sandy Ground Project. We've got the Angels Army present and prepared, hundreds of volunteers raring to go, and a great breakfast spread from "Wide World of Bagels". As 7 AM becomes 7:30… and 7:30 becomes 8… I'm starting to relive the nightmare scenario from Breezy Point. Where in the wide, wide world of bagels is our playground?!?

The truck carrying the playground structure hadn't shown up. I'm thinking there is no possible way that this has happened—AGAIN!

Not after the mess of last time, when the truck had broken down some-where in the Carolinas. After a few phone calls, I come to find out that this situation is even worse. The truck carrying this playground isn't broken down—it hasn't even left Georgia yet! So we're not even talking about car trouble at this point, we're talking a complete dropping of the ball. The truck was never sent.

I lose it. I'm not only embarrassed at this point, but furious. I can't even look our contractors, Toni and Rich, in the eye because of course I was looking to blame someone. Compounding my frustration is the fact that volunteers are showing up in droves... it seemed like every few minutes another 20 people would show up. A brownie troop, a com-munity organization, a busload of students from the high school—they would walk up and ask, "Where's the playground? What's going on?" And with a forced smile, again and again, I'd say, "Nope. Sorry. No playground yet." I was struggling to put a good face on the situation, but inside I was seething. Each time I explained the situation it took more and more of a toll on me.

This was definitely a low point in the project, and explaining what had happened to the community was heart-breaking. They, of all people, had waited so long and so patiently for this day and now the main piece of the puzzle wasn't there. I felt completely responsible. And in that moment even some of our Angels Army were question-ing me behind my back. "Bill can dream the dream, but can he run this project? Do we need someone else?" That sort of thing. No one came out and said it to me, but there were some rumblings and great disappointment. Bob Brower had told me to have the truck arrive a day early but I stubbornly insisted that all would work out fine with the current schedule.

Herman Peters, who is as loyal as they come, came to me that afternoon and told me to snap out of it. "It's going to be okay," he assured me. "We're all here with you." I'd like to say that his encour-agement worked, but it didn't.

Rebecca Kowalski's words, however, did.

Knowing how upset Toni and Rich were about the situation, Rebecca pulled me aside and told me to let it go. "This is not a problem," she said. "It's fixable. This we can work through, and it will be okay."

I was immediately brought back to reality and, frankly, embarrassed that this woman who had been through so much was the one cheering *me* up. I heard my own mother's words in what she was saying. Mom's old adage of: "If everyone threw their problems into a pile, you would be fighting to get yours back." They were both right. As upset as I was, feeling I'd let everyone down, this was not a problem by comparison. We were going to figure this out.

And to their credit, as much of a bust as this day started out to be, every single volunteer stayed.

• • •

Bill Cario is a Connecticut State Trooper who had grown close to The Sandy Ground Project over time. Bill was impacted greatly by the Sandy Hook tragedy as he was one of the first to respond to it. I've had the chance to speak with him at a few of our builds and he has become a good friend.

As fate would have it, Bill was there with us in Mystic the day the playground didn't show. By mid-afternoon, he and Rebecca and I and anyone else who had a contact with the State Police were working the phones with the Trooper contacts within Connecticut and beyond. Since our playground was on its way in a tractor-trailer from Georgia, one could assume the highways it would be traveling on. So he was pulling together an effort to locate the truck and get it to Mystic, CT as fast as possible.

By early evening we had located the truck and it was getting a police escort through the state of Maryland. Then Delaware… then New Jersey… New York and Connecticut. I don't even know if this was legal or what the story was, but every so often Bill had an update for us.

The truck is 4 hours away…

Two and a half hours…

The playground is in Connecticut…

It'll be in Mystic within the hour…

As aggravating as the day had been, this part was sort of thrilling. The playground was going to show up tonight, that was no longer in doubt. But I had a whole bunch of people there, at 9 PM, who had been hanging around for 14 hours. It is Thursday night, we need to get the rubber-surfacing down, there's rain in the forecast, and we've got a ribbon-cutting scheduled for Sunday morning. Those were the facts. Now what are we going to do about it?

"Ok, everybody. We're going to have a night build. We'll go as long as you want or until we get too tired. If you want to stop, tell me. Let's do what we can."

That was my message with the truck 15 minutes away. The Angels Army was all in. The folks from the town, local volunteers, and of course our family and friends from just about every previous build. Lo and behold, at 10 PM, our truck pulled into the park led by a Connecticut State Trooper. All of our volunteers had been on ice for 15 full hours, but each one was ready to rock.

After completing the escort of our playground, a State Trooper named Dawn stepped out of her car. "Ok, I gotta know. What is in this truck?!?" she asked. I realized then that so many people had helped our playground get to Mystic that day and didn't really know what the story was. It could be a nuclear missile for all they knew. But I got Dawn up to speed and thanked her for helping us out.

· · ·

By 10:30 PM, we were moving. The Town and local Fire Department set up lights to illuminate our construction site. A Thursday build was going to be a Friday morning build shortly and the Angels Army was starting to hit their stride. Momentum was building as we headed towards midnight and it was all hands on deck. Given the time of day and the amount of time everyone had been waiting, this build was actually a good chance for a lot of people to shine who hadn't previously been able to. My wife and daughter were given the chance to work the drill, for instance. Those who usually dominate the builds were swapping in and out with more frequency.

At around 1 AM a familiar-looking woman pulled up to the build site and asked what she could do. "Where do I know her from?" I wondered, then quickly realized that it was Dawn (the Trooper from earlier) in civilian clothes. She was so moved by our project that she got off of working a full shift, went home and changed, and came right back to the playground to help us. Dawn worked with us the rest of the night and has been in touch with the project ever since.

Around 2:30 AM we pulled everyone together to assess our situation. "What should we do? Pack up or keep going?" The response was unanimous… "KEEP GOING!"

At 4:30 AM, with everyone's bodies and minds starting to go, we called it a night. A large portion of the playground was finished and it was getting close to 24 hours since we were supposed to have started. I thanked everyone for a herculean effort, clearly like nothing I had ever seen before. The Angels Army had backed up every last bit of its reputation and proved it all night. You even had the guys who stuck around and opened a few cans on the beach, recapping an unbelievable night over a cold one. Tradition is tradition and it was surely five o'clock somewhere. Yeah… here. Five o'clock in the morning.

The plan was for everyone to come back at 8 AM and finish up. The rubber-surfacing process was starting that morning and time was of the essence. As spent as I, and everyone else, was—I thought it would be a victory if half the crew came back.

By 8:15 AM, every single person was accounted for which speaks to the dedication of this group. With less than 3 hours sleep on average, all of them were of the same mind… Don't be the straggler… Don't let each other down… Above all, don't let our Angels down. The build was concluded by 10 AM as the rubber was already being laid out.

Next door, people were showing up for work and their workouts at the Ocean Community YMCA. It was fun to see the faces of those who had gone home the night before (when there was nothing) arriving the next morning to a fully formed playground. The landscape had changed, literally, overnight.

"How many playgrounds have you all built so far anyway?" one woman asked. I told her this was our 19th out of 26. "Wow! You guys must be able to build these in your sleep!"

"You're right," I said. "I think we just did."

· · ·

It rained a lot over the next day or two, which doesn't jive with our rubber-surfacing process. But after what we'd been through together on Day 1 of this build, there was no mountain we couldn't climb. We wound up commandeering just about every leaf-blower in New England and ran them continuously in order to dry out the surface so we could finish.

When it was all said and done, and we rubbed the sleep from our eyes, there was an incredible playground standing on Williams Beach.

The morning of April 27, 2014, was windy and overcast but thankfully rain-free. After some tough moments, and a lot of hard work, we were finally ready to cut the ribbon on Playground #19.

This ceremony featured some great music. There were the performances of local kids—both singing and on violin—who did incredible renditions of "Amazing Grace" and "Still Amazed" (a more upbeat mix of "Amazing Grace").

We also had a dove release to symbolize the peace we hoped would be brought to this community via Where Angels Play Foundation. (And believe me when I tell you we searched high and low for those birds). I was able to convince Dan and Mary Ann Gurrera to take a ride to Rhode Island to pick up the white doves, a two hour ride from the playground. Mary Ann would become famous in our circles for hysterical stories as she was asked to provide last minute props for our ceremonies. Thanks to Anthony Giordano and my future son-in-law Matt Herbert—bird-keepers for a day—it was an incredible moment. It was made even more incredible by the angel-shaped cloud that floated by as the doves circled overhead. Just another Kodak moment for The Sandy Ground Project. Another miracle from above.

Amazingly, just as our ceremony was getting into full swing, the clouds parted and the sun shone brightly on all of us. Having just spent so much time at this park at night and under overcast skies, the contrast of seeing it bathed in natural sunlight was jarring.

After a very special and moving ceremony, all of us headed back to the Engine Room Restaurant once again to celebrate with new friends and new family.

Being smack in the middle of our frantic Sandy Ground spring of builds, we quickly shifted focus to Playground #20. But since it had been such a challenging and transformative experience in Mystic, I was a little more reflective. By now I'd learned that everything connected to this project happens for a reason, and now I was looking deeper into what those reasons were. For instance, why did that playground show up 15 hours late? And why did we stay up all night building it?

Maybe it was to prove that we could overcome anything. We just have to take each challenge as it comes. Whatever happens, happens, and we'll respond with a smile and our best effort.

Or maybe, as Bill Cario had said to me on the playground that night, this wasn't a problem but instead a wonderful opportunity to show these families just how much people care about them. And there is nothing that's going to prevent us for delivering some joy back into communities in need.

Whatever the reason, the Angels Army and I owe the wonderful community of Mystic, CT a great big thank you for accepting us into their community and working alongside us to continue our mission of hope and healing.

CHAPTER TWENTY-FOUR

Playground Celebrating the Life of Jesse Lewis

Stamford, Connecticut

Although our experience in Mystic turned out to be magical in the end, it was clear that we needed to make a change in Sandy Ground policy. Never again would we rely on a truck to deliver one of our playgrounds on the day of the build. From our following build until the end of time, all playgrounds will be delivered the day *before* we have everyone show up to the site to begin construction. I couldn't put another family (or the Angels Army, or myself for that matter) through another 15-hour delay. So as we all drove home from Mystic with that lesson learned, the ribbon-cutting at Playground #20 was only seven days away.

And while I look at that number, 20 playgrounds, I realize that it was not even a considered a milestone at the time. When you're running a marathon, there are 20 miles and then there are 6.2. It's all about the numbers. But in our case, we were so hyper-focused on the family, and the build, and the angel—the numbers were immaterial. So in the long run, no one really remembers "#20". But everyone remembers Jesse Lewis.

• • •

Once again our story takes us back to that ice-cold winter of 2013. Another snowstorm, and another trip up to Connecticut for Brian D'Antoni and me. This time our destination was a small horse farm in Newtown, the home of Scarlett Lewis and her son J.T. Scarlett's youngest son Jesse was lost in the tragedy at Sandy Hook Elementary School. We were there to gauge her interest in having a playground built for him, and to present our vision of The Sandy Ground Project.

We were greeted that day by two of the biggest dogs I've ever laid eyes on. Old English Mastiffs I guess they were (named Remmy and Rhett I'd later learn)—the two of them gave us the once-over as we made our way to the door. Brian and I had been thoroughly slimed by the time we met Scarlett.

It was apparent to us right away that there was something special about Scarlett. She just had a sort-of peaceful, welcoming aura about her. It's hard to describe. She is a very spiritual, hard-working, down-to-earth woman and we were disarmed by the fact that she seemed to instantly trust us. There was no trace of skepticism or suspicion. She seemed to know that our intentions were good and pure before we could even explain what those intentions were.

At one point at the start of our meeting, Brian says, "We feel that these children are guiding us to do this." I couldn't help but cringe. I had no idea where Scarlett was at in her grieving process, what she believed, or how she'd respond to such a statement. She had just been through an unimaginable and tragic ordeal. But, maybe Brian saw something in her that made him say that, because she immediately agreed. "Yes," she answered. "Yes, I am sure of it."

From that point forward, we had an incredible meeting and conversation about her son Jesse. Scarlett talked about how she believed that not only was Jesse an angel now, but he always had been. She had gotten signs from him, both before and after the tragedy at Sandy Hook Elementary. And a playground, she agreed, would be the perfect tribute to her angel. Scarlett went on to actually *show* us some of the signs she had gotten from Jesse.

· · ·

It took a little while for Scarlett to return home after December 14, 2012. She had stayed with her mother Maureen for a few nights until she was ready to go back. When she did, there was Jesse's hand-writing—left on a chalkboard. It read: "Nuturing Healing Love", the words spelled out phonetically yet incorrect, like a 1st-grader would write them. The writing was unmistakably Jesse's. She showed us the chalkboard. And there were the three words, as clear as a six-year-old could make them.

The funny thing was, Scarlett told us, these weren't words Jesse would normally use. He was a rough-and-tumble boy's boy. A little outdoorsman who loved animals and played football. He was tough and brave, patrolling the farm while playing soldier, protecting his family. Jesse was like a modern-day Tom Sawyer. He wouldn't have normally used those words, but nonetheless he had left them to tell Scarlett everything would be okay.

Scarlett also showed us a drawing Jesse had made shortly before the Newtown tragedy. It depicted a small person with angels' wings standing in front of a much larger, darker figure that Jesse described as the bad man. The man's face was scribbled out and obscured. Scarlett, upon finding this picture, felt like Jesse had had a premonition. That the angel drawn was him. When the details of December 14th were released almost a year later, it is hard to disagree. When Scarlett got the details of what had happened inside Sandy Hook Elementary School that day, she knew that her son was always meant to be there.

Jesse Lewis saved the lives of nine children that day. As the bad man in his drawing had his weapon jam (or possibly reload), Jesse yelled for the others to run!—run now! They listened to him and made it to safety. They are alive today because Jesse Lewis was brave. Because of his soldierly instinct to protect others. That had always been his personality. He was their angel in that moment, and still is today.

• • •

Scarlett Lewis actually wrote a book about her experience called "Nurturing Healing Love" and she'd sent me a copy later on that year. I sat down in my living room one evening and read it cover-to-cover, all in one sitting. It was brilliant and the stories contained in it hit me harder than the average person because I knew them to be true. I had *seen* the chalkboard and Jesse's drawing. I had *felt* the presence of these angels on so many occasions. I had been to their homes and bonded with their families.

After a few hours I put the book down, wiped the tears from my eyes, and picked up the remote control. Surely there was a Mets or Rangers game on TV to catch. As I flipped on the Channel Guide, the name "Dr. Wayne Dyer" caught my eye. He had written the foreword to Scarlett's book, the one I'd just put down. Out of curiosity I put him on.

As if Dr. Dyer's show being on wasn't coincidence enough, when I put it on—there was Scarlett! She was sitting front and center in the audience, smiling right back at me. I'd just read her entire book, felt an amazing connection to it, and now here she was in my living room. I couldn't believe it. But when I called Scarlett to tell her about this sign, she *could* believe it. She wasn't surprised at all. "Yup, that's Jesse," she told me. "That's how it works."

. . .

Over a year into The Sandy Ground Project, we finally got down to the planning of a playground celebrating the life of Jesse Lewis. As I had mentioned previously, there was a question as to whether the playground in Milford would be for Jesse.

Scarlett and Maureen (Jesse's grandmother) had originally favored Milford. Maureen owns and operates a store there, so they felt like Jesse having a Milford playground would be home for them. Plus, with Milford being so close-knit and their response to The Sandy Ground Project being overwhelmingly positive, I can't say that I blame them. To be honest, we actually considered doing a second Milford playground because the first was such a homerun.

When Stamford became a possibility, that seemed to jive with a Jesse Lewis playground as well. It was where Scarlett had grown up and the city had been battered by Superstorm Sandy—much like Milford and its other neighboring cities along the Long Island Sound. Scarlett and Maureen were of the same mind—that these playgrounds were going to end up wherever the angels wanted and needed them to be. They were certain of it. They embraced Jesse's playground in Stamford and away we went.

• • •

Throughout the life of The Sandy Ground Project, the Angels Army has had its way of drawing people in. Like a spiritual magnet, it would attract those associated with anyone involved. Certainly my family, immediate and extended. All of the firefighters brought on co-workers or spouses. Some got their children involved. Brian D'Antoni had brought his girlfriend, Gina Aiello, into the fold and she steadily became a full-fledged member of the Angels Army. And, like so many others, she proved to be a vital cog in the Sandy Ground machine when it was her time to shine.

Much like her cousin Nicole had in Mystic only one week prior, Gina took The Sandy Ground Project's Stamford build by storm. Since Stamford is her hometown, Gina had so many built-in connections and so many friends around the city. This included the Stamford Fire Department, led by Bryan Munger and Local IAFF president Brendan Keatley became big supporters of ours and a huge help during the playground build itself.

Gina was also instrumental in piecing together accommodations in the city for everyone, and arranged for all of our meals to be provided by one local place or another the entire time. Brennan's Irish Pub was also a key partner for us there in many respects—food, drink, and fundraising alike.

As Chairwoman of the build, it seemed like there was nothing Gina couldn't find for us somewhere in Stamford. She was even able to hook us up with the school district there, and this kick-started a "Pennies for Playgrounds" fundraiser. Amy Gibson, a wonderful elementary school teacher there who is actually close friends with the Marquez-Greene family, spear-headed the fundraiser. This program alone netted $22,000 in change!! All thanks to the students of Stamford.

It was determined that Jesse Lewis's playground would stand on the sand at West Beach Park in Stamford. Along with Scarlett, we designed the playground to reflect everything that Jesse loved. It would have his favorite colors: turquoise, orange, and yellow. It would feature his favorite toys—army soldiers and rubber ducks—and include his own artwork on the panels. It would also carry the last message he had left for his mom—"Nurturing Healing Love"—in Jesse's own handwriting.

· · ·

The building of Jesse's playground went off without a hitch, basically getting done in one full day. The weather in Stamford was great and the truck carrying the playground was there when it was supposed to be. No issues there. The Stamford build will actually be remembered for the Angels Army getting back to its roots… A straight-up beach build with the sand serving as the playground floor. And if I were to give this build a fancy movie-title name, it would be "The Mud Duck Redemption".

With so many surface-mount builds happening lately, where the playground is secured directly to a pre-poured cement slab, the habitat of the Mud Duck was becoming extinct. They had thrived and honed their craft in places like Sea Bright, Manasquan, and Asbury Park; but since then they'd had to actively seek out opportunities to mix it up and get properly dirty. The Stamford build was old-school in their eyes and they relished the chance.

One such Mud Duck who had come onto the scene was a brother firefighter of mine from Elizabeth—Ronnie Roman. For anyone that knows him, or even been in his presence, the name alone is enough to induce a wide-eyed look that says, "Uh-oh". Maybe it's the lyrical alliteration of the name Ronald R. Roman. But most likely, it's the magnitude of his persona.

Ronnie is a high-energy character that wants to bring everyone around him up to his level. Very in-your-face, sometimes with language that doesn't necessarily go over too well in mixed company. He's a sports fanatic with a New York Yankee logo painted at the bottom of his in-ground pool. Actually, he's probably the prototype Yankee fan the rest of the country has in their mind when they picture one—or see one depicted on Saturday Night Live.

But as maniacal and hard-charging as Ronnie can be at times, his heart is as big as all outdoors. If he loves you, he tells you so and would go to hell and back to help out a friend. He is genuine, and charitable, and loyal to the end. If you met him in passing, you might fancy him a rabble-rouser. He's got the personality of a pirate in a lot of ways. No one has ever accused him of being politically correct. But believe me when I tell you, Ronnie Roman is one of the good guys. One of the best, in fact.

Before The Sandy Ground Project, I'm not completely sure that fact was clear to Ronnie's son Robbie. They are opposites in a lot of ways. While you'd struggle to get a word in edgewise whenever Ronnie's around, Robbie is very much the gentleman. He is reserved, speaks when spoken to, and—as a high school senior—is thoughtful beyond his years.

Ronnie believes very strongly in The Sandy Ground Project. He has poured his heart and soul into it, and works his tail off at the builds. And, as only Ronnie can, he encouraged everyone to get involved and have the same great experience he was having. He would actually go back and forth with me, disappointed and annoyed that only a small amount of our guys from the Elizabeth Fire Department were coming out. I just told him to focus on who's here, not who isn't. "Everyone that is meant to be here, is," I told him. "And it's their blessing. This project is not for everyone."

He agreed with me, but was not about to let his own son miss out.

Ronnie would actually take Robbie out of school to work on the playgrounds of The Sandy Ground Project. He felt there was more to be learned about life working and building outside alongside others for a great cause. It was not a classroom experience, it was real life, and Ronnie wanted his son to share in it.

In that decision, I feel, Ronnie was truly wise. He and his son shared an incredible bonding experience that basically lasted an entire year. From my perspective, it was great to see a father-son team working so hard together. I could imagine on their long drives, from Central Jersey to Connecticut and back, the long talks they'd be having. Whether it was in the car, on the build site, or sharing a drink and a laugh afterwards—I'm sure they learned a lot about each other.

I can safely say that both of their lives, as well as their relationship, have been forever changed by The Sandy Ground Project. Next year, Robbie will go off to college and surely do great things from there. But at least he is heading out into the world having had the chance to see what all of us have always seen in his father—a heart of gold.

. . .

The Stamford build was a family affair all around. Jesse Lewis was the force bringing us all together. For me personally, I was excited to have all four of my brothers in Stamford, working together, mudducking it up. It was the first time in a while the Lavin brothers were all present, accounted for, and working in unison. Jesse's father, Neil Hesslin, also came to the build and put in a lot of hard work. As did Jesse's step-brother J.T., and J.T.'s step-brother David.

J.T., I must mention, is one amazing young man. And although we had been focused on raising funds for The Sandy Ground Project for a year and a half at this point, J.T. turned our attention and support to another great and worthy cause. At 14-years-old, he had started a charity of his own.

In the aftermath of the tragedy at Sandy Hook Elementary, J.T. was really struggling. He was angry. He was withdrawn. He was extremely sad and depressed. A lot of teenagers are like that without having to deal with the immense trauma of such tragedy, so you can't imagine how J.T. must've felt. He didn't want to go to school anymore. He was at a critical point, and now his brother was gone.

And then a grief counselor suggested he speak to a young woman named Chantal. She was in Rwanda, a survivor of the genocide there. The counselor set up a Skype conversation between J.T. and Chantal, where she could express her condolences to him and tell about the unspeakable horrors she'd had to endure. She had lost her entire family and nearly been killed herself.

After telling J.T. her amazing story of survival and perseverance, Chantal's message to him was, in short: "If I can make it, so can you."

This struck an immediate chord with J.T. and put him on the road to healing. Not only that, J.T. started a foundation called "Newtown Helps Rwanda" that raises money to send Chantal, and others like her, to college. He succeeded in raising enough money for Chantal and the effort continues. J.T. is just a remarkable young man and we make every effort to support his foundation in any way we can.

• • •

The wind was whipping across West Beach on the morning of May 4, 2014. Flags were snapping taut and the sea spray was blowing off the water. The Stamford Fire Department was there in full force and in full regalia. The Angels Army was gathered after another job well done. All of the family and friends of Jesse Lewis came out to see Scarlett and J.T. cut the ribbon on his playground—the 20th of The Sandy Ground Project.

We had two of Jesse's favorite things on display that morning. First, we dedicated a little soldier statue to Jesse, in honor of his bravery, his sense of duty, and his desire to protect his friends and loved ones. We were also able to have the biggest rubber duck that any of us had ever seen float by. A giant wooden cut-out of a yellow rubber duck was made—it had to be 12 feet long—and attached to a boat we'd borrowed from someone locally. The boat was then driven across the Sound while the playground was being dedicated. Just a gigantic rubber duck floating on by. Sounds crazy, but the effect of it was perfect.

There was a great musical performance by a group of local children, led by Amy Gibson. They did a great rendition of the song "Payphone" by Maroon 5, which was Jesse's favorite—and even integrated specially written verses about him. They also performed the song "Clouds" which was written by a boy who was dying of cancer about his trip up to Heaven. Very powerful and moving stuff to say the least.

Amy Gibson really went out of her way to make that performance special. The tragedy at Sandy Hook is especially close to her heart. She is a friend of Nelba Marquez-Grace and knew Ana Grace quite well. The emotion and effort she poured into teaching those kids, and the talents of the kids themselves, really shone through and was a highlight of the day.

Given the wind situation, the speeches were difficult to hear. Myself and the Mayor of Stamford both spoke and struggled to be heard through the whooshing sound that was blowing through the microphone. But when Scarlett Lewis addressed the crowd at the end of our ceremony, Jesse made sure that those in attendance heard every word. Scarlett took the mic and the wind immediately stopped. The flags drooped and there was silence.

The message was as clear as the sound coming from the speakers. Scarlett talked about her connection with Jesse, both during his life and after. Her conviction came through in her voice and the audience was enthralled. The moral of the story was: In life and in death, on Earth and in Heaven, love never ends. And Jesse is here with us today.

I didn't catch this until afterwards, but someone caught a snapshot of Scarlett speaking with a rubber duck-shaped cloud floating by above her head in the background. I can imagine that these stories are sounding ridiculous by now, and even I swore that the photo was doctored somehow. But, sure enough, the photograph was true. The signs can be pretty apparent sometimes… if you allow yourself to see them.

As the ceremony concluded, the wind ramped back up and we all headed to a local hall for lunch. Gina Aiello, and the entire City of Stamford really, proved to be first class all the way once again. As always, a great time was had by all. The Angels Army was raising their glasses to Jesse and setting their sights on the next playground. It would be underway in a matter of days. Note: the Rippowam School that sang for Jesse that day, would become the first school to pilot the Choose Love Enrichment Program.

I think back fondly on our experience of building for Jesse in Stamford and maintain a close friendship with Scarlett. The two of them are both great sources of inspiration for us to continually draw from.

And I also think back specifically to a conversation I had with Jesse's grandmother, Maureen. I was working in the firehouse one day and she had called my cell phone. We spent an hour chatting about Jesse's playground, the design and location and all that sort of thing. We hadn't met in person yet, but spoke as if we were lifelong pals.

Then, she told me something I will never forget. It was something I felt, and thought, but never in so many words. It was certainly not something I had said or heard out loud either. But there was no denying its truth:

"I hope you don't mind me saying this, and you might think I'm crazy, but… My grandson chose you to build these playgrounds. Jesse picked you to do this."

I nearly dropped the phone. I felt in my heart she might be right. All my experiences, personally and professionally, had led me to this project, this mission. Jesse *had* chosen me… As did Joey, and Avielle, and Daniel, Olivia, Victoria, Chase, Mary, all of them. There are only a few times in my life where I felt as fortunate, and as blessed, as I did in that moment. My conversation with Maureen allowed me to step back and realize just how lucky I was.

With 20 playgrounds built, there were six more angels that I knew were counting on us. There's no way we would let them down.

Jesse makes his mark on the Stamford Fire Department

Richie in the center of it all

CHAPTER TWENTY-FIVE

Playground Celebrating the Life of Lauren Rousseau

Long Beach Island, New Jersey

Lauren Rousseau's life and future was just starting to take shape. She had just gotten hired as a teaching substitute at a great school, doing a job that she loved. Everything was falling into place for a beautiful young lady, known for her beautiful smile.

Unfortunately, tragedy struck and she left us much too soon. One of the classrooms involved at Sandy Hook Elementary School on December 14, 2012, was Lauren's. She has been an angel ever since.

• • •

I have said many times that the playgrounds of The Sandy Ground Project wind up being where the angels want them to be. It's out of our hands. Well, the playgrounds are also *when* the angels want them to be. They have an uncanny sense of timing.

The original plan for Lauren Rousseau's playground on Long Beach Island was to be part of our "Super Bowl" builds back in December or January. But the NFL felt that the location would not really be appropriate in terms of a New York–New Jersey hosted Super Bowl. Long Beach Island is probably, technically, closer to Lincoln Financial Field in Philadelphia than it is to the home of Super Bowl XLVIII. Hence, Belmar was designated as New Jersey's NFL playground and Lauren's on LBI was pushed back to a later date.

The delay was worth it. Just a few weeks prior we were freezing, building in stiff winds and frigid temperatures. But our week working on Lauren's playground on Long Beach Island was perfect. During construction it was misty and cool, but by the ribbon-cutting it was like full-blown summer. The sky was clear, the sun was burning bright, and some of the Angels Army had to break out the sunscreen for the first time in forever. It was idyllic. Vintage LBI. Just like the summer vacations that members of Lauren's family had enjoyed there with her family for many years.

Early on in the process, I'd had the pleasure of meeting with Lauren's immediate family in Southbury to present them with The Sandy Ground Project concept. We had a great conversation and I got to know a lot more about Lauren at the home of her father Gilles and step-mother Joyce. Lauren's mother Teresa and brothers Matt and Andrew were there as well, and all of them pledged their support for a playground being built in her honor. This is where they told me about Lauren's love of music and Broadway plays, and also mentioned the fact that the family was very familiar with and fond of Long Beach Island. It was the Jersey Shore vacation destination of choice for the many of the Rousseaus extended family. Many of Lauren's aunts, uncles, and cousins visited the island often.

It was still the beginning of 2013 and our initial builds were just starting to come into focus. But I put the Lauren Rousseau–Long Beach Island connection in my memory bank. If the Rousseau's were up for it, I knew the Island had been crushed by Superstorm Sandy and was in need of some rebuilding when the time was right.

• • •

Long Beach Island is a thin, low-lying stretch of land that braces the coast of Ocean County, New Jersey. It's 18 miles long, but not very wide at all. In some places you can easily see right across the island, from the Atlantic Ocean and the Barnegat Bay. There is not a lot separating all that water from all of that infrastructure. Where ever you are, if you look around, the water is never far away.

On a nice day, it's a beautiful thing. I've spent a lot of time vacationing on Long Beach Island myself. But when a strong storm rolls through—particularly Sandy, the most powerful of them all—LBI's true natural role as a "barrier island" comes into full view. The island serves as a barrier, a shock-absorber, basically shielding the mainland from whatever the ocean can dish out. And sometimes the ocean can dish out a lot.

Hurricanes of the past become the stuff of legend on Long Beach Island, a place that is very history-conscious and history-rich. Superstorm Sandy certainly added to the lore as much of the Island was overcome by the storm surge. So many homes and businesses, many of which had closed up for the season a month prior, were devastated. The entire area was evacuated, sending anyone there scrambling for the Causeway—the one land-route off the Island. At one point, LBI's southern portion (Holgate) was actually cut off from the rest and became an island onto itself.

So Long Beach Island had definitely taken more than enough punishment from the Superstorm to qualify for a Sandy Ground playground. And one major factor they had going for them was that Louise Donnelly lives there. The mother of Eddie Donnelly, my successor as New Jersey State FMBA President, Louise had been working and advocating for The Sandy Ground Project to come and build on Long Beach Island.

Not only was Louise getting the word out about The Sandy Ground Project on Long Beach Island, but she was raising funds locally and generating a buzz there. After becoming knowledgeable about the project through her, the people of the Island wanted a playground and wanted to host Lauren. With Lauren being a teacher, we got great support and a sizable donation from the New Jersey Education Association. They had been intimately involved with our first playground in Sea Bright and it was great to have them back in the mix once again.

The big tipping point there, however, was getting the town and the local Policeman's Benevolent Association fully involved with the project. The Long Beach PBA would be able to get us anything we needed to facilitate an island build, and even had a location in mind that was ready to go. Brendan Kerlin the local PBA representative took the lead for us on the island and was an incredible asset to us. Katlyn Forsyth from the Township office also made sure that every resource the Township had to offer was at our disposal.

Right across Long Beach Boulevard from police headquarters stands a bayfront park that was ravaged during Superstorm Sandy. It is in the Brant Beach section of the island and work was just getting started on replacing the bulkhead and gazebo and tennis courts. All that the park needed, it seemed, was a playground.

• • •

The Rousseau family was tremendous in making Lauren's playground, and the week building on Long Beach Island, as special as it turned out to be. Gilles and Joyce pulled their Air Stream Camper into the park mid-week and set up shop on the tennis courts. It was Camp Rousseau for the duration and the two of them poured themselves into the process. Both were at the playground 24/7, literally, with the protection and hospitality of the Long Beach Township Police Department right across the street.

Joyce, I must mention, did construction work on Lauren's playground at an amazing rate. She seemed to be everywhere at once, helping everyone, quickly completing one task and moving right onto the next one. Gilles had joked that Joyce does all the work and he is just there to take the photos. In this case—and I think Gilles would admit as much himself—a lot of truth is said in jest.

Teresa, Lauren's mom, was instrumental in providing so many of the personal touches that made the playground (and the ribbon-cutting ceremony) shine. The theme of the playground was teaching, music, and the color purple—and Teresa gave us all she could to help in designing the structure to reflect that.

Lauren's extended family came out in droves for the week as well, seemingly from every corner of the country and beyond. There were folks from Connecticut, New York, Rhode Island, Alabama, Virginia,

Pennsylvania, Colorado, Quebec, and probably ten other places I'm forgetting to mention. And while they had all suffered a crushing tragedy in their lives, being on Long Beach Island that week gave them a reason to come together and celebrate.

. . .

Lauren Rousseau's Playground—the 21st of its kind within The Sandy Ground Project—was built right into the sand. It was a perfect waterfront location on Barnegat Bay, ideal for watching the sun set. The spot is very peaceful and serene, similar to Chase Kowalski's playground in Normandy Beach. But it also posed many of the same building-related challenges as Chase's did.

Due to the high water-table, the design of the playground itself was constantly in flux. We would drill in one spot and be fine, then drill in the next spot and hit water. The Angels Army, old hands at the process by now, had to continually adjust its methods to get the job done. It was a challenging build, and took every bit of our perseverance and ingenuity to complete Lauren's playground. And believe me when I tell you, we went right up to the minute of the morning of the ribbon-cutting ensuring that everything was solid, safe, and ready for playing.

. . .

And that day of the ribbon-cutting, May 11, 2014, was a special one. It was Mother's Day and Lauren had graced us with the most perfect, summer-like weather you could imagine. The ideal beach day if the ocean weren't still so cold. I could not thank the Rousseau family enough for letting us hold the ceremony on a holiday, and I think they realized that honoring all the mothers and grandmothers in attendance (Lauren's especially) would make it all the more special.

We made sure all the mothers and grandmothers present were recognized and presented with flowers. One in particular—Evelyn Baumgardner Martin, Lauren's grandmother—was presented with a construction helmet in addition to her flowers. At the start of the build, Evelyn had commented to me that she was too old to really help out. So, we decided to prove her wrong and actually made her the honorary foreman of the project and she worked alongside us, enjoying that special designation, for the entire week.

The Sandy Ground Project had gotten tremendous support from the Long Beach Island community to get Lauren's playground built. But on Mother's Day, we found out that the town, the police union, and the teachers were all going to be paying it forward to future stops in our project. Led by the Township's donation of $30,000—all three organizations presented us with monster checks. Mayor Joseph Mancini of Long Beach Township, who had welcomed us that afternoon, was an amazing host for our stay on the island. We were so thrilled that he and his town were paying it forward in this way. He is still a great friend of the project. Mayor Mancini also presented the entire Rousseau family with beach badges in hopes of keeping them coming back to LBI.

The playground was resplendent under the hot sun, purple butterflies and balloons hovering overhead, as the children present waited patiently to take over the grounds. To acknowledge Lauren's love of musicals, we had one of my daughter Kelly's students—future American Idol contestant Courtney Zahn—perform "Castle on a Cloud" from Les Miserables. It was an appropriate song choice for the day a playground was being opened in honor of an angel.

As was fitting for the holiday and occasion, Lauren's mother took center stage. Teresa spoke in detail about her daughter—how much she would have loved the playground and the day's events. She told a story about how, when Lauren was a little girl, she was frightened and nervous to go to school. (Ironic because she grew up wanting to be at school for a living.) So, to calm Lauren down and give her strength and confidence, her mom would give her a lucky penny to hold on to. They would listen to "Any Lucky Penny", one of Lauren's favorite songs, and it would shake the nerves away.

To commemorate this, Teresa had lucky pennies distributed to everyone there as she told the story. She noted that there were several, dated 1982, minted the year Lauren was born. Those were the really lucky ones. Teresa urged everyone to take a penny and keep some of Lauren's spirit in their hearts.

It was an afternoon full of emotion, heightened by the fact that it was Mother's Day. But when the speeches were over and the ribbon was cut, it was all about the kids. They stormed the sand and took over the purple playground. Hopefully they didn't get too crazy and behaved well enough in the aftermath to be good to their moms.

Afterwards there was a reception down the street, our host being the Long Beach Township PBA once again. They had seen us through every step of the way. We got to spend a bit more time with the Rousseau family before going our separate ways to celebrate the holiday with all of the mothers in our lives. Lauren's entire family, particularly Gilles and Joyce, have remained very close to The Sandy Ground Project. They have been at subsequent builds and ceremonies and we stay in close touch.

The playground is well cared for and watched over by Louise and Brendan and Katlyn. The grounds are even decorated on holidays and on Lauren's birthday to make sure she is never forgotten.

We left Long Beach Island knowing Lauren's playground was in good hands. It would be cherished by the families there, maintained by the Township, and watched over by the police officers. Most of all, we know that Lauren is watching over her playground and blessing all who have the privilege of playing on it.

And whether or not the lucky penny from Mother's Day 2014 is still in our pockets, and regardless of the year it was minted, everyone involved in building Playground #21 has gone forward carrying Lauren Rousseau with them.

Ben lights up Ocean City

CHAPTER TWENTY-SIX

Playground Celebrating the Life of Benjamin Wheeler

Ocean City, New Jersey

I t was a whirlwind month for The Sandy Ground Project—everything was coming together quicker than I ever thought possible. As we packed up after a Mother's Day celebration on Long Beach Island, it was already time to head straight to the next build. This one—our 22nd—would be just a little bit further south down the Jersey coast.

By the following Sunday, we'd be cutting another ribbon in Ocean City, New Jersey. It would be our 4th in only 21 days. You'd think the Angels Army would be wearing out by now—people needing to get back to their regular lives, spent from one overload of emotion after another. But it was exactly the opposite. The camaraderie and energy surrounding the project only made them thirsty for more. A Sunday ribbon-cutting was becoming like spiritual clockwork, everyone congregating to be in the presence of something bigger than themselves.

• • •

I felt admiration for David Wheeler from afar—long before I'd had the chance to sit down and speak with him in person. When The Sandy Ground Project was nothing more than an idea, I remember seeing David on television doing interviews in the aftermath of the Newtown tragedy. He struck me as an intelligent, articulate, and thoughtful guy. David had just lost his son, Ben, but still had the wherewithal to be a spokesman for his family and give their perspective. I cannot imagine what kind of strength it must take for him to do that... but according to David, I *can* imagine. And I should.

That was what caught my eye about him, his unique take on peoples' reactions and responses to him after the Newtown tragedy. In an interview, he said, "People come up to me and say 'I can't imagine what you're going through,' or 'I can't imagine if I'd lost my child.' But that is the problem. I want people to imagine. They can imagine. The only way that we'll ever get change in this world is to put yourself in my shoes and imagine what it is like."

This wasn't necessarily what people wanted to hear—and it is, of course, kind of a stupid thing for someone to say to a grieving parent—but I could see where he was coming from. Until people can truly understand, truly *imagine*, what families like the Wheelers are now going through—no one will change. No one will see a tragedy like this from the inside.

So based on these first impressions I'd gotten of David through the television, I knew him to be an eloquent and intelligent guy before I even walked through his door.

I wound up meeting with David one-on-one to present him with the concept of The Sandy Ground Project. His wife Francine and son Nate were out for the day (I would get to know them a little later on), so the two of us settled in and talked about Ben.

Benjamin Wheeler was an extremely bright and energetic little boy. He loved the music of The Beatles and lighthouses. He wanted to be a lighthouse keeper someday and was fond of visiting them whenever he could.

In Ben's honor, his family actually had started up a foundation called "Ben's Lighthouse". It is geared towards helping and supporting the children of Newtown following the tragedy of December 14, 2012. Clearly the kids there are facing a difficult and unique set of challenges going forward. This includes Ben's own brother Nate, who was inside Sandy Hook Elementary School that day and suffered through the great trauma that it was.

So Ben's Lighthouse was built—much like a real lighthouse—to guide and protect all of Newtown's youth and burn brightly in honor of those that were lost.

Right from the get-go, David Wheeler was as impressive to me as I'd expected. He was open and honest in speaking about Ben, as well as Nate who was struggling mightily with the loss of his brother and biggest fan. This brought me to the idea of building a playground for Ben, where Nate could serve as foreman, and maybe we could even build a literal lighthouse to compliment the foundation the Wheelers had built already. David was all for the idea right away. After some discussion with his family, the Wheelers said they would like Ben's playground to be in Ocean City, New Jersey.

• • •

Ocean City, NJ—not to be confused with the one in Maryland—is probably the most family-friendly beach location on the entire east coast. Once you drive over the bay and into the city's friendly confines, you are immediately transported to a different time. The quaint mom-and-pop stores of Main Street… the boardwalk that still has a Music Pier and the food is affordable… the lack of any bars or liquor stores, which keeps the party crowd at bay. It is—to use one of my own personal clichés—a real slice of Americana.

On the opposite end of that spectrum is Atlantic City, which is a mere 10 miles up the road. That is where Superstorm Sandy made landfall on the night of October 29, 2012. Obviously Ocean City would take a hard hit as well. The city was flooded and much of the oceanfront infrastructure was battered. One of the Ocean City Fire Department's firehouses was completely flooded out. The firefighters were still using an adjacent trailer as their living quarters when we rolled into town to build Benjamin Wheeler a playground.

The Wheelers had chosen Ocean City for a number of reasons, not the least of which was the distance from Newtown, CT. The idea that it would be somewhere they could travel to and visit—out of the area, out of state—appealed to them. Also home to one of Ben's grandfathers, Ocean City would turn out to be as far away from Newtown as a Sandy Ground playground would ever get. Ben Wheeler's playground is our southernmost, and it stands precisely 260 miles away from our northernmost in Mystic, CT. There's that number 26 again.

Ocean City is a preferred vacation destination of the Wheeler family and the city proved itself very hospitable to them, and to all the families affected by the Newtown tragedy. Led by the City's Communications Manager, Laurie Howey, Ocean City extended an invite for any and all of them to come down to the Jersey Shore and stay for free in donated vacation homes.

From a standpoint of planning and execution, Ocean City was a slam dunk location for The Sandy Ground Project. We had more support there than in most places, and from all possible angles. Laurie Howey, who I mentioned prior, was our ace asset from City Hall. She was able to arrange for just about everything we needed in terms of food and lodging, and she was our hostess for the week. The Angels Army are builders first, but they are tourists as well.

Our people were staying in hotels and bed-and-breakfasts and soaking up the boardwalk and sunshine in their downtime. It was just a nice, enjoyable all around scene in Ocean City. And while Laurie Howey deserves a lot of the credit for us pulling off a great playground build, she made sure we were all fed and having a great time.

We also enjoyed a great partnership with Chuck Bangle, the owner of Ocean City's famous Manco & Manco Pizza. He donated a seemingly unlimited amount of food (mainly pizza, of course) during our stay and basically gave us carte blanche for whatever we needed. Chuck has become a great friend to The Sandy Ground Project far beyond Ocean City, and we're continuing to work with him on new and exciting projects.

The Ocean City Fire Department was tremendous as well, led by our great friends John Murphy, Steve Costantino, and Chris Vliet (better known as "Cooter"). The OCFD took on a leadership role in bringing The Sandy Ground Project to their city and raised a significant amount of money as well. Even the Chief of the Department, Christopher Breunig, hooked us up with his father-in-law's cement company who did the excavation and cement pad for us. So the fire department definitely came up strong all around.

With all of our plans and resources in place, we broke ground on Playground #22 for Ben Wheeler. It is at 2901 West Avenue, right next door to the fire house.

• • •

The build days are always a flurry of activity. We break ground, the Angels Army storms the area and assumes their positions, and new volunteers are busy finding and being assigned to various jobs. I am always looking in ten different directions at once, trying to make sure things are running as smoothly as possible.

Early in the morning, on the day we began building in Ocean City, I got a text from Connecticut... from Sgt. Bill Cario, the State Trooper who had been instrumental in getting that late-running truck to Mystic and now a great friend to the project and myself. He wrote: "Is Ben Wheeler's playground build today?" I replied, "Yes, just getting started." Then I went about my business.

Bill pulled up to the playground ready to work before Noon. Once he'd confirmed that we were building for Ben that day, he dropped everything and drove about four hours. Straight from Connecticut to the South Jersey Shore. As you'll recall, Bill was one of the first responders at Sandy Hook Elementary School, the first to triage the scene. He felt a special connection with Ben Wheeler, the one child he had carried out of the school in hopes of saving.

He is a very dedicated guy to begin with, but Bill wanted to be there especially for Ben. He loved the other builds for sure, but this one he wouldn't miss for the world. He worked his tail off for Ben that day, with an emotional connection to this particular playground that I'm sure only he could fully know. Then, at the end of the night, with Ben's playground just about finished, Bill got back into his car and drove another four hours home to Connecticut.

With all that going on, I never got a chance to say goodbye to Bill that night. When I realized he was on his way home, I sent him a quick text that said, "Hey, thanks a lot for the effort today. Great to have you here." Apparently he had stopped off on the way home for a late dinner and drink. He replied back with a picture message of a pint and a shot. It read: "My pleasure. Wouldn't have missed it. Here's to Ben."

I got a phone call a few minutes later. It was Bill. His voice was shaking.

He told me a story about how, a month or two prior, all of the pictures and videos in his phone had been erased. Precious photos of his son, video of a performance at school, a couple of years' worth of memories he had been saving for some time. He was devastated when they were mistakenly wiped out.

But when he texted me that picture message toasting Ben, all of the missing photos and videos were inexplicably restored. Every last one of them were suddenly back in their folders. I could tell when he was telling me this that he was sort of in shock. Like *really* freaked out.

It is an amazing story, and still unexplained from the standpoint of how these pictures came and went. But it's obviously not the first time the angels have sent down a gift from above. And that is what we believe Ben did in this case, thanking Bill for being there for him… again.

I guess it should go without saying that angels are cloud experts, living amongst them as they do. But even we, after so many other miracles, were surprised by an angel's ability to influence the iCloud.

• • •

In Ocean City, the construction itself went pretty smooth—which is easy for me to say. It only goes smooth because of the way the contractors and the Angels Army work in unison and streamline their processes. This was the fourth build in as many weeks and we were riding their hot hand.

The one main variable construction-wise in Ocean City was the lighthouse being built. Ben's Lighthouse. And, as I talk about the Angels Army "streamlining their process", I can't believe I haven't yet spoken in detail about Bruce Pollock. He is the Army's streamliner-extraordinaire and the man who would make Ben's Lighthouse shine in Ocean City.

Bruce is one of our best and most dedicated volunteers. He is a Captain with the Millburn(NJ) Fire Department and, out of an eventual 26 Sandy Ground builds, Bruce made 25 of them. It has somehow taken me 22 playgrounds to lay out his importance to the project but, because of his unique set of skills and experience, he has been one of the most vital cogs from the start.

As a member of the Stagehands' Union, Bruce is a really creative guy that can make pretty much anything. He has worked at the Papermill Playhouse in Millburn and the Prudential Center in Newark—making sets for various productions and events. And, being such a versatile craftsman, Bruce has a deep appreciation for his tools. The word "anal" actually comes to mind. But when you've got all different volunteers coming and going, week in and week out, using the hundreds of tools that The Sandy Ground Project has acquired—someone needs to care for them. Enter Bruce "The Tool Man" Pollock.

Our official Sandy Ground truck—which I'll talk more about in a minute—is Bruce's domain. He has it fully decked out with Christmas lights, speakers, flags, and a giant map of all our Sandy Ground triumphs. Bruce is the only one allowed inside the truck, where all the tools, bits, and building materials are meticulously cleaned and in their proper place. The other volunteers are permitted to go as far as the truck's tailgate—stepping up to request a tool from Bruce or placing one they're finished with for him to put back in its spot. He's like a strict librarian in work boots.

Beyond being keeper of the truck, Bruce might be the one member of the Angels Army most responsible for making the builds go as fast as they do. When I say something like "the Angels Army was hitting their stride" or working like a "well-oiled machine", it is due in large part to Bruce. He has created, from scratch, a lot of the custom-made braces and supports that make the process so easy. He meets with the contractors and comes up with a new piece or maneuver to make everyone's lives easier.

And at Ben Wheeler's Playground, Bruce built an actual working lighthouse in practically no time. It would become the centerpiece of the playground, a beacon representing the light that our angels shine down from above. We had a group of kids paint the lighthouse to match up with the playground structure itself—forest green and blue. Ben would be happy to know that his lighthouse is the sharpest looking one on the entire coast.

· · ·

Since right around the second build, we have utilized a truck that was lent to us by Scott Campbell of Campbell Supply. The aforementioned 'Bruce's Truck' is as important as any one of the volunteers and there is no way we can do a build without it. Through Scott's generosity, the truck is ours for as long as we need it. He is actually in the process of gifting it to us permanently, which is amazing.

Campbell Supply is a company that builds and sells fire apparatus, firefighting equipment, and freightliner trucks. Hence the connection to us, the fire service. It is hard to put a price tag on what our partnership with them has meant to the project. They are a family business, and certainly treat us as such.

At one point, during the height of The Sandy Ground Project's building, I stopped to visit Scott and tour Campbell Supply's beautiful new facility in South Brunswick, NJ. As Scott and I chatted and we stepped into his office—overlooking the New Jersey Turnpike—something caught my eye.

It was a picture of the ground-breaking for the very building we were standing in. Campbell Supply was digging in their shovels, but that's not what interested me. It was the date on the frame—December 14, 2012.

On the same day of the tragedy at Sandy Hook Elementary School… and probably as I was driving by, miserable as all could be, on this very stretch of the New Jersey Turnpike… Campbell Supply was starting to build something. As terrible as the feelings are associated with that date now, it was a day that would lead all of us towards building something together.

. . .

Before you knew it, the playground celebrating Ben Wheeler was finished—lighthouse lit and everything. It was blue and green and paneled with all sorts of Ben's own drawings. There were no issues at all with construction, just smooth sailing under Ben's guiding light.

With the structure completed, the rubber surfacing company showed up to seal the deal. They were one man short, however, because one of their guys didn't show up or was let go or something. Not to fear… Rich Picerno, ever the team's leader, stepped in and did it himself. As the general contractor of each of The Sandy Ground Project's playgrounds, Rich oversaw just about every element of the construction. But when it comes time to step up and lead by example, there is no job too small. More than anything, Rich makes sure that jobs get done.

. . .

With Ben's playground ready to officially open the following day, we were invited over to the Wheelers' Ocean City home for a post-build get-together. With such an emotional ceremony on tap for the next morning you would expect a bit of a subdued crowd, but their family was anything but. Kids were running around crazy, eating ice cream sundaes, and we all just had some great conversations and toasted Ben. David and Francine shared so many personal stories with us, it was really an honor just to be getting to know them so well.

Francine took the opportunity to let us know that she was six months pregnant. She talked openly and honestly about how emotional the pregnancy had been considering all the family had been through. And the Wheelers were already looking forward to many visits back to Ocean City after their new baby arrived.

. . .

On the morning of May 18, 2014, Ocean City pulled out all the stops. Streets were closed off and the fire trucks were lined up carrying a giant American flag. It was the day to cut the ribbon and open up Ben Wheeler's playground. Even the weather was cooperative in Ocean City, and we arrived at the park to a picture perfect day.

As I greeted David Wheeler that morning, he confided to me privately that his father had passed away the night before. It felt like a punch in the stomach, I felt so bad. How much can one person take? When I expressed my condolences, David asked that I please keep that news private—he was afraid of taking away from the day's event. Here is a guy who had lost his son and now his father, and he is worried about being a downer at our event. Just a really selfless man, which I couldn't help but admire in that moment.

The ceremony in Ocean City that morning had all the traditional Sandy Ground pomp-and-circumstance. We presented the Wheeler family with the bell that would give Ben his wings. We had bagpipers, a fly-over, and speeches from the local dignitaries. The Wheelers had been vacationing in Ocean City for so many years, and now the city was happy to be welcoming them to their permanent home away from home. The Wheelers had their Pastor bless the playground with waters from the Housatonic and the River Jordan.

Then, in a surprise performance, Francine and David took the stage. Francine is an accomplished and very talented singer, and David was by her side on guitar. She then unleashed the most powerful and moving rendition of "What a Wonderful World" that any of us had ever heard. It was jarring… not a dry eye within earshot.

The performance was an accomplishment in itself, but the fact that Francine could get through it without breaking down was amazing. The deeper meaning of these lyrics, given what the Wheelers had been through and were about to go through, were remarkably poignant:

"I hear babies cryin'… I watch them grow… They'll learn much more than I'll ever know. And I think to myself… What a wonderful world."

Those few lines, under the circumstances, had tremendous impact.

Before we could even recover from such a powerful moment, David was on the microphone delivering a great speech to cap off the ceremony. I had asked him not to thank us, the volunteers, and to his credit he acquiesced. But what he said made all of us associated with The Sandy Ground Project even prouder than if he had.

David said, "Bill always tells us not to thank you all. That it is a selfish project, and your thanks is to us for letting you do this. So I'll honor that. I won't say thank you. Instead, I'll just tell you what this project means to us. You are our reason for getting up in the morning, and living proof that there is more good than evil in the world. And that is what I will leave you with."

Nate Wheeler cut the ribbon. Ben's playground was officially open.

• • •

With Ocean City being a dry town, we all headed back to a local private hall and had a great party with the Wheelers. We said our goodbyes, but we knew they would be only temporary. David and Francine have remained a great addition to the Sandy Ground family. Their ongoing advocacy is how they continue to honor Ben.

By the summer, we were getting pictures of newborn baby Matthew—the latest addition to both the Wheeler and Sandy Ground families... and soon-to-be regular at his big brother's playground down at the Jersey Shore.

Ben's artwork

Karli and Toni, the Spark and the Brilliance

CHAPTER TWENTY-SEVEN

Playground Celebrating the Life of Madeleine Hsu

West Islip, New York

I have talked a lot about the ability of the Angels Army to hone their craft. In terms of the actual building, by Playground #23 it was all a matter of routine. Aside from a few variables in regards to style and surface and layout of the playground itself, we went in knowing our jobs and what to expect. Unless it rains, or the ground is frozen, or the playground itself doesn't happen to show up—you know the level of work and time required to get it done. Over a year into the project, you take it for granted.

I have said many times that the meeting and interaction with the families initially can be very difficult, but I will tell you meeting all the wonderful families has been one of the blessings of my life.

On a cold and icy morning Brian D'Antoni and I met with Donna Arnold, Madeleine Hsu's mom. Despite being complete strangers from another State, Donna welcomed us to her home and allowed me to explain our hope to build a playground in honor of Madeleine. Donna told us that she would certainly consider the idea and was grateful for our time and efforts.

A little more than a year after we had first met, Donna agreed to have a playground built to celebrate Madeleine's life. We didn't meet face to face again, but over the phone she expressed to me that her and her family were in support of it. She was unsure as to whether they would like to be directly involved, but gave us the go-ahead regardless.

We had a playground on tap for West Islip, New York, but what we didn't have was an inspiration for it. That is when Donna and I reconnected and she gave us the thumbs up. She had been monitoring our progress all along and felt that we had done the families of Newtown proud.

Donna carefully worked with Toni Giordano on the playground's design, and was able to share some insight on what Madeleine was like. Madeleine, as we learned, was extremely bright and studious, loved reading, loved running, and loved dogs. Her favorite color was purple.

Donna wanted us to go ahead with the build, but it was too soon for the Hsu family to have any involvement. There was to be no press or media coverage of the playground—a request we would certainly honor. "This playground is not necessarily for us," Donna insisted. "But we love that a community that needs it will enjoy the benefit."

• • •

One of The Sandy Ground Project's biggest champions is Eugene Ambrosio. Known primarily as "Gino", he has been at just about all of our builds and his biggest impact is in the social media realm. He is always on the spot, taking pictures and posting them on Facebook (and anywhere else). Gino played a big part in raising our virtual profile, allowing people from far and wide the ability to follow along with the project's progress.

I knew Gino from my time as a counselor at the Connecticut Children's Burn Camp. He is a very dedicated nurse, treating burn patients and cancer patients at Sloan Kettering and the Cornell Burn Foundation. As I mentioned back at the Normandy Beach build, he had even treated our own Mark Virag during various bouts with mouth and throat cancer. Going forward, he was our information pipeline to and from Mark during his hospital stays.

Ever since getting involved with The Sandy Ground Project, Gino had been advocating for a playground to be built in his home area—on the Long Island coast. Since we were already light on New York playgrounds (compared to Connecticut and New Jersey), I was in favor of this as well. As it turned out, Gino knew a Councilman in West Islip, right near his own hometown. The two of them had scouted out a perfect location—right on the beach at Marina Park. Now it was just a matter of getting the rest of the town on board.

. . .

The waterfront town of West Islip—like pretty much all of its neighbors on the southern coast of Long Island—got battered by Superstorm Sandy. Not only did it deal with the wind damage, power outages, and flooding like so many others; it also got a fair amount of debris crashing its shore from other places. West Islip is located on the bay, and all that came pouring in from the barrier island just compounded the problem.

By the time I had a chance to meet with the Town Council, they had already done quite a bit of recovery and restoration of the West Islip waterfront. But once I had a chance to explain what The Sandy Ground Project was all about, the town approved and embraced the idea of being home to a playground celebrating the life of Madeleine Hsu. From there, the people of West Islip came together and made the build special. The community was truly awesome.

There are so many civic groups in West Islip, all of which were so lively and friendly and outgoing when it came to being our hosts for the week of the build. The one that stood out—possibly because of their catchy name—were the WOWI's (pronounced WOW-eez), the Women of West Islip. They, along with so many other groups, raised thousands of dollars for the project.

Although there were several types of fundraisers and events there, it was highlighted by an affair they called "A Taste of West Islip". Numerous restaurants in town participated and it turned out to be a rather lavish affair. I showed up thinking it was a casual event, but quickly saw that the women were decked out in evening gowns and the men in suits. It certainly did the trick though, as they were able to raise thousands of dollars for The Sandy Ground Project. And the food was incredible to boot.

The West Islip Fire Department were great allies too, as well as great hosts during the build. Many of our Angels Army volunteers shacked up at the firehouse for the duration, and the WIFD was able to provide us whatever else we needed. Many of their members are career guys from FDNY, so they were no strangers to the camaraderie felt between New Jersey and New York City firefighters. Just brothers separated by the Hudson River.

· · ·

Madeleine Hsu's Playground—#23—was built straight onto the beach. It was another throwback adventure for the Mud-Duck crew, so they were in their glory. There was a lot of cement work to be done throughout the whole area actually, as Madeleine's playground slowly evolved into a restoration of the entire beachfront.

The local beach house and restroom building were restored that week, and we had some local kids from town to help with the painting when the work was completed. The Angels Army laid down paved walkways for easier playground access, as well as installed 'reading benches' to pay tribute to Madeleine's love of books. We also had Lowe's come onto the scene and do a full landscape of the entire area. This really polished off what would become a beautiful, peaceful park setting. So while West Islip thought they were just getting a playground out of the deal, the whole area wound up getting a facelift.

The taste of West Islip endured onto the construction site itself, as the firefighters brought in a big grill and kept it fired up throughout. The community, the local businesses, the town itself, they all made sure we were well taken care of. My only hope was that Madeleine's family could somehow feel this outpouring of love for themselves.

· · ·

The Hsu family decided to decline the invitations to the build and the ribbon-cutting ceremony. We certainly respected their decision and desire for privacy, and all media attention was kept clear of Madeleine's playground.

With Madeleine's siblings unavailable to participate, would we be left without an honorary foreman/forewoman for the first time? I thought so originally. But in true Sandy Ground fashion, things would even out. Our forewoman would surface and she would come all the way from Mississippi. As a nod to The Sandy Ground Project's very own roots... Enter: Karli Coyne.

• • •

The little girl who started it all with her heartfelt letter to the firefighters of New Jersey, Karli made the trip up to New York for the building of Playground #23. She was accompanied by her mother, Amy, and the teacher that inspired the 'pay-it-forward' movement at her school, Tammy Raymond. Karli turned out to be the perfect on-site fill-in for Madeleine's sisters. She stepped in as the sweet and precocious leader of the Angels Army and, having seen the news clip of her reading the letter that inspired us all, she was like a celebrity to them. It's amazing to think that this was the first time we had met her in person.

But it wasn't all work for our visitors from the Gulf Coast, as we made sure to give them a taste of The Big Apple during their stay. In addition to West Islip rolling out the red carpet, Karli got to see a Broadway play with the Kowalski girls and spend a day on the boardwalk at Coney Island.

When the job was done, Madeleine's playground was resplendent in purple, standing in the sands of West Islip's beachfront. The area had been transformed into a kid's paradise, with all the personal touches in honor of Madeleine. The statue of a child sitting, reading with her dog. The purple swing set facing the sea. The new walkways, perfect for running straight towards the playground.

• • •

The morning of June 1, 2014, kicked off with the children of nearby Bridges Academy singing "...the sun will come out tomorrow." No doubt it would, but lucky for us it was already out and shining brightly today. The children were great representatives of West Islip, their singing making everyone smile and cry all at once.

West Islip had proven to be a tremendous host with Eugene Ambrosio leading the way as the build's chairman. His mother performed a memorable rendition of "Wind Beneath My Wings" dedicated to all the volunteers of The Sandy Ground Project. Every single person at the park that day was sporting a pinned-on picture of Madeleine. Seeing her smiling face all over the beach brought a lot of joy that morning, and symbolized the joy that Madeleine would be bringing to that playground for years to come.

Our keynote speakers for the day were our guests from Mississippi—Karli Coyne and Tammy Raymond. Even at age 11, Karli spoke beautifully, marveling at how much good can come from one spark of kindness. Tammy brought greetings from Bay St. Louis, MS, and commented how the rebuilding from Hurricane Katrina was still going on all these years later. But that it's the caring from friends in other places—like New Jersey, New York, and Connecticut—that allows them to keep the faith.

Our good friends at the West Islip Fire Department hosted the after-party for us, and we got a chance to toast Madeleine one more time all together. The Mississippi wing of the Sandy Ground family was front and center, and we hoped we'd all be together again sooner than later. Maybe it was Karli being there that made everyone reflect on the whole project—where we'd come from and what we'd done— but it was starting to dawn on the Angels Army that there were only three builds left.

"What are we supposed to do after that?", they were wondering.

• • •

A few months later, the summer was over and The Sandy Ground Project was hyper-focused on the final playground build—the big #26. It was my hope to get all of the families to attend this final event, and I was in the process of personally reaching out to all of them to share the details.

I got in touch with Donna. She said she would see what they could do as far as coming. That was all I could really ask for.

The West Islip playground had been open and operational for a full summer by this point. Surely thousands of kids had played on it by now. And I couldn't help but wonder if Madeleine's family had ever gotten to see it. So I asked Donna.

"Yes," she said. "Just recently, we took a ride to the playground late one night and saw it. I have to tell you… You guys got it just right, and we like it very much."

West Islip Fire Department joins Gino and the Angels Army

"The Kite" Angel in a pink dress

CHAPTER TWENTY-EIGHT

Playground Celebrating the Life of
Charlotte Bacon

West Haven, Connecticut

At what point do you realize you've changed?

Any kind of transformation—whether physical, mental, or spiritual—takes place gradually. You don't notice yourself aging from day to day; it has already happened by the time you can see it. The leaves on a tree don't change color while you're looking. One day it's green, the next day it's red or yellow. Like the old saying goes, "A watched pot never boils."

In my case, I realized just how much I had changed at the beginning of the summer of 2014. It was amidst some political controversy surrounding our 24th playground in West Haven, Connecticut. In my days as a state labor leader, I was no stranger to dust-ups like these. No stranger to City Councils, the news media swirling, or angry mobs (both for and against me).

And I would react to these in vintage Bill Lavin form. Which is to say... aggressively. A fiery speech, forcefully defending my constituents, closing ranks with the membership and going to battle. Who is with us? Who is against us? It's the mentality of politics... the mentality of New Jersey in a lot of ways. It is difficult not to become a product of your own surroundings.

With that being said, the past year-and-a-half I had spent surrounded by our 26 angels, their beautiful families, and the dedicated folks who had taken the mission of The Sandy Ground Project and put it in their hearts. So, as I was about to meet with the Mayor of West

Haven to prepare for a contentious City Council meeting—what did I do? I went looking for a sign from heaven. To be more specific, for a sign from an angel named Charlotte.

Not only did I get the sign I was looking for, it was as clear as crystal.

. . .

The Bacons were one of only a couple of the families that I didn't sit down and have a formal meeting with. At our third build in Ansonia, CT, Charlotte's mother Joann came to the ribbon-cutting and we made our introductions. She had been meaning to get back to me, to set up a meeting of some sort, but things had been hectic. I more than understood. And she told me that day that they'd love for Charlotte to have a playground of her own too… They just needed more time.

And over that time, I got to know Joann—and her husband Joel—over the phone more than anything. This is how I learned more about Charlotte. She loved poodles and was addicted to the color pink. Everything had to be pink.

Joann and Joel also told me about their family's fondness for the West Haven shore, and a seafood restaurant in particular there called "Stowe's". It is a very down-to-earth, kid-friendly place with all sorts of nautical decorations hanging up and "FRESH FISH" scrawled in chalk on a rowboat out front.

Charlotte loved to go to that restaurant and to the West Haven shorefront in general. It was where the Bacons had spent one of their last great times all together, a seafood dinner and gazing out at the water. For those reasons, Joann and Joel felt like Charlotte would love to have her playground right there. On the beach in West Haven, Connecticut. So we went to work on making that happen.

. . .

In kicking the tires on a West Haven build, we had two mainstays of the Angels Army who emerged in leadership roles. You couldn't have two more different guys—George LeMoine and Paul Neugebauer.

George is a an engineer, an idea man of sorts, who felt he could effectively guide us in West Haven from a fundraising perspective.

On the flip-side, Paul is a hard-charging, deeply religious retired Captain from the Bridgeport Fire Department. He is one of The Sandy Ground Project's biggest proponents, even sporting a huge tattoo on his arm of the "Where Angels Play" logo. West Haven is Paul's hometown and he's got a great feel for the community. He is also friendly with West Haven Mayor Ed O'Brien and his son is on the job with the West Haven F.D. All things considered, we began pursuing a playground in the city with a lot of momentum because of both George and Paul.

So we set up a meeting with Mayor O'Brien and the City Council, basically to give them a feel for what The Sandy Ground Project was and explore options for West Haven. They embraced the project right away, and I mentioned the area around Stowe's Restaurant as a possible build site. The lack of adequate parking there was going to prevent that from happening, but we settled on another location that would work better. It was right nearby, still in the section of town known as "Savin Rock". I left the meeting excited that things were falling into place. And I would let the Bacon family know that Charlotte's playground was going to be built where they'd hoped it would be.

Later that night, I got a call from one of the local newspapers. They were looking for a quote from me about the controversial location that had been chosen for Charlotte Bacon's playground. The area we'd discussed, at Savin Rock, was apparently forbidden to be built upon by the West Haven Land Trust. I told them, honestly, that I didn't know anything about it and sloughed it off. I had the Mayor's approval, the City Council's approval, and we were moving forward.

The following morning, the New Haven Register released an article about how the City of West Haven was rejecting The Sandy Ground Project because of the Land Trust issue. I was furious, with the Mayor and Council especially, because they hadn't even given me a heads up about this or given us a chance to sort things out. Most of all, I was upset that this negative attention would affect the Bacon family.

The last thing Joann and Joel wanted was to have their names in the paper. Especially since it put them at the center of a city-wide debate. I felt like I had let them down, but I was truly blind-sided by this becoming an issue. I was especially angry with Mayor O'Brien and told him as much, even though it wasn't his fault and he turned out to be one of the champions of our project. The Bacon family had been through enough.

At this point I had no problem at all if the Bacons wanted to pull the plug on West Haven completely. But when I asked them if they wanted to move Charlotte's playground elsewhere, they said no. If things could be ironed out in West Haven, that is still where they would like it to be.

Knowing this, we resolved to work with Mayor O'Brien and the City Council to set things right. When the newspaper called me back to comment on the story (clearly trying to goad me into saying some fighting words), I simply told them: "I was angry at first, but these playgrounds always end up where the angels want them to be. So I have faith that things will work out."

Mayor O'Brien called me the following day. He said he had another location in mind for Charlotte's playground and asked if I could meet him there to check it out. We agreed to meet there, at Seabluff Beach, at 4 PM.

There was a City Council meeting later that night where the build at Savin Rock was expected to be voted on and hotly debated. The Mayor had asked that I be there. The citizens of West Haven were actually furious with the Land Trust for rejecting our project. They were embarrassed and upset, feeling they had given West Haven a bad name. The Sandy Ground Project had never been booted from any town ever before, and the people of West Haven certainly didn't want their city to have that dubious distinction.

So I head to West Haven, to Seabluff Beach, to meet with the Mayor that afternoon. And I planned to get to the location well ahead of him. I wanted to see the beach alone. I also wanted to see a message from Charlotte.

As I arrive at Seabluff Beach, I realize it's a solid location for all the technical reasons. It's got parking, a nice memorial with flags nearby, and there's people hanging around just enjoying the day. Clearly the local folks are fond of this spot, and I decide to chat one of them up.

Just as a general canvass, I asked the man what he thought of a playground on this beach. He said it would be great. In addition, when I mentioned that I was there to meet the Mayor, this guy vouched for him. He said that Ed O'Brien was solid, had been great for the city, and could be trusted.

As I headed back to my car to wait for the Mayor, something in the sky caught my eye. It was a kite. A little girl, accompanied by her father, was flying it high up in the air. Being a total stranger, I didn't want to address the girl directly, so I introduced myself to her dad. I told him about the project, the playground, the angels, and why I was there.

"As crazy as it sounds, I'm actually here looking for a sign," I told him. "And I'm wondering if your daughter's kite could be it." It looked like the kite might be pink, Charlotte's favorite color, so I asked him.

Having just heard the whole story, the man looked stunned. Not only is it pink, he told me, but just wait until you see what it is.

He then asked his daughter to reel her kite in so that I could see it. She must've been thinking, "Who is this guy?", but she obeyed nonetheless. As this little girl brought the kite closer to the ground, I was able to make out what it was. And I knew, without a doubt, that this was where Charlotte's playground was going to be built.

It was an angel in a pink dress.

• • •

That night, in the City Council Chambers, everyone was expecting a fight. I led off my presentation by saying I don't foresee any problems building a playground in "The Kindest City in Connecticut"—which is what West Haven bills itself as. From there, I told them that they do not make decisions for The Sandy Ground Project. I told them that I do not make decisions for The Sandy Ground Project. I told them that the angels themselves have the only votes when it comes to these playgrounds, and I told them the story of the kite I saw that afternoon.

The battle that everyone expected never came. The City Council put the issue to rest, voting 13–0 in favor of building Charlotte Bacon's playground on Seabluff Beach.

The story that ran in the New Haven Register the following morning was anything but controversial. It told my story of the kite, the vote, and announced that The Sandy Ground Project was on its way to the West Haven shore. I got an excited call later that day from a woman named Heidi. She told me that it was her daughter, Katie, who I'd met the day before. Katie was the girl with the kite and their family was so thrilled that she'd been the one to carry Charlotte's message. I asked her if Katie would be up for being a part of our ribbon-cutting ceremony when the time came and Heidi gladly accepted the invitation for her.

• • •

The initial difficulties experienced in terms of West Haven had been solved by Charlotte. And from there, the building of her playground was nothing but a success. The summer was just about starting on the Connecticut coast so, with a few sprinkles aside, the work was pleasant and bright. We broke ground on Seabluff Beach with Charlotte's brother Guy—our foreman for the week—shouting "Let's get to work!" as he fired up one of our Bobcats.

The Angels Army, keenly aware that the 26th and final build was drawing near, was out in full force. You could see them treasuring every task, relishing every accomplishment together. The West Haven community, proving to be at least *one of* the kindest in Connecticut, came out in droves as well. We had a large group of students from the high school helping out, and the town had a construction company come in and do an awesome side-wall with a monument. The whole area surrounding Seabluff Beach wound up getting really spruced up thanks to Charlotte's playground.

Our volunteers were extremely well taken care of in West Haven. Stowe's Restaurant, being the original draw to the area, came up strong with feeding our crew. Also, since it was getting hotter by the day, the local ice cream trucks and Rita's Italian Ice made themselves available from sun-up to sun-down supplying us with as many cool treats as we needed.

But the coolest perk, from the Angels Army's perspective anyway, was probably being put up in the University of New Haven's dormitories. These were no ordinary dorms though, they were more like newly-furnished townhouses and the Army savored the experience together. It turned into a milder version of *Animal House* to be honest. There were pranks, sneaking into each other's rooms to scare each other, all that kind of shenanigans.

To their credit, the Angels Army were always very adaptable over the last 18 months when it came to sleeping arrangements. One night it's a sleeping bag, the next might be in an oceanfront rental home. They never knew what to expect but dealt with whatever it was. A few builds before, after a particularly rough night on cots in a firehouse, I emailed an apology to the guys to let them know that they were appreciated and we would do better by them. Joe Rainis, replying for everyone it seemed, said simply: "Accommodations were fine. This is an army, not a prep school. We go where we have to go. We do what we have to do."

Either way, it was great to see the Angels Army at their wildest and best—"back to school" at the University of New Haven.

All in all, the West Haven build could not have happened if it weren't for two of our Angels Army regulars—Paul Neugebauer and George LeMoine. Although both very strong and very different personalities, the two of them were able to work together to the great benefit of the people of West Haven and the Bacon family.

At the end of the week, after all the talk and debate and camaraderie that we'll remember West Haven for, we were finally able to gaze upon what it was really all about. It was pink. It was poodles. It was the beach. It was Charlotte's playground and it was exactly where she wanted it to be.

• • •

A month after having celebrated Mother's Day by cutting the ribbon on our Long Beach Island playground, it was now Father's Day and the ribbon to be cut was in West Haven. It was a beautiful sunny Sunday, June 15th, and our 24th playground would be opening in honor of Charlotte Bacon.

We invited Katie, "the girl with the kite", and her entire family to be a part of the day's festivities. After all, she was the reason we were all here on Seabluff Beach—not in some other town or, even worse, still wrangling over whether or not to build at Savin Rock.

Katie brought her pink angel kite to the ribbon-cutting. The very same one I had seen hovering over this very same beach, the tell-tale sign from Charlotte Bacon. Katie presented the kite to Charlotte's brother Guy. It was a very touching moment, between two kids who seemed to understand and appreciate the magnitude of what they were a part of. That kite is probably the most well-known piece of "Sandy Ground" memorabilia there is—if there is such a thing.

Joann Bacon made an amazing speech that afternoon. About the volunteers, about the family's fondness for the area, and most of all about Charlotte. We dedicated the flagstone, a statue of a poodle standing guard with the inscription: "Have a waggin' fun time!" It features the handprints of Joel, Joann, and Guy. We also set the flagstone on a monument labeled "Savin Rock"—a nod to the originally chosen location of the playground. The Angels Army had made a rock of its own.

The day was also extremely special for Joel Bacon. He described the ceremony, the celebration of his daughter, as the best present he could have gotten on this particular Father's Day. And, at the end, his son cut the ribbon and Charlotte's playground was opened.

As we wrapped up the ceremony on the beach, I had the occasion to speak briefly with Katie's older sister. She was overjoyed by the new playground and the role Katie had played in it... that she had been a part of something so special. But what stayed with me was something she said about Katie and their car ride over to Seabluff Beach that afternoon.

"I was telling Katie, 'Today's your big day! You're like the star of the show! It's going to be awesome!'" she said. "But Katie was like, 'No, Charlotte is the star today. Not me.'"

While Katie was right, it did strike me that an 8-year-old would view it that way. When you tell a little kid that they are a star, how often are they so humble and selfless? But Katie seem to have a unique understanding of what was going on. Maybe that is why Charlotte had put that kite into her hands, and high into the air, in the first place.

So while Charlotte was indeed the star of Playground #24, Katie was the messenger who had led us to the perfect spot. And she recognized the great honor that Charlotte had given to her.

Charlotte changes the landscape in West Haven

CHAPTER TWENTY-NINE

Playground Celebrating the Life of Noah Pozner

East Rockaway, New York

It's funny how you keep finding yourself in old familiar places. For me, it was The Blue Colony Diner, right off of I-84 in Newtown. It is where I had stopped so often on my way to and from the Connecticut Burn Camp. It is where I happened to meet several of the families of our 26 angels for the first time.

And here I was again, speaking one-on-one with Veronique Pozner as she spoke passionately about the loss of her son, Noah. I would meet her husband Lenny later on, as well as their two daughters Sophia and Arielle. The Pozners all felt that a part of them had been taken away when Noah was lost in the tragedy at Sandy Hook Elementary, but maybe none in the same way that Arielle felt it. She is Noah's twin sister.

Although the family was struggling mightily at this point, Veronique felt that a playground would be a fitting tribute to her son. He was a fun-loving kid who was especially into "Star Wars". He was always talking about "the force". The Pozners, from all indications, were all in on The Sandy Ground Project and I looked forward to coordinating with them all further.

Over the course of a busy year, I lost touch with Veronique unfortunately. Not long after our initial meeting in Newtown, the family had relocated. Veronique is a professor, teaching oncology nurses, and was starting a new teaching position. In the meantime, the Angels Army was busy building playground after playground. And when we finally reconnected, Noah's playground was lining up to be the 25th, the penultimate, build of The Sandy Ground Project.

As we began piecing together a build in honor of Noah, the first thing we needed (as always) was a place to build it. Veronique had mentioned the Rockaways—a section of Queens, NY—where Noah's grandfather resided in the neighborhood known as Belle Harbor. Having built Playground #16 in nearby Roxbury the previous winter, we were certainly no strangers to the area. But in Roxbury, we had the benefit of circumventing the politics of New York City by being able to work in an area directly controlled by the Breezy Point Cooperative. The Rockaways, however, were very much governed by the Borough of Queens.

As I began to navigate the political channels and explore the possibility of building Noah's playground in the Rockaways, it became clear that the administration there already had their hands full. There had been problems with violence within the community, and I just got the sense that this would not be a safe, stable area for us to build in. While we certainly always focus on helping the communities that need us most, these playgrounds are also very sacred in preserving the memory of its namesake. And it needs to be in a place it will be cared for.

In the end, those inquiries would lead us to the final destination of Noah's playground. The New York connection, the Long Island coast, the very "Rockaway" name—all of it was pointing us towards a town that was ready and waiting and hoping to host Noah and the Pozners.

· · ·

Just outside of the New York City limits lies the bayside village of East Rockaway. Much like its neighbor (and home of Sandy Ground Playground #10) Island Park, it was devastated by Superstorm Sandy and is controlled, essentially, by a cooperative group of homeowners who welcomed us with open arms. In this case, it was the Bay Park Civic Association who would take the lead and make building Noah Pozner's playground a glowing success.

It all began, actually, with Kathy Cleary—whose beautiful email about Island Park, "the little town that could", resulted in Playground #10 being built there. It would turn out that a friend of hers named Dan Caracciolo reached out to us as well, and described East Rockaway in much the same way. He said that the town would be a great host, the playground would be beloved, and it would be free of political interference of any kind.

In terms of Superstorm Sandy, East Rockaway had suffered in much the same way as Island Park and got equally overshadowed in terms of media coverage. The entire village had basically been flooded out, waters rising up to the first-floor ceilings, and it was still in the process of rebuilding almost two years later.

With all of these factors aligned, and most importantly with the blessing of Lenny and Veronique, we examined the beach in East Rockaway that the Bay Park Civic Association had set aside for us. There was *ju-u-ust* enough space for the playground and we really had to study the tidal charts and water-table to make sure it would be high and dry and safely done. When everything checked out and we were good to go, the Association asked me to come back to the town and give a presentation for all of the area's homeowners. We thought they should know the full scope of The Sandy Ground Project's story.

The presentation turned out to be very much a pep rally for Noah's playground. The community was all in and very excited to get the build underway. It would be taking place in July, a beautiful time on the bayshore and an opportunity to bring out the best in East Rockaway. I knew we'd found a great place to build, but a brief conversation with an older gentleman after the presentation confirmed that it was the *right* place as well.

He had clearly lived in the neighborhood his whole life, had seen things come and go. He came up to me with tears in his eyes and told me how much he loved the project and what an honor it was for the town. But the anecdote he added after is what really caught my attention: "I think you should know, there used to be a playground on the beach there in the very same spot. It was lost during Sandy, but before that there used to be a giant ship for the kids to climb on and play in. The funny part is, all the children referred to it as 'Noah's Ark.'"

So now, in its place, another Noah was coming to town.

• • •

In order to make this playground a real reflection of our angel Noah, we needed to learn as much about him as possible. This is where Lenny Pozner, Noah's dad would be an invaluable resource for myself and for Toni Giordano, our chief playground designer. The difficult task of pouring through precious photographs and generously sharing all of Noah's remarkable traits with us was left to Lenny. This beautiful story of Noah entrusted to us by Lenny is why these playgrounds are considered so sacred to us and reflect the care and respect with which our entire project is built.

The building of the playground itself went great. There were no problems at all, and that was thanks mostly to the leadership role taken on by Theresa Gaffney—a trustee with the Bay Park Civic Association. She was our liaison to all things East Rockaway, matching up every resource with every need. Theresa handled the accommodations for the Angels Army and arranged for all the meals to be provided by various businesses around town. The biggest of which was a waterfront bar/restaurant called "Reel". They played host for numerous meetings, meals, and even our ribbon-cutting after-party. The folks at Reel made our lives a whole lot easier.

A Sandy Ground build on New York soil always means bring in our great (and high-powered) friends from Hallen Construction to lend a helping hand. They had started working with us in Island Park, and here they were for our final New York build. Island Park and East Rockaway are not exactly close to one another when you're on land—but by boat they are only ten minutes apart. It would turn out that Caroline's playground and Noah's playground actually face one another, separated only by water.

The East Rockaway community came out in droves during the build and we were able to meet so many great people there. With the Association's "beach house" being right on the grounds, we had a lot of the creature comforts that are not available on a lot of these builds. It was a sort of headquarters for us, and it allowed people a forum to meet and greet one another, hanging out as one as the build progressed.

The Sandy Ground Project had basically taken over a two-block section of town. When you were inside that radius, you were with us, and it was tough to navigate your way out. There were just so many people, the volunteerism was booming with only two builds to go. As far as the Angels Army, they were sensing that each time they did a certain task that it might be the last. Noah's playground was an old-fashioned beach-build too, so the Mud Ducks were savoring all the dirty work as only they could.

• • •

The Angels Army was experiencing a lot of raw emotion at this point. There was a sense of inner-conflict, and almost dread, as we all neared the climax of what was a tremendous collective accomplishment. The Sandy Ground Project had really become a way of life for a lot of these people. No one wanted the project to end, and at this point we didn't even know that we wouldn't be building again until the fall. With the 26th playground being our biggest all-around undertaking, it would actually take the rest of the summer and early fall to piece it together.

So for months people had been asking, "What's next?" And by the time we were working on Noah's playground—#25—that answer was starting to come into focus.

I had been floating the idea to the families for a while now, asking if there was another location they'd like to sponsor a playground build. It would be like a post-Sandy Ground pay-it-forward, from Newtown to the rest of the world. And as construction was happening in East Rockaway, I had gotten my first answer in that regard from Joann Bacon.

It turns out that she and Charlotte had been involved with the Pine Ridge Indian Reservation in South Dakota. Honestly, I had never heard of it before she mentioned it, but it is a very impoverished area that struggles with various health and social issues. I thought it was a great idea, but would need to learn more about it.

As we were building Noah's playground in East Rockaway, right across the street was a group of kids from an organization called "Next Step". They were traveling around the region to assist in rebuilding Sandy-damaged areas. They just so happened to be rebuilding the community center across the street when we were in town.

We wound up inviting the group over to our side of the street for lunch one afternoon and we all got to talking. There was a lot of mutual admiration for each other's projects and we invited them back for the weekend's big ribbon-cutting event. But as I spoke to the Next Step supervisor, it caught my ear that they have a headquarters in South Dakota at Pine Ridge. I couldn't believe I was hearing of the place twice in a matter of days after never having heard of it before. One thing leads to another, and we're now hoping to bring a playground to the Lakota Sioux people that live on that reservation. Another small miracle connected by The Sandy Ground Project.

• • •

Another great connection we made in East Rockaway was with a young woman named Dawn Castellano. She happened upon the playground as it was being built and was especially moved by the mission of the project. As it turns out, she had lost a child of her own about six months prior—an infant that was only a few days old. Her and my brother Bob, who had suffered the loss of his own daughter many years ago, got to talking and bonding over their experiences.

Dawn became part of the landscape in East Rockaway, and it was clear that the Sandy Ground playgrounds could directly help more than 26 families. They had become sort of a rallying point for those looking for inspiration and hope—the loss of a child, or a parent, or a home.

Dawn also got us involved with the TEARS Foundation, which is an organization that helps new parents in dealing with the unexpected loss of a newborn. Being of like minds, we support them any chance we get and presented Dawn with a donation at one of our East Rockaway fundraisers. We also invited her back for the ribbon-cutting so that she knew, for sure, that she was a part of our family now.

. . .

One of the most prominent visual effects from any Sandy Ground playground was built right onto the bay's surface in East Rockaway. We had a group of children paint four gigantic letters—each probably about eight feet tall—making the word NOAH in gold to match the playground. We then took the letters offshore, by boat, and lashed them to some pilings where a dock had probably stood before Superstorm Sandy blew through.

The result was really cool. Looking at the playground, Noah's name appears to be rising up out of the water in the background. Just striking to look at, and it wound up being a permanent tribute. Those four letters are still there, standing on the water's surface, to this very day.

All of the work done at Noah's playground was exemplary, including by his own family who assisted at the build. Lenny, Noah's dad, did a lot of work alongside the Angels Army and our little forewomen, Sophia and Arielle, were the bosses. Unfortunately, Veronique was hung up with some teaching duties, so by the time she arrived in New York the playground was nearing completion.

While we would have loved to host Veronique for the duration, the reaction we got when she did arrive was literally priceless. She was completely overwhelmed, taking in all of Noah's playground in one fell swoop. The golden structure on a beautiful beach, the Star Wars touches and flag, the little Yoda statue. And most of all her son's name sitting out on the water as a constant reminder of who had made it all happen.

Veronique expressed her sincere thanks in that moment, as did Lenny. Veronique said she couldn't believe anyone would do all this for her little boy, and they were honored by all the love and attention. She actually apologized for not staying in better touch with me, but obviously no apology was necessary. If this project has taught me anything, it's that everything happens in its own time and as it's meant to be. The truth was Veronique and Lenny would have no idea how much their trust and strength and courage has inspired us to continue to try and make a difference for others.

Of course, there is no way to comprehend all that the Pozners have had to endure since Noah left this physical world or any of the families for that matter. I can say, however, and have witnessed the courage and commitment, that the Pozner family have shown in an effort to make sure that Noah's life, spirit and legacy is accurately portrayed and protected. Notwithstanding the evil conspiracy theorists and truthers who attempt to spread hate and vile falsehoods, the Pozners, Lenny in particular, have made sure the beautiful life of their son Noah continues to shine as a force for good. We at Where Angels Play Foundation are, and will continue to be, humbled to play a role in the celebration of Noah's life.

With Noah's playground complete and a ribbon-cutting ceremony slated for the following morning, I enjoyed an incredible Italian feast with an incredible Italian family. Anthony Proto, the Bay Park Civic Association President (and now great friend of mine), had been kind enough to have me in his home to dine with his family. Anthony and his wife and in-laws had helped with every single aspect of the project and now were welcoming me into their home.

These were people who'd had their lives turned upside-down during Superstorm Sandy, having had to take up temporary housing, still trying to rebuild. And here they had all been so great in taking us in during the playground build. Now, on top of it, they were feeding us an amazing Italian dinner.

Oddly enough, as we sat eating, there was a mysterious knock at the door. When Anthony answered, no one was there. Just a 6-foot-tall cardboard note addressed to me. It was a little disconcerting that someone knew that I was there, but the message on the note was a positive one. It paraphrased the Broadway musical "Wicked" and said that because the town of East Rockaway knew me, it had been changed for good.

I knew it wasn't because of me, necessarily, but I agreed with the sentiment just the same. It was because the town had embraced Noah that it had been changed for good. We never did find out who left that note though.

. . .

The morning of July 27th was a breezy but sunny one in the Bay Park section of East Rockaway. It was time to cut the ribbon and officially open the playground celebrating the life of Noah Pozner. This being the 25th installment of this kind of ceremony, you would think it would become routine to a degree. But you would be wrong. Each one takes on its own special meaning, and reflects the spirit of the angel being honored.

For Noah, there were his favorite Star Wars characters roaming the grounds and a beautiful cake wishing that the force be with all of us. Most notably was his mother, Veronique, speaking powerfully about the positive impact and the hope that The Sandy Ground Project had injected into their lives.

East Rockaway was a place where, thanks to Noah, a lot of new friends had been made. Anthony Proto gave a great speech on the meaning of community there in Bay Park. The folks from Next Step came out to support us and, through the efforts of Karen Burke, Dunkin Donuts presented us with a whopping $25,000 donation.

But the one new friend I was happy to see come out for the day was Dawn Castellano. After the actual ceremony, I introduced her to Veronique and then stepped away as they got to talking. It was a touching thing to watch as, although I couldn't hear the exact conversation, Veronique was counseling Dawn about the one major (yet heart-breaking) thing they had in common. You could see Dawn healing a bit from Veronique's words of counsel. You could see Veronique healing a bit from being able to help another grieving parent.

The Sandy Ground Project was, in the very simplest of terms, a network of people helping one another. In a whole slew of ways, it was people getting to know each other and changing for the better. And although the building had wrapped up for the summer, that element of being there for one another had not.

• • •

Since building Noah's playground last July, we have stayed in touch with Veronique and Lenny—probably even more so than we had before the build. We would reach out on Noah's birthday, which is Arielle's birthday too, a situation that I am sure is difficult to navigate for the entire family. Lenny continues his tireless work to defend his family and the legacy of Noah every single day. Their love and dedication to their son's memory continues to be a source of inspiration for us all.

Shortly after an amazing weekend in East Rockaway, Veronique was back at work getting ready to teach her class of future oncological nurses. (A profession that takes immense toughness and brains I might add.) As we texted back and forth thanking one another for what was a great experience in Noah's honor, Veronique lamented having to go and lecture with all of it so fresh in her mind.

So I suggested just taking the whole class and dedicating it to Noah. Talk about him, his playground, what she'd experienced over the weekend. It was just a passing suggestion, as I don't know the first thing about teaching such a class.

But a few hours later I got word back from her, thanking me for the idea. The students' reactions were incredible, she told me, and it was a cathartic class period for her as well. She really came away feeling like that conversation with her students had changed their lives, much more than anything else she could have taught.

• • •

And so, with 25 down and only one to go, the Angels Army prepared to—appropriately—head back to Connecticut to put the biggest, and final, piece into the Sandy Ground puzzle.

CHAPTER THIRTY

Playground Celebrating the Life of Dawn Lafferty Hochsprung

Watertown, Connecticut

There is no greater tragedy that can occur in one's life than the loss of a child. Nothing that can prepare you to deal with that kind of pain. But maybe, having been in the presence of so many strong and inspiring individuals, being a dedicated member of the Angels Army helped Billy Valentine through the worst time of his life.

Along with Alan Ballester, Billy was one of two guys that made every single playground build of The Sandy Ground Project. He was 26-for-26. He knew every town. He checked every nut and bolt. He met every family. He heard every speech. And he wondered how they did it. If he were in their shoes, could he even get out of bed in the morning?

During the layoff between playground builds 25 and 26, in August 2014, Billy lost his 21-year-old daughter Christina to suicide.

All of the Angels Army had their family and friends involved in The Sandy Ground Project to some degree. Billy and Christina were certainly no exception. Billy was a mainstay, part of the very backbone of the group, so he naturally included his daughter. She was a familiar face to us, having come to some of the builds with her dad. And so this tragedy rocked the Angels Army to its core.

While there is no cure or solace for heartbreak like that, it seemed as though his involvement with The Sandy Ground Project is what had prepared Billy to cope. Maybe the angels had blessed Billy with a schedule allowing him to make all the builds? Maybe it was to prepare him, in some small way, for the most difficult time in his life? He had helped and connected with so many of the families from Newtown and now they were there for him in his time of crisis. That is, after all, how families work.

It was remarkable to witness people like Scarlett Lewis, Rebecca Kowalski, and so many others, reach out to Billy and step into the role of counselor. The pain is unbearable, but Billy's attitude and resolve have been remarkable. As I'm sure he would tell you himself, it is because he has been able to draw strength from all of these families he had gotten to meet and know and love.

Billy would often reference a ribbon-cutting speech by Sandy Previdi. She had expressed gratitude for having gotten to spend six beautiful years with her daughter Caroline. Billy thought, "If Sandy can consider herself so lucky to have six years, how lucky am I to have had twenty-one?"

In a sad but wonderful way, the families had become his role models—the examples of grace in the face of unimaginable tragedy. He, along with the Angels Army and the Where Angels Play Foundation, put his building efforts towards paying tribute to his daughter. We designed and completed a project in his hometown of Jackson, New Jersey. The "Garden of Hope" was dedicated in Johnson Park in May 2015—in memory of Christina Valentine.

• • •

As the summer of 2014 gave way to the fall, our final build of The Sandy Ground Project was upon us at last. The three-month layoff had given us extra time to plan, of course, but it also gave us a chance to look back on all that had been done. And in doing that, I thought it was important get everyone who had helped us along the way up to speed. In the end, we couldn't have done it without every last one of them.

So I sent out the following letter to my entire email database, all the veterans of Playgrounds 1 through 25 (and soon to be 26). They needed to know how special they were to the project… and that we were going to make it to the finish line.

September 24, 2014

In just five days from now, you, the Angels Army, will begin construction on Playground #26—which will complete The Sandy Ground Project. What I thought might take 5 to 10 years to finish, you have done in under 19 months. I cannot begin to thank you for your dedication towards this effort, or explain what this project has done for so many.

I write this short message to you. Specifically YOU! If you're receiving this email, you ARE Where Angels Play. You may have been at all of the builds, or one of the ceremonies. You may have been a supervisor, or you may have been a soldier. You may have served coffee, or cooked, or chaired a build, or silently carried some metal, plastic, or cement. You may have raked a beach, repaired a sign, designed a playscape or scheduled a flyover. You may have organized a fundraiser or sold a t-shirt. You may have counseled a family member or simply shared our story with a stranger.

I have tried to share as many stories, quotes, and miracles with as many of you as possible. I'm sure you haven't heard them all, and I'm sure I know only a fraction of the stories that reflect all of your individual experiences. But I look forward to hearing them all eventually.

You have given families hope. You have given communities a much-needed boost. You have restored peoples' faith in mankind. You have been an example of selflessness. I will spend the rest of my life trying to find a way to thank you for all that you've meant to this blessed project... and to me.

For now, however, I will ask you for one more thing...

That you take the time this week to drink it all in and take full measure of what you have accomplished. Enjoy every conversation, every step of the build, every hug and smile, every ache and pain, every beer and every cup of coffee. The Where Angels Play community, the Newtown community, and our heroes—the moms and dads who represent the families of our angels... we will come together this week like never before. Enjoy every moment and every sense of accomplishment. You have earned it.

Where Angels Play will build again. In fact, I believe our 26th playground represents the beginning rather than the end. There will, however, never be another project quite like The Sandy Ground. I believe in angels, and these 26 have chosen you in particular to spread their message of hope and healing and love.

Please enjoy this week. Laugh and cry and soak in every last moment. You deserve every thank you and every special moment headed your way. As much as I have tried, no words will ever aptly describe what you've meant to these 26 families... and to one another... and to so many people you will never know.

I look forward to an amazing week and sharing it with the most amazing group of individuals I have ever had the privilege to know. I am humbled to work alongside all of you.

I love you, and hope to see you in Watertown!"

• • •

We had waited until the Fall to get all our ducks in a row for the big finale of course, but also to be sure that everyone who wanted to be there could. Everyone's summer vacations would be over by October, so we could have one gigantic dedication. School would be back in session and we wanted to welcome the entire Newtown/Sandy Hook Elementary School crowd. Playground #26 would, after all, be built in honor of their Principal—Dawn Lafferty Hochsprung.

Dawn was a big educational activist who strove to instill a life-long love of learning in every one of her students. She was the leader of Sandy Hook Elementary School and made it her mission to create a positive place for all of the children to spend each day. Her last moments on Earth were spent trying to keep it that way, as she confronted the disturbed trespasser who was looking to do her kids harm.

Mrs. Hochsprung's motto, her message to her students, was always: "Be kind to each other. It's all that really matters."

In the lead-up to the final build of The Sandy Ground Project, I had the pleasure of getting to know Dawn's family. Her husband

George. Her daughters—Erica Lafferty and Tina Hassinger. Her mother Cheryl—affectionately known to all as "Gee-Gee"—and her four beautiful grandchildren.

Through them, we were able to get a sense of Dawn's personality and all the things she liked that could be reflected on her playground. She loved sailing, dogs, and pirate ships—all things we'd certainly be able to incorporate. And with the build-up for The Sandy Ground's ultimate project being bigger than ever, Erica and Tina were awesome spokeswomen for both their mother and The Sandy Ground Project. They couldn't have been more accommodating when it came to doing interviews and they were intimately involved throughout the planning process. Their enthusiastic participation is one of the big reasons that Dawn's playground wound up being where it is.

• • •

In my initial brainstorms when the idea of The Sandy Ground Project was formed, the thought was to have the 26th and final playground in Newtown itself. But this was in January of 2013 which, to be honest, feels like it took place in a past life by October 2014. Literally everything for me, personally and professionally, had changed. As had my thinking on the location of Playground #26.

Over that period of time, I'd gotten to know and love the families who had been affected by the Newtown tragedy. We had been building and laughing and crying together for a year and a half. So as we moved towards the end of The Sandy Ground Project, I knew what they thought about a playground being built in Newtown. It wouldn't fly, and I understood why.

So many of the families had wanted their playgrounds far away from the town, outside of the fish bowl that Newtown had (in a lot of ways) become. The playgrounds were their escapes, a place to remember their loved one's life instead of their death. A playground in Newtown would just be another reminder, another focal point in the community for "tourists" to zone in on. In the families' minds, The Sandy Ground Project was something that ran counter to all the tragedy and controversy and media attention. It was something apart from Newtown. Playground #26 would have to be built elsewhere and I was in full agreement.

• • •

Here is a trivia question you should be able to answer by now: If you go on the website MapQuest and ask for driving directions from Newtown, CT to Watertown, CT—how many minutes would the trip take you? If you said "26 minutes", this book has taught you a little something. And that is not why Watertown was chosen for Dawn Hochsprung's playground… but it didn't hurt. Just another sign that we were on the right track.

Three grandsons and a granddaughter, Dawn's pride and joy, all call Watertown home. Tina and her husband Ryan are raising their children there and we all thought it was a great idea for them to be able to play on a playground, in their hometown, dedicated to their grandmother. With Tina and Erica leading the charge, we were quickly able to get the ball rolling on a Watertown build.

Tina and Erica were the ones who set up the meetings to facilitate The Sandy Ground Project coming to Watertown. As a result of that, we received great support from the administration there—including the Mayor and Town Council. The go-to guy was Chuck Frigon. He was instrumental in clearing the way for us and making Dawn's playground a reality. Lisa Carew, director of recreation became our liaison to the city and was a magnificent partner as well.

The Watertown Fire Department and Police Department were both huge supporters of the project as well. It was a rare thing to have both on board in a given town throughout The Sandy Ground Project's life, but things were coming together in a special way for #26. Everyone was relishing being a part of it. Kudos are also in order for Ron McClellan, President of Carlos Soto's local of the Service Employees International Union. He was basically the facilitator of all the food—delivering it, cooking, cleaning up—all of it done right at the job site in the picnic area.

As the actual build drew near, Dawn's daughters and I did a presentation at a local firehouse in Watertown. It was really just to drum up support and energy for the week-long playground build that was to come. The people of Watertown really responded, and gave us a standing ovation by the end. Watertown was clearly all in, in every possible way—the administration, the businesses, public services, and the people. The Mayor made available whatever he could in terms of materials, food, transportation, and even provided all the landscaping that we would need.

All in all, Playground #26 for Dawn Hochsprung was shaping up to be a beauty. The only thing left was to execute and, as always, we had our ace in the hole—the Angels Army—to carry out the mission.

• • •

Playground #26 is, area-wise, slightly larger than all of the other playgrounds. We wanted it to be an all-encompassing tribute, so we would need a bit more land to get that accomplished. There would be 20 swings surrounding the playground structure, one for every child. There would be six riding toys—two each to honor the firefighters, police, and EMS workers, as well as six personalized panels presenting each one of the heroic teachers. The location of the playground is in a beautiful park on top of a hill, and after moving a few rocks out of the way the Angels Army started taking care of business.

It was like their graduation in a lot of ways. The playground in Watertown, by chance for the most part, required just about every element of the first 25 builds. There was a cement pad for our technicians, courtesy of Connecticut Tank Removal once again. But there was also a lot of MudDuck work to be done. There were walls to be built, walkways to be laid down, earth to be moved, and it all needed to be decorated in some fashion. It was amazing to see what everyone was able to do to reshape the entire area.

This was truly the culmination of all the hard work the Angels Army had ever done together. Every skill they'd learned, every idea they'd come up with, every trick of the trade—it all manifested itself as one in Watertown.

Early one morning, while we were in the midst of building Dawn Hochsprung's playground, we held an informal memorial service for Billy Valentine's daughter Christina. The Angels Army had not all been back together, in its element, since her passing. And this was an opportunity to honor Christina, say a few prayers together, and make sure that Billy knew we were with him as brothers and sisters.

I was surprised to see George, Dawn's husband, come to be with us early that morning. He was a new member of our Sandy Ground family, but a member nonetheless. And he graced us with a beautiful speech and left us all with some words that we won't soon forget. He said: "I don't know that there is any group of professionals—teachers included—that could have pulled off this project other than firefighters. In all my life, I have never met a more special, or more selfless, group of people."

Amidst a week filled with emotional moments, I felt like George had really set the tone and hit the nail on the head. The Angels Army, for all they had done, deserved a sincere and reverent pat on the back.

• • •

While most of the playgrounds built over the past 18 months had taken one, two, or maybe three days tops... we allowed ourselves a full week to build our 26th. This had less to do with the size of the playground or the actual work required, and more to do with everyone's desire to savor the moments together and make them last.

It was a reunion really, working alongside people we hadn't seen since maybe the first or second build. Just about everyone came back, knowing how special it had been and knowing it was their last chance. Each day, the work went well into the night—not because there was any urgency, but simply because nobody wanted to go home and call it a day. When it started to get dark, people pulled out their cell phones to light up the twilight. When that wasn't enough, we pulled the cars around and put the headlines on. It was the Angels Army's finest hour and they wanted to work a full 24 of them.

Towards the end, we had Dawn Hochsprung's four grandchildren come and put their handprints into the cement. It was a family affair and Dawn's legacy would live on in those kids, and in all the kids that would come to her playground for generations to come.

When it was all complete, we raised five flags over the playground as a tribute to where we'd all come from and where we'd all been. One for the American flag. One for the Canadian flag. Three more for the State flags of Connecticut, New York, and New Jersey. And, for the first time ever in public, we raised the official flag of the foundation that this project had given birth to: "Where Angels Play".

• • •

Almost a year ago to the day that we broke ground in Watertown, NBC Evening News ran a piece about The Sandy Ground Project. One of their reporters came to Island Park, New York—to Caroline Previdi's playground—to show our story to the rest of the nation. Brian Williams, a Jersey Shore guy and probably the country's most famous anchorman, introduced the "Making a Difference" segment at the end of his telecast.

Brian was struck by the project and said that he would like to come out and see us personally when The Sandy Ground Project was complete. We were at playground #10 at the time. Now here we were a year later at #26. And sure enough, Brian Williams came to Watertown.

Led by Brian, the NBC people put together an amazing piece that briefly chronicled the life of our project. They interviewed some of the Angels Army, some of the parents from Newtown, myself, and Dawn's grandson Robbie. Brian talked to Robbie about the work he had personally put into his grandmother's playground. He was as well-spoken as a kid could be, and you could see that he was proud.

• • •

The morning before the ribbon-cutting ceremony, the Executive Director of The Sandy Ground Project strolled around our final playground. This strip of land had been a buzzing hive of activity for almost a week straight, but now it was quiet. It was just her and her boyfriend, alone, and suddenly he was down on one knee.

This happened to be my daughter MaryKate and her boyfriend, now-fiancé, Matt Herbert.

A week before we all headed up to Watertown, I was at home in Woodbridge, New Jersey. I was working on turning my ramshackle old garage into a high-tech "man cave". Matt, who is a police officer in town, had come by to give me a hand with some sheet-rocking. More importantly, he had come to ask for my blessing and my baby daughter's hand in marriage.

To Matt's credit, he realized the great significance that The Sandy Ground Project held in our lives now. MaryKate had gone from secretary at the New Jersey State FMBA office to the project's Executive Director in less than a year. These playgrounds were not only her job now, all those involved with building them had become her second family.

With all that in mind, Matt's idea was to propose at the final playground when it was done. The Sandy Ground Project was coming to an end, but it was a new beginning in a lot of ways. We were embarking on new adventures with the Where Angels Play Foundation. They were embarking on a new life together. Every new beginning comes from some other beginning's end. And, so as not to take anything away from the culmination of the project at Sunday's ribbon-cutting, Matt graciously proposed on Saturday morning.

As if we needed more emotion injected into our week in Watertown, the news of the engagement ripped through the Angels Army and the Sandy Ground family like wildfire. There were hugs and happy tears, bottles of champagne, toasts all around. This was a group of people who had come to truly appreciate how fleeting life is and how valuable these types of special moments are. Life-changing events like these—the birth of a baby, an engagement, a wedding—they had taken on a new and deeper meaning. The future is so precious and there is so much to celebrate.

There would be plenty of celebrating the next day as well. Playground #26, celebrating the life of Dawn Lafferty Hochsprung, was complete. It was expansive, taking over the park and glowing a bright purple and yellow in the sunshine. There were all her themes—pirate ships, dogs, sailing—and 20 swings embracing it all. The Sandy Ground Project was complete and the Angels Army family had one more victorious, yet emotional, day to be together.

In his follow-up segment on NBC News, Brian Williams described the afternoon of October 5, 2014 as "startlingly beautiful". The weather, courtesy of Dawn Hochsprung, was yet another gift from our 26 angels. All of them now had a playground. The ribbon opening our final one was to be cut at noon that day in Watertown.

Up above, an airplane was circling, carrying Dawn's message: "Be kind to each other. It's all that really matters." Down below, the largest crowd ever assembled for a Sandy Ground event was gathering at the playground. There were so many people—roughly 2,500—that most had to park remotely and get bused to the playground site. Many people were bused directly from Sandy Hook Elementary School in Newtown. We had a special viewing area set aside, decked out in green balloons, for all of Dawn's students and fellow teachers who had made the trip.

Between Dawn's family, the Sandy Hook Elementary School community, the Watertown community, and all the faithful Angels Army that had come together over 18 months—we really had the perfect storm for a wonderful event. So many of the families from Newtown, whose own playgrounds were being played on in other towns and states at that very moment, came out to support us. Some of them spoke at the ceremony, and all of them were presented with our newly-minted "Where Angels Play" flag. Flags were also presented to Connecticut Tank Removal and Old Castle (makers of Sakrete)—two of our most loyal sponsors that the project could not have done without.

There were bagpipers. There was Dennis Bourke playing our Sandy Ground anthems. There was Erica Lafferty reading an excerpt from her mother's favorite book. There was not a dry eye in the house. And while this ceremony was very similar to the 25 others we had been blessed enough to hold throughout the tri-state area, something was different.

The weight of the moment, the finality of the event, seemed to amplify everything. Everything was harder—the hugs, the laughs, the handshakes, and eventually the goodbyes. As I spoke at the ribbon-cutting ceremony, the emotions were just beneath the surface but ready to burst at any moment.

And while trying to put some kind of capper on all that The Sandy Ground Project had meant, I closed by saying that today's event was not an ending. It was the beginning of the families of The Sandy Ground Project paying it forward by building playgrounds for others. They would be extending their goodwill to Boston, and Oklahoma, and Colorado, and South Dakota, and Mississippi. Through the Where Angels Play Foundation, the building would not end here in Watertown.

When Dawn Hochsprung's playground was officially opened and the ceremony of the day officially closed, we enjoyed a huge lunch right out on the picnic grounds. It was compliments of the SEIU, who had come up strong for us all week and was doing so one last time. While we knew we'd have a more formal celebration together at a later date, this was the last time the Angels Army would be together like this. In its current form and in its familiar surroundings.

The person I was, perhaps, the happiest to see there that afternoon was Mark Virag. He was the heartiest soul in all of the Angels Army, battling mightily against cancer for the entire lifespan of The Sandy Ground Project. As his fight became tougher and tougher, he made it his mission to get to this point... To Watertown, Connecticut... To Playground #26... To finish what he had started alongside the brothers and sisters who loved him.

Thanks to Mark, and the 26 angels who were in his corner each and every day, the Angels Army had arrived at the finish line intact. Everyone present and accounted for.

Before starting what would become a very tough round of goodbyes for all of us, the Angels Army assembled in front of Dawn Hochsprung's Playground for a last picture. It was graduation day. We stood shoulder-to-shoulder, a sea of blue, all of us smiling through the tears that were about to come.

After the impromptu photo shoot was over, a bunch of the guys hoisted me up onto their shoulders. I was very moved by this, but it was embarrassing for me. For all they had done, and with their hearts in the right place as always, the Angels Army guys deserved this moment of celebration.

But it was never about me and it was important to be respectful until the end. While it was a happy occasion, there were still 26 incomplete families out there. Some of them were too emotional to even come to Watertown that day, so I didn't think it was right to be celebrating on a memorial site such as that. The day, simply put, was the very definition of bittersweet. Because their pain, and their loss, is permanent. The Sandy Ground Project was never designed to be a cure. It just provided one ray of light—one good day in a vast sea of very difficult ones.

In the end, we all left one another with an incredible sense of awe and satisfaction. And I say "we" as in everyone. We the Angels Army. We the communities devastated by Superstorm Sandy. We the families of Newtown, Connecticut. We the angels who made it all possible. We had become one-in-the-same over a year and a half span that profoundly changed us all.

The Sandy Ground Project could be boiled down to one sentence, really. It was just a bunch of people being kind to one another. Which, in truth, is the only thing that really matters.

• • •

Driving home that day, it was impossible not to have a lump in your throat. The goodbyes were said, the tears inevitably came, and there was Playground #26 getting smaller and smaller in the rearview mirror.

26... that was always the number. 26 miles... 26 towns... 26 on the back of a jersey or catching your eye on a digital clock... 26 buckets... 26 miracles...

And, above it all, 26 angels.

There will never be another playground build for The Sandy Ground Project. The 26th was always going to be the ultimate in that respect. But that doesn't necessarily make this the end. In fact, the exact opposite.

Our next playground will not be #27. It will be #1.

With the Where Angels Play Foundation, and its loyal Army of Sandy Ground veterans, this is only the beginning...

An angel's view of Watertown, CT

Epilogue

"December 2015"

To attempt to capture with the written word a summary of what the Where Angels Play Foundation and Sandy Ground Project has been, is now, or will become, is quite impossible. The book you have just read represents only a fraction of the stories. The ones remembered by me. I have tried to highlight some of the miracles and blessings that took place as best I can.

While my son, Charles "Smitty" Lavin, has used his incredible talents to relate our story, there is no real way to capture it all. Because the unabridged version, all the blessed moments that have taken place, lies with each and every volunteer, friend, family member, financial supporter, corporate executive, or casual observer. That is the real phenomenon of Where Angels Play.

Just as this project has meant so much to me and changed (maybe even saved) my life in many ways, there are countless others out there like me. Those who will tell of the unexplainable messages and blessed happenings that can be attributed to being introduced to these Angels.

Which brings me to the source and energy behind the Where Angels Play Foundation. I, and many who work daily on our mission, are often thanked, acknowledged, and sometimes even honored for the work that we do and the beautiful nature of all that is our organization. The truth is, I will spend the rest of my life trying to thank all of those selfless individuals who make up Where Angels Play and spend even more time trying to explain the blessing that is manifested within this amazing group of people.

However, the unmistakable source of energy and inspiration comes from the families of the angels. The Moms and Dads, spouses, daughters and sons, brothers and sisters and Grandmothers and Grandfathers of these young Angels—who somehow find the strength to trust us with the memories and legacies of their loved ones—continue to leave us in awe of their strength and courage and generosity.

Imagine the privilege it is to be able to be a part of the lives, if even in a small way, of young mothers and fathers who have suffered the worst personal tragedy imaginable. And witness their grace and courage and strength and love in order to trust complete strangers enough to not only honor their Angel but to lend their Angels' spirit to a community that sorely needs joy and hope and recovery. As described by one of the cameramen covering one of our builds, this for so many is a "triumph over tragedy" story. A hopeful moment in time in a lifetime of grief and loss.

It is my hope that Where Angels Play will continue for generations to come and its mission will continue to be fulfilled for so many who need to experience joy once again. I hold so dear to the notion that as communities are rebuilt and playgrounds are constructed and children have a place to laugh and play and be happy, the Angels who are responsible for these gifts will forever be remembered and therefore forever be with us in a very real way.

Finally, my hope is that through the example of our Angels families, we can appreciate every blessing that is in our lives. And know that no matter how dark our lives may appear at times and no matter the difficulty, we have witnessed the strength of Angels and that through community and faith and charity nothing is impossible. Love does endure in this world and the next.

Thank you for taking the time to read our story. If it has impacted you in a fraction of the way it has impacted those who have lived it, I respectfully request you share it with someone you love or a complete stranger. They will be better off for knowing Angels are real and live and work and play all around them.

May God Bless you, the Angels, and the families of Angels who have given this gift to us all.

The following names are many but not all of the members of the Angels Army. Without their dedication and selflessness, this project would never have been completed...

A playground for Sean Collier "Super Cop"

Angel Update

As of this writing, Where Angels Play Foundation has completed 36 projects. Builds are being planned across the U.S., Ontario, Canada, and discussions are underway to build as far away as Rwanda on the African continent.

Bringing joy to communities in great need, and with a desire to heal and inspire, the men and women who make up the Angels Army have grown into a close-knit family of brothers and sisters. They consider themselves blessed to be a part of a phenomenon where the grateful become the thanked, and the thanked become ever grateful.

One of the second generation of playgrounds we were privileged to build was in Wilmington, Massachusetts. It was built in honor of M.I.T. Police Officer Sean Collier. Sean was a wonderful young man, very popular with the children in his community, and wanted nothing more than to be a police officer when he was growing up. Sadly, Sean's life was cut short in the aftermath of the Boston Marathon bombing. It was at Sean Collier's playground that we were told a story that probably best underscores the very essence of the Where Angels Play mission.

Kelly and Joe Rogers, Sean's mom and dad, proved to be amazing supporters of ours and the project in Wilmington was an absolute joy and blessing for our entire team. It was several months after the build, however, that Kelly shared a heart-warming story with me on the eve of Thanksgiving.

Apparently, a family with three young boys (ages 10, 8, and 6) who lived near the playground became very fond of the new park. The boys loved it so much that they created a game called "Sean Collier: Super-Cop". The game always ended with whichever youngster chosen to be Sean as the hero. According to their mother, the boys would argue so much over who got to be Sean each day, she had to make a calendar just to track whose turn it was.

Sean's mom was so touched by this story. She told me that no words could express what it meant that her son's legacy is living on at the playground, through the imaginations of these little boys. Kelly asked me to tell all of our volunteers that they had provided a gift to her family that they would never forget. I suppose this story may be the best example to describe exactly what the Where Angels Play Foundation is hoping to achieve. Continuing the work of the Angels we honor.

We, of course, wish that very bad things did not happen to very good people—or to anyone for that matter. But as long as pain and grief exist in the world, there will be the need for healing, hope, and recovery.

Mark Virag and Dennis Bourke, two heroes of the Where Angels Play Foundation written about in this book, are now Angels themselves. We have no doubt that their work, like all of our Angels honored with these playgrounds, continues to this day. To make a difference like they did is our individual mission. To tell their story through our work will continue to be our collective goal for generations to come.

May everyone blessed to hear the stories of "Where Angels Live, Work, and Play" be inspired to "pay it forward" to someone in need.

If you remember nothing else you read in this book, my hope is that you will remember the words of my hero:

"If you threw your problems into a pile with everyone else's, you would fight to get yours back!"

– Elizabeth Dwelle Lavin

Forever Grateful to

GOD

ANGELS

FAMILY

FRIENDS

What else could I possibly need!

Supporters including but not limited to: